IF YOU WANT TO BE Rich & Happy DON'T GO TO SCHOOL?

Ensuring Lifetime Security for Yourself and Your Children

Robert T. Kiyosaki

With Hal Zina Bennett, Ph.D.
Supported by Marji Trued Collins

Aslan Publishing
2490 Black Rock Turnpike #342
Fairfield CT 06432

Published by
Aslan Publishing
2490 Black Rock Turnpike #342
Fairfield CT 06432

Library of Congress Cataloging-in-Publication Data

Kiyosaki, Robert T., 1947–
If you want to be rich & happy, don't go to school?: ensuring lifetime security for yourself and your children. / Robert T. Kiyosaki. -- Rev. ed.
p. cm.
Includes bibliographical references.
ISBN 0-944031-59-5 : $14.95
1. Business education. 2. Success in business. 3. Self-culture. 4. Educational change -- United States. I. Title.
HF1121.K59 1993
332.024'01--dc20

92-39775
CIP

Printed in USA
Revised Edition

10 9 8 7 6 5 4

214 7697277 TASHA CELL P

WHAT READERS SAY ABOUT THIS BOOK:

"The most inspiring book ever written! It has helped me find a great job and inspired me to make some well-needed changes. I want to learn more!"

Graphic Designer

"Saw it in a bookstore I thought: 'That's just what I think.' I agree, I agree, I agree!!! I want something better for my 14 year old son. I want him to learn — I want to learn."

Mother

"Excellent. Based on actual real-life experience. Understandable writing style. Relatable concepts. Practical."

Network Marketing/Account Manager

"Worth its weight in gold."

Bartender

"I have learnt so much by reading this book, and I am now interested in learning rather than memorizing."

Just Left School

"Congratulations! Finally someone articulated the education problems and has a positive plan to address it."

Information Technology Consultant

"It is a great book — thank you for writing it — the book puts into words what I have been thinking for a long time. This will be my last year teaching in the 'system.' There is another way and I agree with all you have to say. Thanks again."

School Teacher

"This book explains why the world is the way it is."

Attorney

"I would like to see all students read the book before enrolling for university."

Restaurant Owner and Land Developer

"Having read the book, everything I've seen and experienced in my working life clicks — at last! Robert has given me hope and sounded the bugle which calls my spirit to act. This is mind-snapping stuff and I want more."

Hydrogeologist

"Finally someone has discovered the truth about the current education system. When is the next book coming out?"

Student

"As a parent of four and an infants' school teacher, I could not believe how true the statements are and I only wonder why I could not see this to be so — maybe I am a great product of the system. . . ."

School Teacher

"I was enraged, upset and excited while reading the book, and left me wanting to know more at the end."

Small Business Owner

"An excellent articulation of much of my experience during 30 years of teaching."

Retailer/Teacher

"I have fallen out with a lot of my children's teachers over what is taught and the system over many years. The author has confirmed in his book what I have been saying for years — fabulous book."

Financial Planner

"Very enlightening and in line with the way in which our thinking on a whole range of issues has been developing over the past few years."

Married Couple — Teachers

Dedication

This book is dedicated to my father,

*Ralph H. Kiyosaki,**

former Superintendent of Education, State of Hawaii

—the best teacher I ever had.

** Ralph H. Kiyosaki was one of two persons to be awarded an honorary doctorate degree from the University of Hawaii in August, 1991, for his contributions as a leading educator. The award was given at a celebration marking the 150th year of public education in the State of Hawaii.*

Acknowledgments

This book would not have been possible without the loving support of the thousands of graduates who trust our work, invest in their own ongoing education, give of their time to assist others in classes, recommend our courses to their family, friends and business associates, and do their best to leave behind a better world for the children to come.

There are countless people who make our work possible, but I would especially like to thank the following for their direct professional and financial support of our work: Darrell and Rachel Mullis, Dwight and Merle O'Neill, Mike and Judy Salnek, Jaime Danforth and Julie Belden, Bill and Linda McCarley, Betty Pearce and John Cook,Vince and Yve Betar, Ian and Lya Shaked, Denis Cooney, James Caldwell and Liana DiStefano, Peter Johnson, Diane McCann and Robert Mathews, Stan and Jane Jordan, Irene Schoenfeld and Mike Healey, Rasa Warr, Lynnette Webby and Ian Dempster, Laura Humphreys, Gary Clements and Lucy Walter, Patricia Reed, Idoya Torres, Lyall Jones, Graham Harvey, Bev Burdett and Sue Saliba, John and Liz GilbertGrant, Harry Baruhas, Dianne Filipenko and Eileen Darwin, Jacqueline Seow, Nancy Bekhor and Catriona Rogers, Brian and Ann Bieler, Joel Seiden, Keith and Nancy Cunningham, Paul and Wendy Buckingham, Margaret Wright and Floyd Geis, Doretta Massa, Carol Maero, Judith Orloff, Ken and Jane Windes, Kayt Campbell, Burge Blanton-Smith and Donna Summers, Heather and Doug Johnson, Sudy Saunders, John and Bonnie Dean, Mary Noyes, Bobbi DePorter and Joe Chapon.

Thanks to my fellow teachers: Blair and Eileen Singer; Krystyna Spicer, Pauline Katz; Wayne and Lynn Morgan; Brendan and Annie Nichols; Dominique and Mara Lyone; Brenda Saunders and Leanne Lemmer; Tony Fogarty.

To the following teachers who inspired me: Dr. R. Buckminster Fuller, Marshall Thurber, Anthony Robbins, Dr. A.A. Norton, Sondra Ray, Landon Carter, Marcia Martin, Randy McNamara, Robert Pante, the Roths, Jenny Kaye and Allen Wright, Marianne Hagen, Lawrence West and Jayne Taylor-West.

To Larison Clark, for being the best of friends.

To my parents, Ralph and Marjorie Kiyosaki, and the parents of my wife Kim, William and Winnie Meyer, for being role models of marriage and family...Thanks for allowing us to grow with love, guidance and freedom.

To my partner in my life's work, D.C. Cordova, for being the best business partner I could have asked for.

To Marji Trued Collins, for without her support the writing of this book would not have been possible.

To Hal Zina Bennett, whose editorial skills have allowed me to truly communicate my message.

And to my wife, Kim, for making my life complete.

CONTENTS

Introduction 9

Chapter 1 Charting a New Course 13

Chapter 2 Education's Biggest Mistake 27

Chapter 3 What Do You Want to Be When You Grow Up? 37

Chapter 4 My Child Is Doing Fine 45

Chapter 5 Where Is My Paycheck? 67

Chapter 6 If I Have All the Right Answers, Why Can't I Think? .. 81

Chapter 7 Money Is Evil 89

Chapter 8 What Is Financial Security? 97

Chapter 9 Who Says Women Are the Weaker Sex? 105

Chapter 10 Teaching People to Be Mindless Parrots 117

Chapter 11 When Being Wrong Is Right 133

Chapter 12 God Doesn't Create Stupid People — Our Educational System Does 145

Chapter 13 Why Most People Die Poor 153

Chapter 14 How Rich People Can Be Poor 159

Chapter 15 When 1 + 1 Doesn't Always Make 2 165

Chapter 16 It Is Not the Teachers 173

Chapter 17 The Courage to Change 177
Chapter 18 The Wapakununk Factor 185
Chapter 19 How to Become Wealthy on a Small Budget 195
Chapter 20 I Deserve a Raise 205
Chapter 21 Who Causes Poverty? 217
Chapter 22 Unlearning the Lessons that Keep You Down 229
Chapter 23 If I Could Change the Schools 237
Chapter 24 Should I Send My Child to School? 247
Chapter 25 What to Tell the Children 259
Chapter 26 Embrace Your Own Genius 263
Epilogue Sure, Anyone Can Criticize—Here's What We Are Doing 271
Bibliography/Recommended Reading 288

INTRODUCTION

It is time for our society, and particularly our educational system, to stop playing the game of winners and losers with our children's minds, hearts, and financial futures.

In our own school years, most of us were subjected not to a system of education but to a system of elimination—and that system sadly continues even to this day. Rather than helping us develop the very best in each of us, this system has pitted us against each other in a tragic struggle where only those whom the system defines as the "fittest" have survived. In this system less than 15 percent of us are defined as winners. The rest of us are left with a diminished sense of our own self-worth.

Instead of leaving school with confidence that we have the skills to do well in life, all too many of us have graduated crippled and hurt. What's even worse, most of us are shamefully unprepared for the challenges that we meet in the adult world. Do we want to continue perpetuating this pattern for our own children and for the generations to follow them?

In this game of winners and losers into which we've been thrown, even the so-called winners ultimately lose since we end up with a society where only a small fraction of our human potentials are ever discovered or utilized. The cost to all of us is immeasurable—in terms of financial pressure, low productivity, crime, emotional stress, and a continuing diminishment of personal satisfaction.

So destructive is the system that one is tempted to seek comparisons in the experiences of war. In his book, *Mastering the Art of War,* James Cleary's translation and commentary on the classic by Sun Tzu, we read:

When you have killed many people,
You weep for them in sorrow.
When you win a war,
You celebrate by mourning.

For many generations now, we have been celebrating by mourning—and the time has come for change. That change can begin within each of us. We can unlearn the crippling, self-defeating habits and ways of thinking that we have been taught. In the process, we will enjoy success in our own lives, and we will provide our young people with the models they require to find success as they move into adulthood.

Our increased awareness of what has happened to us as individuals, and of what we must do to overcome the damage inflicted upon us by the educational system, will filter out into society as a whole. If we do nothing else, we can influence the world by overcoming our own wounds. The success we will then enjoy can have a major impact on society in general and on our educational system more specifically.

However, those of us who work more directly with the educational system itself—parents, teachers, administrators, volunteers, custodians, etc.—have a special responsibility. We can work from the inside, making changes that will help the coming generations appreciate themselves more. We can help them develop their own inherent gifts so that they may break the deadly cycle of winners and losers once and for all.

The purpose of this book is to shed some light on how the educational system has affected each of us individually and how it is affecting young people today. It is intended to shed light on why it has been difficult to change both ourselves and the system, and what we can do now to change both with only a little effort from each of us.

In this book, you will find that the focus is on money. This focus is fundamental. In our society an understanding of money is absolutely required. Without this basic knowledge, anything else we might teach in our schools is undermined. Given the structure of modern society, the neglect of this information is comparable to neglecting to teach farming skills in an exclusively agrarian society.

It is my belief that the first duty of any society is to teach its people the basic skills necessary to be successful, happy, contributing citizens. Judging by what I have observed, our educational system has a long way to go before we can give it a passing grade. In most schools, students can get straight "A's" throughout twelve, sixteen or more years of education, yet still not have even a basic understanding of those money-oriented skills that we need to survive and prosper in our society. Moreover, they do not have the skills of cooperation and goodwill that we must have if we wish to create a society that lives up to the ideals of our forbears.

As adults, our task is twofold: First, to overcome the wounds that our educational experience has inflicted upon us; and second, to do whatever we are each capable of doing to change the educational system that will serve the younger generations. I believe we are all in favor of greater success in our own lives and happier kids all around us. I believe we are all in favor of creating a society that is excited about lifelong learning. I am for each person living up to his or her greatest potentials. I am for economic prosperity for more than just a few people. I am for reducing crime and poverty, since they go hand in hand. I am for preserving our planet's environment. I am for peace. These ideals describe the mission of this book, a mission that begins with education—our own as well as the education of our coming generations.

Let's begin. And let's get it right this time.

1

Charting a New Course

All persons are hypnotized from infancy by the culture in which they grow up. The prime task of adult life is dehypnotization, enlightenment.

—WILLIS HARMAN AND HOWARD RHEINGOLD

Let's pretend for a moment that we can travel 200 years into the future. We have just arrived at a forum where a large gathering of scholars is discussing a period of history known as the 20th century. It is a time that still puzzles these learned men and women.

They have been together for days. Time capsules have been opened and studied. Everyone has watched videotapes, and has looked at artifacts, documents and literature from this period. As you take a seat at the back of a great hall, one scholar stands up and turns to address the others.

"Well, all this study of the 20th century has been most enlightening, but I am confused."

"Why are you so confused?" the chairperson asks.

"Can the conclusion I am drawing from the evidence presented here possibly be correct? Is it true that during those years of monumental economic turmoil, back in the 1990s, the educational system completely refused to change, that it miserably failed to meet the needs of the times? Judging from these volumes of evidence, it appears to me that education failed in the one thing it must do to justify its very existence within society; it failed to respond to the times. It failed to provide people with the knowledge and skills they needed to deal effectively with the problems of their time."

The other scholars nod their heads silently, gloomily.

The first scholar continues. "And their society failed to educate its people about the principles of money, when these principles were absolutely essential for survival within their system! They only taught their people to study for specialized professions that soon became obsolete! Why, this is like an ancient hunting and gathering society failing to teach its people where to look for the plants that would nurture them or how to track the game birds and other animals that would provide them with meat!"

Another silent nodding of heads.

"If the educational system didn't teach the masses about finance, credit and investments, who did?"

A second scholar, who has studied this issue carefully, answers simply, "The banks and other financial institutions did this."

The first scholar shakes his head in disbelief. "You mean the very same people who were profiteering from the mistakes and ignorance of these people were their educators?"

Again, heads nod in agreement.

"And these very same institutions, themselves directly responsible for destroying the economy—many of which went broke in the process, I might add—provided the key people responsible for teaching the rest of the population about borrowing, investing and saving?"

The other scholars begin speaking among themselves, concurring that this indeed had been the case. The rumbling of voices continues in the room as everyone exchanges comments about how unbelievable this seems.

"It must have been like leading lambs to slaughter," one man notes.

"Or the blind leading the blind," a woman sitting next to him adds.

"Or maybe a little of both," comes another comment.

The scholars chuckle, amused but nevertheless fully aware of the tragic implications of these revelations.

After a long pause, the first scholar stares at the group with a perplexed look. "What is most inconceivable of all to me," he says, "is that educators of this period actually punished young children for making honest mistakes. And the masses went along with this! Could it actually be possible that they didn't know they were violating the fundamental principles of human learning?"

A deep stillness spreads over the room. Everyone knew, only too well, that this was exactly what had happened. By punishing young people for the honest mistakes that were so vital to learning, they essentially slammed the door of future opportunity in the faces of everyone in that culture, robbing them of the rewards of a successful and happy life. The hush that falls over the crowd attests to the consternation of everyone present.

"My God. They must have been barbarians!" someone says, voicing the sentiment felt by every person in the room.

• • •

This short parable of the future unfortunately illustrates a reality that is happening throughout the modern world today. It depicts a truth which you and I, and every single one of our loved ones, are facing right now. Each and every one of us whose life is less than we would like it to be is living the nightmare expressed in this story. It is a nightmare created not by our own lack but by an educational system, supported by our society, that has taught us not how to succeed but how to fail.

It's a grim picture, I'll admit. But I have purposely presented it in this dramatic way to alert everybody to the facts and give them a chance to do what they can, starting right now, to change the course of history, beginning with themselves.

Now that you know the bad news, let me tell you the good. The good news is that by reading this book and allowing your life to be guided by the principles you'll find here, you can undo the damage that's already been done. In these pages you will discover what thousands of others have discovered before you, that you can create the life you want and have always dreamed you could one day enjoy for yourself and your loved ones.

This book strips away the veils that hide some very basic truths about all our lives. In these pages you will explore why many of the limitations you thought were just the facts of life are not. You will discover how many of the disappointments and frustrations you may have experienced in your life aren't the result of your personal shortcomings; instead, they are the shortcomings of an educational system that promised you a map to successful living but in fact delivered just the opposite.

But don't get me wrong. This isn't a bad news book. Above all else, you will find in these pages a brand new map, one that allows you to plot a new course, to achieve wealth and happiness beyond your wildest dreams.

Planting the Seeds of Failure in Children's Minds

The seeds of failure are planted all too early in our lives. As often as not they come in the form of phrases that few of us would find objectionable:

"Be good."

"Do as you're told."

"No, you're wrong."

"This is the right answer."

"Don't make mistakes."

"If you do well in school you're sure to succeed in life."

As a young child, wanting to please, you responded dutifully. And deep within the fertile soil of your innocence the seeds of your greatest potential, which you inherited at birth, waited for the sun and the rain and the gardeners who would nurture and cultivate them as they sprouted. But thirty years later, only a few rare seeds had blossomed. Many of the seeds withered and died, rotting away deep within, giving birth only to anger, bewilderment and pain. And life became tougher, not easier, with each passing year.

Why?

We find answers to this question by taking a close look not at what we failed to learn in school but at a hidden curriculum that we have learned only too well. In our later years, long after we've left school, we begin to discover that some of those tender, early seeds of our potential have somehow been transformed into the viruses of an epidemic of self-defeat whose crippling symptoms have touched all our lives. We are living in the midst of a plague of self-defeat that all but guarantees our failure if we don't wake up and learn how to save ourselves.

We like to believe that education makes our lives easier. For a few, it does. But for most, it doesn't. We are taught that if people do well in school they will also do well in life. The bitter irony is that what we are taught in school can actually shrink our innate capacity for achieving financial security and happiness.

There are growing numbers of people in our society who are earning less, attaining fewer of their goals and who have been crippled in their pursuit of happiness, not because they were bad students, but because they were good ones. Our educational system is teaching people to be failures later in life, this dark plague attacking even those who graduated at the tops of their classes. However, the greatest failure of the educational system is that it too often rejects the people who should be benefitting the most from it—the so-called "slow" students.

I know that what I am saying is going to contradict what most of us would like to think are immutable truths about our society. Many will ask how could it possibly be that success in school could lead to a life of failure? And why are the "slow" students so often victims?

To answer these questions, we need to add the perspective of time. The repercussions of what we are taught in school do not show up in a person's life until around age 35, nearly 20 years after graduation from high school. It does not matter if you were an excellent student or a poor one. It doesn't even matter if you went to private or public school, community college or Ivy League. And it doesn't matter whether you were a high school dropout or have a series of doctorates from the world's most prestigious graduate school. The silent, insidious viruses of modern education infect almost every aspect of your life, long after school is behind you.

The negative effects are created by a school system established to serve the agrarian age, or what author Alvin Toffler called the "First Wave." It is still tripping all over itself with methods designed for a stable, slow-changing society, for people whose average life span was about 40 years, not for the average life spans of today which have practically doubled. And it was designed to accommodate the needs of farming families: school out in the mid-afternoon so that children can help with evening farm chores, closed during the summer months when labor on the family farm was at its peak. The fact that our schools still adhere to these old schedules, dismissing children from classes hours before their parents are home from work, and setting them free during the summer months when little or no adult supervision is available, describes only one area where our schools have failed to respond to the changing times and needs of our society. The result is a society of peers, where children raise children, their lives devoid of the greater wisdom and experience of caring adults.

This arbitrary clinging to a bygone world is only a token of what's wrong in public education. The world has changed dramatically since the 19th century but our educational system has not kept up.

How Shall We Measure Our Schools?

We cannot grade our schools by our accomplishments and failures during those years of our attendance up to the day of graduation. Instead, we must start evaluating them according to our lifetime accomplishments. We should be asking "How has my education helped me live my life? Can I look back over my years with a sense of accomplishment and pride? Can I honestly say that my education has helped me live my life to its fullest? Did it teach me how to make the world a better place? Did I spend my life at a job I enjoyed? Did I earn enough money to provide well for myself and my family? Did education teach me skills that truly helped me to enjoy a high quality of life?" If you are anything like the overwhelming majority of people in our society today, you will find the answers to these questions perplexing and troubling. And you will no doubt find that judged by these standards, our schools are a dismal failure.

While greater numbers of people enjoy a higher standard of living, there is also a disproportionately greater number suffering economically and professionally. Judging by current trends, with the number of jobless and homeless rising throughout our country, we are facing an epidemic of people living on some form of government assistance, barely surviving. Increased numbers of people are living lives of desperation, with broken or unfulfilled dreams. And at the root of it all are the educational system's archaic methods which, like cancer, silently eat away at what should be the vast, unlimited promise of humanity's potential.

Our educational system has planted seeds of failure, frustration and financial disaster in our society which will prevent most people from ever coming close to achieving their true potential. Antiquated methods applied so early in our lives, under the guise of education, virtually guarantee an unhappy adulthood.

The seeds of limited success, or even failure, are continuing to be planted in our children's minds every day. And our kids know it. Every day they experience the contradictions between what they are taught in school and what they see in real life. Why does Madonna make $20 million a year and a college-educated teacher only $25,000? We look at these obvious contradictions and instantly know that something isn't right about what we are taught. We stop believing the myth that education is the road to success, and those young people who are the hope for the future lose respect for school. They quit trying or they drop out. At least in terms of what earns the biggest financial rewards, school certainly appears to be a waste of time.

By now I hope you are asking some probing questions such as: "What are the long-term negative effects of our failed educational system? And how do the things we have learned in school undermine our innate ability to be successful, fully to realize our greatest potentials?"

You may be a victim of education's hidden curriculum if any of the following scenarios seem true for you:

1. **Income Plateau.** You lack the ability to generate more income, though you want to buy a home, pay for your children's education, put money away for retirement, or pay medical bills. You may work harder and longer, but the growing needs of your family far outstrip your outcome.

2. **Promotion Plateau.** You are beginning to notice that people younger than you are getting promoted while you seem to have gone as far as you can go. Your new supervisor is someone with less seniority than you, or was recently hired from outside the company.

3. **Professional Obsolescence.** You studied hard to learn a skill, trade or profession. But suddenly, the need for your special qualifications or skills is diminishing, or there is a growing number of people with your training, thus increasing the competition for your line of work and reducing your value in the workplace.

4. **Right Ladder, Wrong Wall.** You have carefully planned your career path and have committed your life to one company. Your ladder to the top of the corporate structure is strong, but there is one big problem. The wall where you placed your career ladder is crumbling.

5. **Low Pay but Love the Work.** Your work is satisfying, but your family is paying the price. They are afflicted with the proverbial "sacrificial lamb" syndrome. You are often heard saying, "Money isn't everything." Meanwhile you and your spouse lie awake at night wondering how you're going to pay the bills. You feel guilty about your inability to provide a better life for your children. And you know that your retirement will be a nightmare—not the dream you were taught it should be.

6. **High Pay, Hate Work.** Three types of people fall into this category. But they all share certain themes, characterized by statements such as: "I can't afford to quit," or "I'm doing it for the kids," or "Only a few more years until I retire. I can put up with anything that long."

   The first type is the "prostitute syndrome." If you are a member of this group, you sacrifice your body, soul and mind for money. You do not care what you do, as long as it brings in a lot of money.

   The second type is a little more complex. This is the "lost interest" group. If you are a member, you may make a lot of money, perhaps even at a job you once enjoyed. The only trouble is that your interests have changed. Many professional people belong to this club. If you're a dues-paying member you probably excelled in school and made your career choice early in life. Maybe you're a doctor, dentist, accountant or lawyer. You went to college with a specific career in mind. Then, past the age of 30, your interests began to change, often precisely at the time your career accelerated and your income started going up.

   The third type is the "traditionalist." Members of this group followed in their parents' or a close family member's footsteps, taking up a line of work or a business either because of family pressures to do so or because they just never stopped to seriously consider any alternatives. If you're a member of this group, you probably find yourself lying awake at nights realizing you never pursued any of your own genuine interests.

7. **Low Pay, Hate Work.** The worst casualties of the educational system fall into this category. Unfortunately, this may be the largest group and the main reason our methods of teaching require emergency attention. These people spend their lives at jobs which they

hate, and for which they receive insufficient compensation. Sometimes called "the working poor," they live one step above slavery. This book will give examples of how the teaching system is directly responsible for creating this large group.

8. **The Perennial Freshman.** When the promotions don't come or their dreams don't immediately materialize, life becomes boring for these people. They become impatient and decide that the solution to their problems is to go back to school. However, no matter how many times they go back, they never seem to get anywhere. If you are a member of this group, the only thing you have to show for all your efforts is a wall full of degrees and educational certificates, and a growing list of disappointments.

9. **The Future Lottery Winners.** For this group, the only thing resembling "financial planning" starts with the lottery, race track or casino. Psychologists have discovered that the more people feel frustrated in their efforts to be successful, the more they are encouraged to "play the long shots." It is not that successful people do not take risks. On the contrary; as a group they are the biggest risk-takers of all. But as Charles A. Garfield points out in his book *Peak Performance: Mental Training Techniques of the World's Greatest Athletes,* our highest achievers are, "by their nature, educated risk-takers." They only take risks calculated to work in their favor.

    You are a member of the Future Lottery Winners if you live your life hoping that luck will come your way and bless you with a big jackpot at the casino, in the state lottery or at the race track. You are a member of this group if you believe that it is only through a "lucky break" that you will ever realize your fondest dreams. There is no way of knowing for certain how many people are caught in this trap but, judging by the number of tour buses that line the streets of Las Vegas and Reno every weekend, packed with pilgrims to these meccas of glitter and hype, a conservative estimate would be in the millions.

    It is interesting to note not only the increase in the number of state lotteries, but also the size of the prizes. Ironically, the more depressed the economy, the more the "future lottery winners" get into the game.

10. **The Criminal.** There are street criminals and white-collar criminals. Many white-collar criminals are highly educated, greedy people working in important businesses and in government. In the 1980s, with the public exposure of the financial and sexual scandals of people like Jimmy Swaggart and Jim Bakker, we saw that even religion has its share of swindlers and con artists.

    No doubt there are people who consciously choose crime as a way of life, as a career path, and they should go to jail. However, we also know that desperation forces many innocent people into lives of crime. The tragedy is that if people only knew how easy it is to make money we would have far fewer criminals in our world. Education could be our greatest deterrent to crime. Yet, as you'll be learning in the pages ahead, much of what is taught in our schools today actually increases crime.

11. **Options Diminish With Age.** This is possibly the most insidious of all long-term effects of education. Instead of life getting more exciting as we grow older, opening up greater options and more freedom, life gets narrower with age. Retirement income can't keep up with inflation. The costs of clothing, food, and simple home and car repairs all continue to rise, becoming major financial burdens.

    Health care costs weigh heavily on the minds of people as they age. For this group, the world seems to get larger, faster, more expensive and more threatening by the moment. When these people recall their youth, their memories are usually prefaced with phrases such as, "If only I had..." or " I should have..."

12. **Leisure Class.** This group has plenty of time and money on its hands. The largest portion is comprised of people over 50. In his book *Age Wave,* the world-famous expert on aging, Ken Dychtwald, states that this group numbers 60 million and is growing rapidly. They control "70 percent of the total net worth of U.S. households—nearly $7 trillion of wealth." Yet in the highest income brackets, all too many contribute little or nothing to the society which has made "the good life" possible for them. There are thousands of notable exceptions, of course, people who give generously of themselves and their resources. But our society desperately needs even more of their help: their knowledge and wisdom as well as their personal time and financial support.

All too often, those in the highest income brackets of this population spend their time frequenting country clubs and cruise ships, talking to their stock brokers or running "cute businesses" to fill their time. "I've done enough, let someone else handle the problems" is a recurrent theme for this group. They often donate money or are seen at gala fund-raisers, but they give little of themselves. This distance and alienation from the problems of society is a by-product of our educational system's teaching methods. The problems we face today need money, but even more they need personal involvement and genuine compassion.

13. **Living Life Through Your Children.** Many parents, unsuccessful themselves, put pressure on their kids to accomplish what they failed to do in their own lives. When they feel these pressures, many kids rebel. They know they are not being valued for themselves but only for their utility in fulfilling their parents' dreams. Their rebellion may surface in any number of negative and self-destructive ways, by turning to drugs, crime or sex. They don't know what else to do to escape the pressure and the not-so-subtle denial of who they are, and there is nothing in their education that helps them to make better choices.

14. **Love Work, Lots of Money.** This is a small but growing group. Many people claim to be in this category. But we have to ask, "What is it they really love? Do they love work because it brings in lots of money?" How many would answer yes if asked, "Would you continue to work if you were not paid?" We might get a few convincing yesses to this question, but also much hemming and hawing, with justifications such as, "Well, nobody works for free."

We must face the fact that none of these issues has suddenly appeared on its own. These problems are not "facts of life" that we simply must endure as part of the human condition. And they are not the natural outcome of an overcrowded planet. They are, instead, the result of our society's adopting beliefs that are either patently wrong or were based on needs of a society that no longer exists.

We must keep in mind that education is nothing if it fails to teach beliefs and skills that prepare us to live successfully within our times. Each of us comes into life with gifts for living happily and successfully.

But we need to back up those gifts with knowledge and skills that will tell us how to employ them most effectively. When our educational systems fail to do that, we don't lose our gifts, we simply wander about like lost souls, unable to appreciate or use what we have. And it is at this point that most of us sit up, begin to question what we have been taught, and thus start looking in earnest for a better way.

There Are Solutions

No one questions the great benefits of education in the modern world. It has brought us all much good, particularly in technological advances that in many ways have increased the quality of our lives. Through our study of the human body and health education we have extended our average life expectancy, almost doubling it from our great-grandparents' day. And it has brought us conveniences in our homes, reducing the hours we must spend at daily chores such as preparing meals, doing laundry and cleaning house.

The problem is that while society and technology are changing, education simply isn't keeping up. It has tragically fallen into a stagnant state that, like a polluted pool, has become a breeding place for some of the worst ills society is facing today.

On the positive side, education is under tremendous pressure to change. Thank goodness! It must change or our troubles will only expand and deepen. If it fails to change, a growing portion of our population will be subjected to lives of constant struggle, marginal success, violence, frustration, financial instability and deepening despair. The roots of a revolution such as this country has never experienced are already burrowing deep into this dark soil of the future. And unless we pay attention now, and make the changes that are required, those roots will undermine and collapse the very foundation of our society.

The trouble with knowing the shortcomings of our educational system is that the problems just seem too big. How can any single person like you or me even begin to do something about them? Well, the biggest step any of us can take, drawing us all toward lasting, effective solutions, is to become informed, to start thinking about what's wrong and what we can do to correct it. The hope for our own future is found in sharing information such as you'll be reading in the pages ahead. Furthermore, by unlearning the self-defeating, hidden curriculum which has thus far limited you, you can begin to experience the success that you know, deep down inside, can be yours. Your new success can then become a beacon to inspire others.

If you ever lie awake worrying about money, if you believe you could be richer and happier than you are right now, read on. If you are concerned about your children and their futures, read on. Much of what you'll find in the pages ahead will surprise and possibly even shock you. But rest assured that you'll find answers here that will help you more fully realize your dreams and fulfill all the potential that you know you have.

If you are like the thousands of people who have already read this book or attended our lectures and workshops, the knowledge that is soon to be yours will change your life. As the quotation at the beginning of this chapter says, we are hypnotized from infancy by the society into which we are born. In adulthood, our prime task is dehypnotization and enlightenment. Given that this is so, let us begin.

2

Education's Biggest Mistake

The reason I know so much is because I have made so many mistakes.

—R. Buckminster Fuller

Not long ago I ran into a classmate I hadn't seen since high school. We had a couple of beers and talked about the adventures we had since graduation. His name was Glen, and he had been the class brain. He told me that he had attended college and afterwards had gone to work for the state government. While he initially enjoyed his work, at 42 years of age he now felt stuck in middle management. Although he had no fear of losing his job, the pay was only enough to get by, and he saw no opportunities for increasing his income.

Glen had bought a small house 10 years earlier. But he remarked that on his present income he would not be able to afford to buy that same house today. He worried now that he couldn't afford to buy a bigger house to meet the needs of his growing family.

He asked how I was doing and, not wanting to make him feel bad, I hesitantly told him that I was financially secure and in fact was in a position to retire if I chose.

He thought about this for a moment, and it was obvious that he was having some trouble with it. At last he said, "I don't understand. In high school you were the class clown and your grades weren't so great, as I remember."

I had to admit that all this was true. In fact, I had often failed. The only courses I excelled in were football and lunch. Most people didn't think I'd ever amount to anything.

"How did you do it?" my friend asked. "And why do I feel so financially and professionally trapped when I did so well in school and I work so hard now?"

It was difficult for me to come up with an instant answer. Instead, I asked how old his children were. He said he had a son, 16, and a daughter, 15.

"I'd like to talk with them," I said. "I think I could show you how I did it much better than I could explain it."

We agreed to meet in a couple of weeks. The day we got together again, I met his family and asked his children about school.

"What was the last test you took?" I asked his daughter.

"History," she stated.

"How many questions were there?"

"About 100."

"Well, how did you do?"

"I got a B, 85 right answers out of 100."

"So you missed 15?"

"Yes."

"What caused you to miss 15?"

"I don't know."

"Do you know what the 15 mistakes were?"

"No. But I don't really care. What I care about is the ones I had right."

I turned to Glen and said, "That's the key right there. Kids care more about grades than they do about learning. Our educational system teaches that being right is more important than learning what you don't know. It rewards right answers and penalizes us for making mistakes."

"I'm not sure I understand," Glen said, looking puzzled.

"Look at it this way," I said. "It's really important to look at the wrong answers. It is from them that we best learn about our mistakes and how to correct them. Mistakes are much more important than right answers."

"I'll have to think about that," Glen said. I could tell he was skeptical.

"The main reason I'm very happy with my life, and don't ever worry about money," I said, "is that I have learned how to fail. That's the reason I have been able to make progress in my life."

Glen stared at me blankly. I think he was trying to decide if I was serious or if I was still clowning around, as I did in high school.

"In school you got good grades because you gave mostly right answers on tests and were awarded an A or B. Am I right?" I asked.

"Yeah, you're right."

"Do you remember all those right answers today?"

"No, most of them I don't."

"So you were rewarded for memorizing answers that in time you would forget?"

"Yes. No doubt about that!"

"Like your daughter, you probably didn't find out why you made mistakes, did you?"

"No, I didn't."

"So what did you learn?"

"What do you mean?"

"Well, let me see if I can explain it. My biggest complaint about the educational system is that students are not taught how to learn from mistakes. They are conditioned to believe mistakes are bad. In real learning, however, mistakes are essential. A person rarely has the right answer the first time around, so learning is accomplished through trial and error.

"When you learned to ride a bicycle, did you just get on and ride away, or did you fall off a few times before conquering the problem of balance? I know I had my share of skinned knees, but boy, was it worth the pain! Learning to ride greatly expanded my world. I didn't have to memorize anything, either. I knew how to ride or I didn't. Learning that way was frustrating, but also exhilarating. And that's what learning is—it's exciting and you want to learn more. Once you truly learn something, your world expands and you feel great!

"If you walk into a classroom today I doubt you'll find much excitement. Too often you only find boredom and fear. Students are bored because the excitement of learning has been excised from school. Creative thinking, curiosity for more knowledge and the exhilaration of discovering something new no longer exist. The old is still being crammed down their throats. In addition, many students suffer from stress associated with the drive to be right all the time. They are driven not by the excitement of learning but the fear of being wrong. Education has become a boring, fear-driven process that deadens minds instead of breathing life into them.

"Do you remember sitting in class afraid to answer a question because you feared being ridiculed if you were wrong?"

Glen nodded. "I even remember trying to hide because I was so afraid of not knowing the right answers. But I'm not sure I understand why that happens." He thought for a moment. "You know, what I'm beginning to realize is that I was so afraid of being wrong that I began to blindly accept any answer that an authority told me I should learn. I think I just stopped questioning what things really meant. I learned to give the teachers back what they wanted."

"Unfortunately, we don't leave those old habits in the classroom," I reflected. "Most of us take them right out into adult life."

"So, are you saying that this fear of being wrong still runs me as an adult? Do you mean that it is this fear that prevents me from achieving personal happiness and financial success? And that it is also this fear that is holding my family back?"

"That's right. And your children are in school seeking right answers because they are taught if they get good grades and don't make waves, they will find secure jobs and be happy. Our whole society has been brainwashed into believing only right answers matter. Anything other than a right answer is wrong, and 'wrong' is 'stupid.' And who wants to be called stupid?

"Education leaves out the crucial process of questioning what you don't know. Do you remember ever being taught that it's not what you know but what you don't know that's important? Only when you find out something you don't know will you gain knowledge. To punish people for making mistakes actually prevents them from gaining knowledge. Learning is simply a process of making mistakes, finding out what you don't know and correcting."

Our educational system would teach riding a bicycle by lecturing on the subject for fifty hours, giving a written test and then punishing any student with a bad grade for falling off on his first try! This is backwards thinking. It leaves students exactly at that point where real learning begins—where they have discovered what they don't know, and where they can begin using their own resources to figure out how to correct their mistakes and grow from them.

When schools teach the belief that mistakes are wrong, we end up robbing students of the skills they need to gain more knowledge. We rob them of both the frustration and the exhilaration that accompany true learning. In the end, is it any wonder that fear, boredom and blind memorization rule supreme in our schools?

When we study the world's greatest achievers, the artists, scientists, businesspeople, musicians and writers who have made a real contribution to our lives, we find their lives were filled with mistakes. But they learned from those mistakes, then continued to make some more and learn from them, too. Thomas Edison, for example, was no stranger to mistakes. Branded as retarded, he was actually kicked out of school. Later in his life, after many failed attempts to invent the light bulb, he was accused of failing 9,999 times. His reply: "I did not fail 9,999 times. I successfully found out what did not work 9,999 times." And out of all those failures, I might add, he discovered what did work. History tells the rest of the story. Edison went on to become a wealthy entrepreneur whose inventions make our lives a little easier, inventions which perhaps never would have happened if he had been afraid of making mistakes and learning from them.

Avoiding mistakes makes us stupid, and having to be right all the time makes us obsolete. When I finally discovered that I learned more by making mistakes than by having the right answers all the time, I set out to perfect the art of making more mistakes faster. I no longer even think of it as making mistakes any longer; rather, they are "learning experiences," or "taps on the shoulder," alerting us to the fact that there's something we are missing and must further explore.

One of the most important teachers I ever had was R. Buckminster Fuller.* "Bucky," as his friends called him, was sometimes known as "the planet's friendly genius." He was an architect, mathematician, author, designer, cosmologist, scientist, inventor, philosopher. He invented the geodesic dome, coined the term "spaceship earth," developed the concept of synergetics, and was known the world over for his creative contributions to our thinking and the technology of the future.

* Please see note at the end of this chapter.

He had also been a dismal failure in school, finding the educational process frustrating and limited.

I had the privilege of studying with Bucky and got to know him quite well. It was he who taught me about "taps on the shoulder" and "getting hit by Mack trucks." If for some reason we ignore the first gentle "taps," signalling us to change something in our lives or expand our knowledge, the tap may escalate, getting harder and harder until it becomes a Mack truck, threatening to run us down. Some people have a lot of Mack trucks in their lives, but when they look a little closer they nearly always find that those Mack trucks came along only after they'd been ignoring the subtler taps for a long period of time.

I was 32 when I encountered my first Mack truck. I discovered money missing from our company and I brought up the subject in a meeting. One of my partners said he would look into it. I had a funny feeling about it but ignored that early message, that little tap on the shoulder.

I continued to keep an eye on the money but could no longer detect anything missing. Yet I still didn't feel right about something. It wasn't long before I discovered what was going on. The partner who'd taken on the responsibility of looking into the missing funds had done that, all right. He had taken my request as a signal to do a better job of covering his own tracks. In the end, he ran off with the money and the company folded.

For a year or more I blamed my ex-partner. I called him every bad name in the book and was convinced that the whole thing was his fault. I swore I would never have another partner. I was absolutely convinced that I could trust nobody but myself. I lived with these feelings for a long time, and doing so was extremely uncomfortable. And then one day it dawned on me that as long as I blamed my old partner, or anyone else, I would never be able to learn anything from what had happened.

So I asked myself what it was I didn't know that had allowed someone to steal from my company. I sat for hours, reflecting on my upset. Suddenly, the lights came on and I realized two things:

1. I needed to use my intuition more. I had known in my gut that my partner was dishonest but I had never had the courage to confront him. Instead, I just took a nice guy approach and hoped things would work out. Today I trust my gut feelings, my intuition. I

choose partners with whom I feel completely comfortable having open, honest discussions. Trust is everything—worth the search or the long building process, no matter how long it takes.

2. I realized that even though I'd taken accounting classes, I had only a textbook knowledge. I knew that if I was to be successful in business I had to learn more. I hired an accountant from a Big Eight firm who taught me accounting not simply from textbooks but from applications in real life.

These two corrections alone increased my ability as a businessperson and have been worth literally millions of dollars to me.

No doubt, the most valuable lesson I learned from that mistake was that I really didn't want any more Mack trucks in my life. I'd act when I felt the gentle tap on my shoulder from then on. Now I pay very close attention to my mistakes, and to mistakes that other people around me make. Each time I start learning sooner, I get the lesson more quickly and everything runs much more smoothly in my life.

But don't get me wrong; I'm no saint. Each time I make a mistake I still get upset. And my initial reaction is still to blame other people, make excuses, try to justify what's gone wrong, or simply ignore the fact that a mistake has been made. This first reflex of denial seems to be a deeply ingrained human response. I'm not sure I can ever feel good about making mistakes, but I know that it is possible to change how we respond to them. I have made learning from my mistakes easier on myself by having friends who enjoy laughing at me when I screw up. They have all learned to ask me, "What have you learned from this?"

I do the same for them. I remember my friend and teacher, Marshall Thurber, telling me that "all upsets are opportunities to learn something." A child learning to walk takes a step, falls down and begins to cry. The child is certainly upset by each fall. Learning can be frustrating. What we aren't taught in school is that this frustration is part of learning and should be looked upon in a positive way, not a negative one. Our children are learning that falling down (making mistakes) is not cool, so they should avoid doing so at all costs. As a result, millions of people are adopting the belief that "looking good" and not making mistakes is the only way to go. Well, they might be looking good, but they sure aren't going anywhere. Our corporations are filled with people like that, people who learn how to run the treadmill with the least amount of energy. How can you learn if you are afraid of making mistakes? What can you gain if you never risk? That's why good, intelligent people grow numb and stagnate in their jobs.

A few years ago, it seemed that our society was having a great purge of religious figures, politicians and bankers who had cheated the public in one way or another. Every time we turned on the television there was more news about someone's trial. As I sat and watched the news every day I was amazed that even the people who admitted being guilty continued to insist that they had been right. One person even voiced his lifelong motto, "Never make a mistake."

Likewise, in education, we make being right so superior to being wrong that people become rigid and self-righteous about it, living their whole lives in fear of ever being proved wrong. In today's world being wrong has become a worse "sin" than cheating the nation's taxpayers out of millions of dollars or violating our constitutional laws!

Bucky Fuller once said, "A mistake is only a sin when not admitted." He believed that a mistake was one of God's ways of saying, "You don't know everything." He also contended that when humans admitted to making mistakes they were then closest to God, or "The Great Spirit" as he preferred to say it.

When we can say, "I screwed up," instead of insisting above all that we are right, people are willing to extend more sympathy to us. Perhaps one of the toughest lessons we have to learn is that only people who do nothing don't make mistakes! Thus, knowing how to make mistakes may well be one of the most valuable lessons we can learn for traveling the road to success.

Sitting down with my friend Glen that day was at least as valuable for me as it was for him. It gave me the opportunity to put into words some of the lessons I'd received from my own teachers over the years—most of them people like Bucky Fuller and others from the U. of H.K. (University of Hard Knocks). At one point during our visit, however, I started worrying that perhaps I had gotten a little carried away with myself. I almost expected Glen to be dozing off. But instead, his eyes were bright and I could see something there I hadn't seen before: his anger building.

"So what can I do so that my children don't end up afraid to make mistakes?" he asked. "I don't want them to wind up like me."

I understood what he was asking and I could empathize with his anger, but I also didn't want him to give up on himself. I told him, "I believe it is important, first, for the parent to be an example. Be the model for what you want your children to become. Encourage them to understand that the only way to progress in life is to learn new things, and that new things can be learned only by making mistakes, through trial and error.

"The difference between a rich professional golfer and an amateur is the number of balls they've hit. In sports, mistakes and correction are called practice. Any way you can lessen your children's fear of making mistakes would benefit them.

"Or, as one of my wiser teachers once told me, 'If something is worth doing at all, it's worth doing poorly.' In other words, action, correction, perfection! I believe we need to teach our children to be more like Columbus — to question conventional wisdom and risk making mistakes — otherwise they will never know what is out there or how far they can go."

I sometimes wonder how many millions of people get stuck in jobs for most of their adult lives, wondering what happened to those early dreams they might have had. They follow all the rules of the educational system, and things don't turn out as they thought they would. They study hard, make good grades and secure a good job after college. But now they feel trapped and unhappy, emotionally, professionally and financially defunct.

If I were asked how to build a brand new kind of educational system, one that would truly prepare people to be successful and happy in life, I'd say build it around making mistakes. I don't know of any more valuable single lesson than that in the world. I sometimes laughingly tell my own students that they get a Master's Degree in the science of making mistakes. The ability to make mistakes and learn from them really is a science, and I'm glad I've studied it.

Education needs to emphasize the rewards that can be found in making mistakes. Mistakes show initiative. They are proof that we are sincere about learning instead of merely echoing back answers memorized from a book or from a teacher's lecture. They are proof that we aren't trapped in doing nothing because we're afraid of being wrong.

I am not trapped in a dead-end job, and in fact I am financially independent, because I made more mistakes than most people do, not because I instantly had more right answers than anyone else.

Far too many people are leading lives in which their real potential is never discovered, never put into action. They look back and mourn lives of unfulfilled dreams because "don't make mistakes" is the only lesson they ever learned in school.

Ask yourself this: "What dreams of mine have gone unfulfilled because I was afraid of failing?" And then get ready to change all that, recognizing that a life of unfulfilled dreams is hardly worth living. You can change all that and fulfill even your wildest dreams if you are willing to unlearn some of those early lessons that are presently holding you back.

***About R. Buckminster Fuller**

R. Buckminster Fuller, known by many as "the planet's friendly genius," and perhaps one of the best known American thinkers of the 20th century, was an architect, mathematician, author, designer, cosmologist, scientist, inventor, and philosopher. He coined the term "spaceship Earth," developed the World Game, invented Synergetics, created the geodesic dome, and was recognized throughout the world for his creative contributions to technology and the future. Many people predict that by the year 2000 he will be placed alongside Einstein, Copernicus and Newton for his tremendous contribution to the well-being of humanity and our planet.

3

What Do You Want To Be When You Grow Up?

I don't like work—no man does—but I like what is in work—the chance to find yourself. Your own reality—for yourself, not for others—what no other man can ever know.

—Joseph Conrad (1902)

A few years ago I was at a dinner party with about twenty-five people. At about nine o'clock, the hosts' ten-year-old son came downstairs to say good night. After a few questions about hobbies and schooling, one guest asked him, "So what do you want to be when you grow up?"

The young boy smiled and said, "I want to be like Tom Cruise and be a Navy fighter pilot." The guest said, "Oh, good!" But another said, "Oh, Billy, you don't want to be that. Don't you want to be a doctor like your Uncle Ted? You know, doctors make a lot of money. That's why Uncle Ted has a big house and lots of cars..."

But the boy knew his own mind. "I want to be a fighter pilot."

"Are you sure? It's an awfully dangerous job and doesn't pay that well. If you get good grades in school and study hard you could become a doctor and be wealthy."

The boy began to look confused. "Well, okay," he said, "I'll think about becoming a doctor." Then he ran off to bed.

I thought back to when I was a kid and remembered that I had based my career dreams on fantasies, just like Billy. Our dreams are important, far more important than most of us realize. They are the core stuff that motivates us to learn and develop in our lives. Choices made only on the basis of money or status, or on somebody else's recommendation, tend to go stale for us. Halfway through the educational process to become, let's say, a doctor, we grit our teeth just to get through. We're no longer interested in learning as much as we're interested in getting to the end so that we can start reaping the rewards. If we have had the courage to risk pursuing our dreams, they sustain and motivate us even through the toughest of times.

But I am the first to admit that dreams change. Will Billy always want to be a pilot? Maybe someday he will be as motivated to become a doctor as he presently is to be a Navy pilot. If it's true that our dreams change, how do we educate the Billys and the Barbaras of the world? What should we teach Billy so that he could, in his lifetime, be both Navy pilot and doctor and perhaps enter a few other professions along the way? Let us see if my own story won't provide us with some clues.

I imagine I was a lot like Billy at his age. I read books about men who went to sea in wooden ships, sailed from port to port around the world and returned to tell stories of their fascinating adventures. I read Joseph Conrad, Herman Melville and Richard Henry Dana. I dreamed of those faraway exotic islands in the Orient and the Pacific.

At 15, when my guidance counselor asked me what I wanted to do when I left high school, I naturally told her I wanted to be a sailor. She replied, "Wouldn't you like to make a more appropriate career decision?"

I got the message. She was basically telling me to wise up. But I stuck to my decision and told her I really wanted to be a sailor. I said I wanted to travel to faraway ports, to sail wooden ships to Tahiti. I wanted to have beautiful maidens paddle out in their war canoes with nothing on but flower leis yelling, "Hi, sailor!" I told her those were the dreams of my life. Realistic or not, that's what I wanted to do when I left high school.

"Well," she said, looking disgusted, "you don't have very high aspirations, do you, young man?"

"No, I don't," I replied resolutely, half smiling, "but it sure would be a lot of fun."

Her next response surprised me. "Okay," she said, "if you really want to be a sailor, why not be the best?" She pulled out a book listing schools that trained people to be sailors who would also earn decent salaries.

Well, the world seemed to open up for me. For the first time in my life I had a purpose for studying. Even though my advisor had informed me that I would have to face some pretty big hurdles along the way (for example, to become a ship's officer you had to get a congressional nomination to enter some of the most highly selective schools in the U.S.) I didn't get discouraged. And in 1964, I received two nominations: one to the U.S. Merchant Marine Academy in Kings Point, New York, another to the U.S. Naval Academy in Annapolis, Maryland. I accepted the Kings Point nomination.

However, following graduation, and at the age of 22, I had fulfilled my childhood dream. I had sailed a tanker into Tahiti and had met the beautiful natives. Even though I was being paid a tremendous amount of money, and doing the thing I'd always dreamed of doing, I was bored. The problem was that the only thing I could do was what my training had prepared me to do: be a ship's third mate. Without knowing it, I had become a specialist, unemployable except in that single job area. I would have to get training in another profession if I wished to be paid the kind of money I was already making.

As a result, I decided to follow another childhood fantasy, to become an airplane pilot. Off I went, joined the Marines, became a fighter pilot and went to Vietnam. I loved flying, was paid miserably and probably enjoyed combat more than most pilots ever do. But when I came back in 1973, I again found I was a specialist. I had very special skills which gave me only two choices: I could drive a ship or fly a plane. Neither one interested me anymore.

It was then that I began to realize that schools actually decrease our potential for success because of the way they are geared to specialization. And the kind of specialization we've become accustomed to in this country leads straight into career traps that rob us of our dreams and rob the world of our greatest potential.

There are literally millions of people between the ages of 28 and 45 who are grievously dissatisfied with what they are doing. The attraction they may once have felt for their careers has faded, or they have gone as far as they can go on that particular career path and feel they're at a dead end. This dissatisfaction is the reason so many people make career changes in mid-life. The problem with changing careers, however, is that we lose seniority. It's just like starting all over again, even though we have other experience that we will apply to our new career.

Studies show that the average person will make at least five career changes in his or her lifetime. Given that this is so, why does our society require kids to specialize so early in their lives? Part of the answer lies in the fact that we are still running our educational system as if it were serving an agrarian society. And we are designing our educational programs as if the average life-expectancy was only 40 years or so; few would argue that with the shorter lifespan we would have little need for more more than one career. Besides, in that agrarian society, there weren't many career choices available. A person really didn't have to know much to get through his or her life.

For children today, who may work as many as 60 years, the idea of specializing is ridiculous. As R. Buckminster Fuller said, "Overspecialization leads to extinction." We need an educational system which teaches general principles that would be transferable to any specialized profession. This would permit people to switch careers with an absolute minimum of retraining.

In 1973 when I left the Marines, I wasn't interested in developing another specialty as much as I wanted to become a generalist. As a generalist I knew I would need broad skills such as sales, accounting, marketing, finance and production in order to be better prepared to handle changes in the future. I didn't want to make a decision that would narrow my future growth as I had done in the past.

One thing I had discovered as a specialist was that every career advancement meant that I would have to become more specialized. Although sometimes advantageous, that road also becomes narrower, limiting our options. If I were a dentist, for example, and wanted to make more money, one option would be to specialize in orthodontics.

One area that makes the world go around is business. While I realized that the world of business had negative connotations in some circles, the more I thought about it the more I realized that every home is a business. Money comes in and money goes out. A church or a charity is a business. Government is a very large business. In fact, I can't think of anything that isn't a business in some way. Like it or not, our contemporary world runs on money, production, sales, marketing, finance and accounting.

So my decision in 1973 was to become a generalist in business. I began choosing jobs not for the amount of money I could earn, but for what I could learn. When I left the Marine Corps, I decided that I wanted to learn what for me was the hardest aspect of business: sales, since I am basically a shy person who has very little tolerance for rejection.

I researched several companies, searching for the one with the best sales training program. Eventually I selected a multi-national corporation which also marketed its sales training package as a separate product. I should mention that at this point in my life I felt that salespeople were the scum of the earth. I had grown up in academic circles and had been taught that salespeople were unethical, immoral and would do anything for a dollar. The picture I had was of a man wearing patent leather shoes and dressed in a polyester suit, selling used cars. I had a lot of personal prejudices to overcome!

The first lesson I learned was that there isn't much in the world today that doesn't involve sales. A teacher in front of a classroom is selling ideas, curriculum and learning. A minister sells religion or God. And a mother is constantly trying to sell her child on better behavior. Similarly, managers of large companies are selling whenever they attempt to motivate their employees.

What I realized was that the more competent a person is in sales, the easier one's entire life becomes.

Not long ago, my postman complained to me that he didn't earn enough money. He knew I taught businesspeople and asked me what I thought he should do. I suggested that if he didn't want to go back to school he should find a job in sales. He said, "I hate salespeople. I'd never be one." I told him he already was selling his time to deliver mail. His response, "Yeah, yeah, but that's not the same. Salespeople are crooks." In the end, that limited attitude kept him and his family at their present income plateau.

I'm not sure where people get the idea salespeople are bad. Perhaps it is because the stereotype of the seedy, aggressive, used car salesman offers such an entertaining image for the media and popular sitcoms. But to get stuck with those stereotypes can be greatly limiting. We project these limited beliefs onto the whole profession even when every one of us, nearly every day of our lives, seeks the help of salespeople every time we purchase a product or service.

The important point here is that professional sales work epitomizes the kinds of skills that are applicable in virtually every career position. I have known people who are doctors, lawyers, teachers, heads of large corporations, even psychotherapists, ministers and rabbis who say that their early sales experiences were perhaps the most valuable schooling of their lives. Their years as salespeople taught them how to talk with people, how to pace their energies and their time, how to meet people and get important points across quickly, effectively and persuasively.

Don't misunderstand me. I am not saying our educational system should encourage everyone to go into business and sales. What I am suggesting is that there are skills, like those of the salesperson, which are applicable in a variety of jobs and professions. Let's look at these careers as models for educating the generalist. Rather than encouraging young people to become specialists right away, wouldn't it make sense to establish a program which educates them to do their very best in whatever career they choose? Let's teach people to communicate well with other people, to motivate, to manage their own and other people's time, and to be able to employ their reasoning skills, their creativity, and all their personal resources in a variety of ways. The human mind is a miracle of adaptability when we know how to employ its capacities broadly instead of narrowly.

Education of the sort I have in mind would open all our horizons tremendously, instead of narrowing them. Whether we are children or adults, a generalist's education can help us grow in any direction we choose, at any time in our lives. With the world changing as fast as it presently does, specialization is dangerous. How could we possibly prepare ourselves for a future that we can't even imagine? We all need to keep in mind that education is a lifetime learning process and that it doesn't end when you leave high school or college.

In my own life, what I learned through my years in sales has been invaluable, but it was also one of the toughest educational challenges I ever faced. I started out, as most people do, afraid of sales because I believed I could never stand to be rejected, something that happens over and over again in this profession. Rejection goes with the turf. I began working door-to-door, one of the toughest of all sales positions. I went to every sales seminar that came to town. It took two years of being a blundering idiot, making very little money and struggling, until I finally caught on. Then it became easy. Next, I got good at it—really good at it. It was just like learning to ride a bicycle. When I at last got the hang of it, the world opened up to me. No matter where I went, I became valuable, since almost every company needs a good salesperson. I found my income was directly related to my skills, that is, my ability to sell my product. For the first time in my life I felt truly free because I knew I could go virtually anywhere and get money in exchange for my skills. I cannot begin to describe what a liberating feeling that was.

Today I own an educational company. When people ask what I do, I answer that I am a teacher. In reality, I think of myself as a generalist first. Secondly, I am a teacher since this is just one of the professions where I can apply my skills. I could just as well answer that I am a businessperson, an administrator, a speaker, a manager...the list could go on and on because I am all of these, thanks to my education as a generalist.

A Global Perspective of the Generalist

We in the United States would do well to look at how other countries view the issue of specialist versus generalist. Few countries in the world emphasize specialization as much as we do, and I would argue that this emphasis is at the root of many of our present economic problems. When Japanese companies train people for executive positions, they put much less emphasis than we do on their previous educational background. For example, I met a young "fast tracker" coming up in a large Japanese company. His formal education was in languages (French), not business. This surprised me, and I probed to find out more. He said that within 10 years he would probably be president of the company.

The young man told me that his company first looks for people who have social graces and can learn quickly. Then the company spends 14 years training that person in every aspect of the business. When this person finally takes over, he or she has hands-on experience in virtually every operation in the company. This is true generalization, a far cry from the kind of specialization we find in most American companies of today. In most American companies, managers are hired from MBA programs in the top universities, with little or no hands-on experience. Rarely is a new person diversified and competent in departments outside his or her own. The skills of the generalist are not even recognized in most cases.

So what do our colleges and universities presently offer the person who wants to be a generalist? Long ago, a degree in liberal arts was intended to serve that role. But it certainly doesn't today. In most universities, the liberal arts program is little more than a smorgasbord of specialties, offered like a huge banquet so that undecided students can get a taste of a variety of possibilities. And in all too many cases, the liberal arts programs offer only academic background, providing no practical skills whatsoever.

Becoming a Ph.D. Generalist

Do you feel trapped because you are too specialized? Do you know how to get out of your present job and into something new without giving up too much?

My suggestion is to begin looking for jobs where you can learn, not just earn. Commit a number of years of your life to increasing your generalized skills in business as well as in whatever specialized skills you may presently have. Specialists must work for generalists unless the specialist is also a generalist.

Today, if you're an adult, you're probably going to have to create your own program for becoming a generalist. But perhaps that is as it should be, since knowing ourselves and knowing where we need to grow is one of the most important skills of the generalist. The world is filled with opportunities ranging from free lectures at colleges and local service clubs to jobs that offer training in areas that will expand your skills.

Along the way, we can pass our lessons on to the younger generations, either by just being models for them or by actually going into the schools and helping to make some changes. Hopefully, this book will help you accomplish either or both.

4

My Child Is Doing Fine

The biggest problem is education.

—R. BUCKMINSTER FULLER

I was listening to a colleague of mine at a company board meeting. He was saying:

"I think the educational system is great. I enjoyed school and did well. My son is just like me. He loves it and is at the top of his class. Some university is going to be lucky to get him. His future is very bright. I don't understand why people are complaining so much. I think the education system is doing an excellent job."

"But what about the kids who aren't doing well in school?" I asked. "What about the children who drop out? What will happen to the children of these children? And what about the kids who will not have your son's opportunities?"

"That's not my problem," he said coldly. I felt like leaping across the table to choke him.

As I travel the world speaking about educational reform, I run into people who staunchly defend the current system.

"Leave the system alone," they say. "I did well and my kids are doing just fine. The teachers in our school district are the best."

To questions concerning the welfare of less fortunate students, the responses can be very disheartening: "That is just the way things are." "I can't help it if there are kids who are not as smart as mine." "Talk to the parents of the kids who aren't doing so well, not us." "What do you expect me to do about it?"

However, the most disturbing underlying message is one that is always quite clear: "Leave us alone. It's not my problem and don't you tell me it is."

What has shocked me over the years is the oversight, the callousness, the ignorance, the apathy, the blind disregard and the lack of awareness by many adults who defend the system. We are all overjoyed when we find children who like to learn and who do well in the current system. Many of us who are doing well today survived and even learned from the system as it is today. Unfortunately, that's not true for the majority of people.

When I meet people who want the system to stay the same, I ask them the following questions: "What will it take for you to realize that education is everyone's problem? Which of the following problems, the roots of which are education-based, will it take for you to wake up and begin to care about others?"

1. How many homeless adults and children will it take to realize that you and I have a stake in making our educational system work for everyone?

2. How many people losing their jobs, after years of dedicated service, will it take to realize that something is missing in our present curriculum?

3. Have you ever experienced the emotional turmoil that kids go through when someone in the family is laid off? This, too, is a product of the ills in education today.

4. Will it take a burglar breaking into your home for you to realize that we have an increasing problem with desperate people turning to crime for economic survival?

5. How much more in taxes are you willing to pay in order to build more jails? Do you realize that jails only mass-produce more criminals?

6. How many more jails will it take for you to realize that it is not the prison system that is breaking down, but that our society and educational system are failing us? Do you realize that the largest-growing sector of government employment is prison guards? What does that say about our society?

7. How many adults and children taking drugs will it take to show that people are unhappy and lonely deep down inside, and that much of this could be remedied by education?
8. What will happen to people who cannot afford medical benefits?
9. How many people who cannot afford respectable retirement years will it take before we act?
10. How high will we let the national debt rise before we start teaching our kids what is causing it and what we can do to change our government?
11. How much of our best real estate are we going to let foreigners buy before we realize that education can play an important role in teaching us to value our own communities above easy profits or being a slave to our own greed?
12. Who will your children work for? Will your children be fulfilled?
13. While foreign-owned companies provide jobs, to which country do the profits flow?
14. How many families are torn apart by arguments over money, arguments that would never occur if their schools had delivered on what should be the first priority: to teach people how to be economically secure in this society?
15. What do children learn when parents fight over money?
16. Although you did well in school or your child is doing well in school, have you ever counted the number of children that the system is failing, even if they remain in school?
17. Do you have any idea what goes through a child's mind at the age of seven when an adult classifies him or her as "not as smart as?" Have you ever thought about how that must feel, or about how many years the child carries that emotional scar around, or about what effect that must have over a lifetime?
18. How many dreams are crushed and forgotten in school when a child learns that only the "smart students" get showered with attention?
19. How many geniuses are lost because they are forced into conforming to the system or are forced out of the system? What is the price

of that for all of us? How many new inventions or patents will our businesses miss out on?

20. Must the problems land directly on our own doorsteps before we can care?
21. If our educational system is a reflection of who we are as a society, what does that tell us about ourselves?

A Story for Our Time

At the risk of sounding immodest, I'd like to share with you some of the early educational experiences which motivated me to write this book.

On a hot August day in 1965, I entered the U.S. Merchant Marine Academy at Kings Point, New York, one hour outside of Manhattan. At 18 years of age, this was one of the proudest moments of my life. To be accepted into this school I had to be nominated by a U.S. Senator, as well as have a physical evaluation, take several competitive exams and pass personal interviews. There were only two students from the entire state of Hawaii who were allowed to enter this school each year. Only men were allowed into the academy in those days. (That has since changed.)

Administrators paraded around in bright white, starched naval uniforms. We were all welcomed into the school auditorium. The administrators were very polite to the new entering class and their parents. We were told we were the finest our country had to offer. For every one student accepted, over three hundred had applied. Punch and cookies were served while guests were escorted around the beautiful grounds of the school. Soon it was time for the parents and guests to leave. We said our good-byes. The party was over.

The upperclassmen soon mustered us into groups. I do not know how we got into these groups, but I guess we just responded to our names being yelled out by a person a year older than we. Standing in the hot sun in my civilian clothes, sweat seeping through my sport coat, I began to wonder what I had gotten myself into. I remember hearing someone standing somewhere behind me say, "When does the fun start?" Immediately another voice responded, "Hell is just about to begin."

We were soon marched to the school's barber shop where we received our new hairstyles. The special that day was called the "bald look," and considering that the Beatles were the current rage, the haircut was a little tough to accept. I knew that getting a date with a girl was going to be a challenge—not only because I had no hair, but because the war in Vietnam was just becoming unpopular. Needless to say, men in uniform weren't being fought over by young women.

The next stop was the basement. My section of 30 men was lined up under the boiler pipes at what is called the "brace" position. This meant your back flat against the concrete wall, chin on your chest, eyes straight ahead and no moving. The August heat was bad enough, but the stuffiness and the heat of the basement made it worse. We stood there for what seemed like hours. I could sense people beginning to wobble and I was sure I was hallucinating. Our upperclassman section leader just paced silently in front of us, glaring into our faces, demanding that we not look at him. Standing nose to nose, he would say, "Don't look at me, mister."

I remember feeling perspiration running down my legs as I did my best to unfocus my eyes. What made it worse was that his breath was bad and my socks were wet.

After a long silent pause, our section leader yelled out, "Eyes left." We all responded immediately. "Eyes right." We snapped our heads to the right. There I was, staring at the back of two hairless heads of two strangers. "Eyes front." I returned to staring forward at a hostile-looking section leader in a hot, stuffy, barren basement.

"The chances are, gentlemen, that come graduation day, two out of three of you will not be here." He was almost right. Four years later only a little over half of us graduated. The others had gradually disappeared over the years.

One cold winter's day in 1968, I looked out of my third-story window and watched my best friend and roommate walk slowly across the mustering square, bags in hand. Ed was much smarter than I was and was more able to grasp many of the mathematical and engineering courses we had to study. He would explain our calculus problems with a depth of natural comprehension that would leave me with my jaw hanging open. But he "choked" on tests If you do not know what "choke" means, just ask a golfer who has missed an easy shot due to emotional pressure. In our last few months as roommates, I sensed that

Ed's spirit had been crushed and I felt like I was watching a person slowly die. When he was put on academic probation, the panic set in. We would sit and study together, but the more he worried, the worse he would do. He could explain everything to me, yet he could not do it for himself on the test. I would "cram," pass, and immediately forget while he comprehended, "choked," and was eventually dismissed from school.

We were a military school. After each quarter's grades were posted, our section would line up in formation and one student would read off the grades. Some students cheered and others cried. We all knew that those who were expelled were often drafted and sent to Vietnam. While this was great incentive to do well, the failure rate was still high. But it wasn't because we didn't study. And it wasn't because we didn't want to do well. Nor was it because all of us weren't smart. After all, the admissions standards are some of the most difficult in the nation. No, it was because failure is designed into the system. Does failure have to be part of the system? No. Failure is part of the system only because it is the motivation used to educate. And it is this very same system that we send our children into today, whether it's a military school or the neighborhood public school down the street.

Children don't fail. It is the system that fails because it requires that a certain percentage of children must do poorly every year, year-in and year-out, starting the moment they enter kindergarten. When someone is proud of the fact that they did well in school, we need to start asking, "How many others had to fail so that you could feel good?" When parents brag that their child is smart, we need to ask a similar question. "How many kids are at home right now feeling miserable because your kid is doing well? How many kids are beginning to give up hope for their futures right now? How many kids think they aren't smart? How many kids are thinking, 'what's the use, I can't make it anyway?' How would you feel if we stacked the deck, put your child in a class with the most gifted kids in the nation and then ranked performance?"

Some parents will respond by saying, "Well, that's life. There are winners and losers. Better prepare these kids young."

No one can seriously argue that life is fair or that the real world is not harsh. Yet why not make it our duty as adults to provide the best environment for as long as possible so that children can grow strong mentally, spiritually, emotionally and physically? Children of today must confront the "real world" far sooner than you and I did. What effect does that have? Should we expose them earlier or protect them longer?

Spend a little time with young children who are doing well in our schools today and you'll discover that most of them are very proud of the fact that they are excelling. Certainly there's nothing wrong with excelling; it's a wonderful feeling to accomplish things and know you're doing well. But within the school setting, excelling doesn't just mean doing your best; it means doing better than somebody else. The measure of success comes not from each person's accomplishments so much as from other's failures. Perhaps it seems like a subtle difference until we dig a little deeper.

In my travels I have visited schools and asked the kids who are at the tops of their classes to tell me a little about the kids who aren't doing quite so well. Those top kids begin to fidget, obviously uncomfortable with the answer. It is apparent they don't like to think about it. Most just skip over the subject or make light of it, sensing something is wrong but not understanding exactly what it is. They just know that something doesn't feel quite right.

In our current system of education, we are teaching children that the weak become the pawns and victims of the powerful. Built into our system is a belief (and this is an important part of the hidden curriculum) that if I am to succeed there must be some sacrificial lambs. Others must fail for me to make it. This belief system is so ingrained in all our minds, beginning from the day we enter kindergarten, that it is difficult even to imagine a different way of thinking.

Because this system is based on fear, students learn to prey upon each other. Instead of the strong standing up for the weak, we teach our children to turn their backs on those who do not do well. The current system teaches us that the goal of education is getting good grades or high scores on a test. Within the system that goal becomes more important than love, friendship, loyalty, trust or even one's own personal dignity. Our children are taught that personal survival is of greater value than personal ethics. We teach children to succumb to this tyranny by committing all these little atrocities that we, as a society, have come to accept as permissible. These little atrocities become habits that students carry with them into adulthood. Often without giving it a second thought, we nourish the system that is ultimately bringing us all to our knees.

Jerry B. Harvey, author of *The Abilene Paradox*, develops this idea by giving us a quick tour of history. He points out, for example, that during the early days of World War II, Winston Churchill warned the other countries of Europe of the fate that awaited them if they did not stand up to Hitler. Many countries simply wanted to appease Hitler. Churchill said, "Each one hopes that if he feeds the crocodile enough, that the crocodile will eat him last. All hope that the storm will pass before their turn comes to be devoured."

The day I read these words I immediately recalled my own school experiences. I remembered that when I was in school, I rarely studied because I knew there were a lot of others who weren't as "smart" as me. I had joined the party feeding the crocodiles, feeding fellow students and friends whose "failures" became the foundation for my success. It was difficult to admit, but I was discovering that I had been following the same kind of belief system that Harvey describes in his book.

After psychiatrists interviewed Adolf Eichmann prior to his trial, they found him to seem "normal" and to have a desirable attitude towards his family, relatives and friends. A minister who visited him regularly found that he was a man with positive ideals. It seems that Eichmann was not, in person, the madman people made him out to be. What's more, it was discovered that no one, not a single relative, friend or fellow officer ever confronted him on the morality of his actions. No one stood up to him. He is quoted as saying, "Not a single person came to me and reproached me for anything in the performance of my duties."

The example of Eichmann is an extreme one, of course, since he fed some of the most heinous and perverse crocodiles in all of human history. But how many of us are equally guilty of supporting a system whose evils, though much subtler, are still a very destructive element in our society?

Both Eichmann and Hitler would not have had the power to do what they did had they failed to rally the cooperation of the German people and, in a few rare instances, the Jews who conspired against their own people to save their own hides. Many of the German people who were against Hitler from the start committed sins of omission by remaining silent out of fear.

Our modern corporate world has its own Eichmanns who find it easy, given what they've been taught, to do their jobs. They are the necessary "ax-people," usually the most eager corporate ladder climbers who, under the direction of the CEO, execute the weakest workers in the organization. Joe the ax-man is told, "Profits are down and we need to let a fifth of our workers go. If you do a good job, I'll make sure your division gets extra funds for the next quarter. That will really make you shine in the company. You'll be at the top of the ladder sooner than you think. Just make sure the blood-letting is quick and quiet. We don't want any adverse publicity." So with visions of a promotion to a vice-presidency dancing in his head, Joe slaughters friends and fellow workers alike.

Why doesn't Joe stop and ask, "Isn't there another way?" Because he knows that questioning his superiors is not the way he will get to the top of the ladder. And he also knows that for him to get to the top rungs somebody ahead of him has to get knocked off. Wherever people subscribe to this Eichmann mentality, it is every man for himself. "Doing well" in such a world means doing it at somebody else's expense. The trouble is that the expense is never just the other guy's; we all pay the price. In 1990, a friend of mine who consults for a large accounting firm told me the following story which illustrates this point.

In one company, my friend told me, profits were way down and the employees were given the choice between a 20 percent pay cut across the board or laying off 20 percent of the entire company. Employees voted for the reduction of the work force rather than the pay cut. After the pink slips were handed out, my friend talked with the people who'd been let go. The comment he heard most often was, "I didn't think it would happen to me!" The lesson here is that they had learned their early lessons so well that they gave no thought to the hardships "other people" would suffer as a result of their decision until they suddenly discovered that they were the "other people."

In Harvey's book, he points out that during Hitler's rise to power the people of Denmark refused to be stampeded by fear. The history of this terrible time was that Hitler and Eichmann did not start out immediately murdering Jews. They started with "little atrocities" such as requiring all Jews to carry ID cards. Once they got the Jews to do that much, however, they took the next step. They required the Jews to wear arm-bands for external identification. After that was accepted, then came the murders. Strangely, millions complied, and millions of non-Jews fell in behind Hitler to target the Jews as a national threat.

When Hitler and his war machine occupied Denmark, however, the King of Denmark refused to go along with the Nazis' demands. Instead, he ordered that if Jews had to wear yellow Stars of David, then all Danes, regardless of race, had to wear them. The Danes continued to stand up to the tyranny and the Jews of Denmark were spared. The belief system that forces so many of us to sacrifice others for our own safety simply wasn't part of their thinking. The Danes valued others' lives as much as their own and were unwilling to let friends, neighbors and fellow citizens suffer.

•••

There are few of us who don't understand the lesson, and yet we continue to teach a belief system based on fear and the sacrifice of those around us for our own benefit. Is there a single person among us who doesn't already understand that no autocracy, whether in school, at work, at home, or in government, can exist unless there are subordinates willing to collude with that person? There can be no victimizers without victims. Our corporate world, upon which our civilization is so dependent, is filled with people terrified of making waves. They fearfully hold their tongues when it comes to stating their beliefs and refusing to conform...too often at the cost of violating their own personal ethics and morals. During the 1980s, when our country was being shaken to the core by the feeding frenzies of "leveraged buy outs" and "mergers and acquisitions," the raiders used money from employees' pension funds to finance their own greed. This resulted in the employees' hard-earned retirement money being legally stolen from them by "smarter"people who were driven only by greed. As a result of these greedy few, millions of men and women who believed they had planned well for their retirement now face their later years with despair. Many will be destitute, dependent on government assistance, friends, family members or continued employment to get them through.

Where does such inhumane behavior begin? Is it "human nature," the "law of the jungle," as we are often taught? The fact that whole countries like Denmark don't follow this way of life should tell us that it's not a natural course. Instead, it is a way of looking at the world and our own lives that we continue to teach through the educational system. Once we become aware of this, how can we continue to send five-year-old children into a system where the chances are great that they will get slaughtered, a little bit each day, over the next twelve years? How can we continue to send our children to a place where the system demands that some students have to fail? How can we send our children to a place where humanity is sacrificed for a grade that ultimately is a measure of nothing lasting?

In education, do some people have to fail so that others can succeed? The answer is a resounding "No! Definitely not!" Failure only occurs in education because that is how the system was designed. But since we created the system, don't we have the ability to change it?

Why don't parents and teachers stand up to this system that is set up for students to fail? Who authorizes the system to brand your child smart or slow, gifted or not gifted? Why do parents whose children aren't doing well allow them to be the "less than smart" underclass so that privileged "bright" students can look good?

Go into virtually any classroom in the country today and observe how many children are "tracked" into being good students or bad students from the day they enter. Even five-year-olds are placed in special reading groups according to their skill level. If you think that children do not realize they are in the "fast" group or the "slow" group, think again. However, in the peer society that develops in such environments, "fast" and "slow" quickly gets translated into "smart" and "dumb." How does one measure the emotional pain that slips into the subconscious and haunts children, both the high and low achievers, over their lifetimes? We cannot afford to be careless about our judgments and thoughts around children.

It is important to note at this time that there are some schools, mostly private ones, that understand the problems we are describing here. They are making strides to improve the methods by which we educate our children. Three examples are the Montessori, the Waldorf and the Rudolph Steiner methods. These three systems are doing progressive jobs of teaching. And there are others, of course.

Traditional education, however, is still set up to reward the students it deems smart while systematically weeding out the undesirable, less intelligent, "stupid" students. It is not a system set up to educate all the people that come in to it. It is set up to look for the smartest and to educate them. That's why there are tests, grades, gifted programs, remedial programs and labels. It is a system of classifying, discriminating and segregating.

If there is a single message that we must understand from all this, it is that *the current system of education will not change until we let go of the idea that there is such a thing as a stupid human being.*

Many Native Americans use the phrase "The Great Spirit" instead of the word "God," as most religions do. I contend that The Great Spirit would not create a "stupid" human being. The concept of a stupid human being only exists in the mind as a subjective judgment, the view of an arrogant and fearful person who is not yet free of the exploitative belief system we've been describing here.

On many occasions I have presented this idea to groups and have immediately been challenged by smart, well-educated and intellectual people. I particularly remember a dialogue I had with an intellectual from a local university. He jumped up from his chair in the audience with his bearded jaw trembling. He couldn't speak fast enough to express his outrage at what I had just said.

"How dare you say that!" he bellowed. "I have my doctorate degree. What degree do you have?"

"I have a B.S. degree," I replied. "And I think B.S. quite accurately describes what it means."

"How dare you make light of the institution of education!" he shouted. "Less well-educated and less intellectual people like you should never be graduated. You give education a bad name and you have no right criticizing. You are not an accredited teaching professional. By the way, what are your credentials?"

I decided to ask a few questions. "Do you think you're more educated than I am?" I asked.

"Of course I am," he said. "I have my doctorate degree."

"Do you personally think you are smarter than me?" I asked.

With that he began to back down a little. "Yes, I do. I had very high scores on all my tests."

I then asked him if he had a car. He nodded yes.

"Do you take it to a mechanic or do you repair it yourself?"

"I don't know how to fix a car."

"Does that make you stupid in comparison to the mechanic?"

He thought for a moment. "No, not really. I guess we are both just smart in different areas. In fact, I've always been amazed at how knowledgeable my mechanic is, even though he has no degree."

I nodded my head. The professor and I smiled at one another. For a moment, at least, we were beginning to look at the subject from the same set of eyes.

During my lifetime, I have sat on the boards of a number of businesses. These boards are usually made up of people with very different backgrounds and areas of expertise. I am always impressed by how much each person knows about his or her work specialty. Yet, I have never left one of those meetings feeling stupid because someone knew more than I did. Each person simply adds something from his or her own vantage point which ensures that the whole of the company does well. It is called cooperation. Unfortunately, in too many schools this kind of cooperation is known as cheating.

As a professional instructor, I consider it extremely important to keep my personal judgments of other people to a minimum. I do my best to hold the thought that everyone in the class is smart in his or her own way. My job is to validate and encourage each person's brilliance. When I don't do that, or when I slip and start speaking to them from my own subjective point of view, I quickly notice that problems come up. When I speak from the point of view that I know more than they do, they either fight me or cave in. If I begin to treat one person as my "pet," other problems arise. Therefore, I do my best to become one of the class, someone who is on the journey of learning myself, someone who has only experiences, not answers, and someone who encourages the class to find their own answers and their own strengths.

The Great Spirit does not create stupid people though it is certainly true that each of us is smart in some ways and less smart in others. I can always find someone smarter or someone less smart if that's where my focus is. And unfortunately that's where the educational system's focus usually is. The current system eliminates the masses and focuses instead on the chosen few who learn quickly, easily and with the least challenge to their teachers. The system is judge and jury about who is smart and who isn't. What we need always to keep in mind is that it is possible to create a system that educates everyone and inspires them to learn, without judging what they are capable of and without forcing the "right" answers down their throats.

One belief in the current system of education is that the "smart" people, the students who get the best grades, are always the winners in life. But is this true? No, it isn't. In any closed system, nothing is ever only one way. If a person plays a game with a focus on winners and losers, then he or she must experience both winning and losing. As with most other things in life, the win-lose paradigm is merely a point of view.

To explore this further, let's look at sports which does have an apparent winner and loser. When I competed in the martial arts, for example, I lost many times. But each time I lost, I also learned, improved, and was soon fighting as a black belt. The problem was I had to fight other black belts and some of these guys were very frightening. There were two people I particularly dreaded fighting. And yet I also looked forward to these matches. One fighter was Charles, the other William. We were all three about the same size and weight. Each time I climbed into the ring with either one of them my heart pounded with fear. Neither of them ever smiled as we took our preliminary bows before the fight. In all the tournaments I fought against them I never won. I was always severely pounded and often had to limp away after our final bows of respect at the end of the match. Once the match was over, though, both men were always eager to stand off to the side and talk to me about the match, telling me what my weak points were, what their weak points were and the opportunities I missed in hitting them. After every match, both men willingly told me how to beat them. Our love and respect for each other grew. We all wanted everyone to get better.

That's not an experience many of us have in school. Children are required to watch quietly the gradual elimination of friends and classmates in the name of finding out who is the smartest. Students take tests alone and most often fail alone.

When I was in high school, I played on a wonderful football team. We were one of the most powerful teams in the state. We regularly beat our opponents with ease. We loved it, and the more games we won, the more excited and strong our team became. Until one game. Our coach had a personal vendetta against the coach of our rival team. I do not know what caused the rift, I just knew it was a serious one.

Before the game our coach shrieked with excitement, anticipating a "kill." He demanded that we beat the rival team as no team had ever been beaten. By halftime, the gap in the score and the mounting humiliation of our opponent were evidence enough that the game was more than over.

In the locker room, however, instead of congratulating us, our coach demanded that we "run the score up. Give them the beating of their lives, one they will never forget." We complied with cold precision.

We won that day, for sure, but our team had lost something quite valuable. A few sports writers criticized us for running up the score. We argued, calling their position sour grapes. Our coach continued to keep us pumped up about our wins and we practiced harder and continued to win. Yet, most of us knew in our hearts that we had lost something. We had sacrificed our humanity that day.

I hope it is not true that we have lost our humanity where teaching our children is concerned. We need to maintain love as the foundation of education. On a playing field, a team that cannot love its opponent is not a complete team. This does not mean that you don't do your best to beat them. It just means you never lose your love, respect and compassion for the opposing players. The best part of the game of rugby union, which I took up after my college days were over, was sitting around drinking beer with the opposing team after the game. My love and respect for those men was immense, yet it did not preclude me warning them that I would be back next Saturday to teach them a lesson...especially if I had lost the game. In sports, ideally, you may lose the game, yet you should never lose the love of the other team's players.

In China during the Cultural Revolution, hundreds of thousands of people had to receive new training all at the same time. There was new farm machinery to master. People had to learn about building new homes and farm buildings. Others had to learn folk medicine, teaching, and even parenting skills. The pressure was so great to rebuild the culture that every single person had to make a contribution—tiny children, teenagers, young adults, and even the very old. If a group of people came together to learn, for example, how to drive a tractor, the class wasn't over until every person had mastered the skill. The students who learned fast helped those who needed more time. Although there is much I might criticize about the Cultural Revolution, the slogan for this period of China's history was "Friendship first, competition second."

In modern academia everyone competes for the top grades. When the class ends, scores are totalled up and people receive either passing or failing grades. Some learn from the experience, others don't. The "losers" suffer alone in defeat...the victorious ones celebrate. You may have noticed that oftentimes the very best of academia are social introverts, brilliant within the academic system but socially lacking. They stick to themselves or with others of their kind. They are the ideal smart people that schools praise. Students like these conform well and abide by the rules. They learn early that to love and help your classmate is not allowed; it's called cheating. They avoid forming close relationships where helping a friend could mean losing their own position as the "smartest" in the class.

It is not a coincidence that many people who staunchly defend the educational system are both elitist and lonely. They seem to have a need to prove to everyone around them how smart they were in school or how many degrees they have. Having completely bought into the system, they perceive education as little more than a game of one-upmanship. When one has been so thoroughly indoctrinated by the educational system, knowledge soon takes a back seat to how many framed degrees we have on the wall, trophies that "prove" we are better than other people.

The more we learn about the infrastructure of our schools, the more we realize that there are only three basic types of people in our institutions of higher learning. First, there are those who are the pure academics. They study because they were born to study, and they love it. The second group consists of people who are in school primarily for the "piece of paper" that qualifies them for a better paying job. They attend school, get their degree, show it to an employer as proof that they have earned their right to a particular job, and thus get to work in the real world. The third group includes students who attend school and collect degrees in the hopes that the degree will give them a backbone. Of course, rarely does a diploma make up for no spine. Instead, all too many of these people hide behind their titles, seeking refuge in organizations that judge each other and the world around them according to the educational degrees they hold rather than by actual performance.

When I was in the military, I met many such people, particularly in the officer corps. For all too many officers, the only way they could get respect was by the bars worn on their uniforms, not by earning it through their actions. Without the ability to "pull rank," many would never have been given the time of day by the men and women whom they commanded.

The movie *Good Morning, Vietnam,* starring Robin Williams, all too accurately portrays the Vietnam experience. The general in the movie reminded me of my experience of top officers: very smart and big thinkers. In between the generals and the troops were officers who were threatened by the Robin Williamses of the world, the people who, through their own actions, won the respect of men and women around them. All too often, officers who abused their power in this way were shot in combat from behind.

But we needn't look to the military for men and women who abuse their power over others. Most large organizations in our society are swollen with such people. They seek titles like vice- president or major. Or they boast to others of their degrees to bolster their own low self-esteem. They seek others to look down upon so that they can feel good about themselves, a recipe for living that never quite works because no matter how high you get it seems there's always someone above you. This group, often called "perpetual middle managers," are most effective at carrying out orders from above. They do not think well on their own, yet are quick to carry out others' orders. That way, they can always pass the buck if something goes wrong.

We could easily overlook those who crave power and get it only through rank or title, if were not for the fact that they are often quite destructive, particularly when it comes to individual creativity. In business, the military, religion and education, middle management is filled with people whose first impulse is to crush creativity wherever they find it.

Ask most school teachers who these people are and what positions they hold. You'll discover quickly that most teachers want changes and have some great ideas that are squelched by higher-ups who slam doors in their faces. Our world needs creativity more than ever before if we are to solve our problems. But this creativity will never surface and flourish if our current system of education is maintained in its static state by people whose only interest is gaining power to bolster their own ego needs, rather than to make a genuine contribution to the human community. Our educational system cannot change as long as we allow it to be dominated by people whose top priority is maintaining their power. This is true not only of our schools, of course, but of virtually every bureaucratic organization upon which our civilization depends.

Those who want our educational system to stay the same are generally motivated not by a need to serve and create a better world, but by a not-so-hidden need to maintain a position where they can look down on other people. They cling to the status quo not because they are convinced it is right or effective, but because they have no other way to deal with their own sense of inferiority or inner powerlessness. Meanwhile the educational system perpetuates itself, its hidden curriculum teaching everyone it touches to stay disconnected from others, thus making them unable ever to experience the tremendous strength they could all enjoy through cooperation and love.

Some years ago, when travel restrictions were removed from mainland China, I jumped at the chance to visit. It was interesting to talk to the plump, rosy-skinned Chinese on the Western side and the dark, gaunt, sometimes emaciated Chinese on the Communist side. They were like two completely different races. Yet the only difference was the government. What I remember most clearly was how the dark Chinese, some living in mud huts, were able to look across the border at the plump Chinese on the Western side. They were angry at their rich counterparts for not sharing their wealth. Meanwhile, over on the Western side, the "rich" Chinese complained that their Communist counterparts had no comprehension of how hard they worked to achieve their higher standard of living.

Each side had its own grievances that kept them sadly separated from one another, not just by physical boundaries but by the thoughts in their own minds.

But are we any different in the U.S.? The alarming truth is that we are not. We are engaged in an undeclared economic war that affects every one of us, regardless of color, race, religion, gender or national origin. Those at the top want to believe that everything is fine just the way it is. They give to their local charities, but keep their hearts to themselves. They pretend that the suffering beyond their own borders is not their problem, and so they do their best to keep themselves isolated.

It is difficult to cast blame on them, or any of the rest of us who both suffer from and maintain our isolation from one another. We have all come through an educational system that fosters this kind of thinking, doing it in a way that is almost invisible as we are taking it in. When we are taught from the tender age of five that there must be winners and there must be losers, we have been thoroughly indoctrinated long before we've developed the critical ability to see what has happened to us. Winners and losers exist because we are taught to think that way, but the teaching starts so early in our lives that by the time we're adults it has taken on the look of an absolute truth, a fact of life that no one in his or her right mind could refute.

If we humans are to evolve to enjoy our greatest potential, we need first to change this old and outmoded way of thinking. If we are to come together, we need to gain the ability to suspend judgment and see other people simply as people. This evolution will not take place, however, if we continue to turn our backs on the little atrocities being daily committed in our schools. Year after year, our children are being shoved through a system that sorts and classifies them arbitrarily. The "dumb" ones are identified early on. Then the "smart" ones are taught to numb themselves to their own feelings as their less fortunate friends are eliminated or shunted off into the corner, where for all intents and purposes they are ignored. They may be put in special classes, given special help to "bring them up to speed," but the underlying message is always the same: the system values them far less than it does those at the top of the class.

After a while, all this becomes so commonplace that the children accept the consequences, even support it. As a result, we create callous people, most of whom yearn for deeper emotional connections just as the rest of us do. The kind of competition we learn in the schools fosters loneliness and a sense of being separate and alone, not just for those who've been rejected by the system but for all of us. We too often go through life having never experienced the joy of true friendship or either giving or receiving real support from another human. Think about the last time you felt the pain of saying good-bye to someone for whom you cared deeply. Most of us learned long ago how to insulate ourselves from such feelings. Without that insulation, the ability to turn our backs and walk away from a friend, we never could have succeeded in school. Yet, while we watch all this happening, we sit off in the distance committing the same "crime of silence" that dehumanized the people of Hitler's Germany. Maybe we are not filling as many trenches with bodies, but we are surely abandoning as many hearts.

Only now through a growing awareness of our global environmental problems are we at last beginning to realize that we are all, indeed, interrelated by virtue of our sharing this singular, closed ecosystem we call planet Earth. Not long ago we heard people in the north saying that cutting down trees in South America was none of their business. It had nothing to do with them. Now we are all beginning to think in broader terms, seeing that what's happening in South America affects the whole planet.

Then why is it that we still hear people say that they have no interest in where the government and various corporations dump our nuclear waste "as long as isn't in my neighborhood!" These people have not yet realized how we are all one, living together on one little planet. Thank goodness we have devoted, caring people who patiently work at informing those who think that the health of our planet is not their problem.

When I was 15, I failed English and had to repeat my entire sophomore year. My dad asked me how I felt about that. I told him I didn't have a problem with it. He then asked me if I thought I deserved the F. I said no. After all, the teacher had failed over a third of his students. I just happened to be one of them. And we all knew that it wasn't our failure to learn that had earned us these bad grades.

Well, my poor father hit the ceiling. "Never stand idly by while people commit what you know to be an injustice! Injustice only leads to more injustice." He was furious with me, not for getting the F but for not standing up to an obvious injustice.

Just as Harvey states in his book, little atrocities lead to bigger ones. My father taught me how important it is to fight back, even when I could not be absolutely certain if I was right or wrong. He taught me a valuable lesson about rules, ethics and morals: that we need to discover them for ourselves, not merely accept the so-called truths that others might foist off on us.

Teachers learned to dread me. They knew I wouldn't lie down and accept the grades they gave me. But my father's lessons didn't stop with school. They continued to serve me many years later, when I went to Vietnam. One day I found a little boy in my helicopter, which was parked just outside Da Nang. According to military rules I had every right, if not the duty, to shoot and kill him on the spot. This was the code of war we were taught as military officers. I was defending both U.S. property and my own life. But just as I took aim and started putting pressure on the trigger, I looked into that boy's eyes. What I saw, for the first time, was the soul of another human being, not a Communist as I had been taught to think. I put my gun away that day forever. I committed myself to finding new ways of doing things, instead of simply responding to what I'd been told to do by a person who supposedly had more authority than I.

Three weeks after my encounter with the boy in my helicopter, our aircraft carrier was at anchor in Hong Kong Harbor. Our squadron received an emergency message that we were to return immediately to Vietnam. We were about to engage in a large military operation near the DMZ, the border between North and South Vietnam. I never returned to my ship. To this day, that was one of the hardest decisions I had to make. I trembled for hours as I walked the streets with my mind screaming. I was called a coward and a traitor by some of the other pilots. I realized it was not the most honorable way to handle my refusal to fight any more. But I also knew I could not fight and kill simply because I had been ordered to do so. What the other pilots never understood was that for me to fly and kill again would have been the coward's way out.

Looking into that young boy's eyes that day had been my wake-up call. No longer would I just go along with the crowd because it was the popular thing to do. I would listen to my ethical self first, before selling my soul or spirit for the approval of my friends. And no longer would it be okay with me to stand silently, looking out the window, as a friend was eliminated by a cruel system.

Since that day in Vietnam in 1972, I have looked earnestly for alternatives to the system by which we think about our global problems. After the war with Iraq and all the parades were over, I began to wonder how the U.S. was going to address the problems at home: our poor and homeless, our angry and disadvantaged, our health care crisis, environmental pollution...the list goes on. We can't bomb these and make them go away. A show of force isn't going to solve them. Hopefully, we humans are evolving, moving closer to the realization that our problems can no longer be solved by killing and maiming others.

I am convinced that the most profound solutions will come through changing the way we educate our children. It is possible to create learning environments where people are excited about learning and where everyone is a winner. As my teacher, R. Buckminster Fuller once said, "Don't change people, simply change the environment."

We begin changing the educational system by changing our own thoughts. It is important that we begin to drop the idea that there are stupid or smart people. It is all relative. As a child from the Special Olympics said, "We are not stupid, we are just slower in some subjects."

And so it is for all of us. We are ~~we~~ all slower in some subjects, faster in others. That is what makes our world operate. Each person has a unique gift. The purpose of education is to inspire and nurture that gift until it blooms. These human gifts do not bloom in environments where creativity is crushed and where memorizing facts, figures and formulas that adults deem necessary takes priority. What would happen if we had a school with no tests and no curriculum? Could we, as adults, trust that inside each child is a God-given guidance system that would allow the child to seek out all the knowledge the child is designed to acquire? Could we trust enough and leave them alone—or are you thinking right now that we must play God and attempt to mold and control that child's mind and what goes in it?

How often are we only imposing our own personal fears, beliefs and desires on young children in the name of education? We must learn to trust our children to think for themselves and to ask when they are ready to learn something new.

The belief that "my child is doing fine," accompanied by a disregard for those children who aren't, is costly. If we do not realize soon that we are in a closed system, and that the plight of the poor, the uneducated, the criminal, the unhappy, the lonely and the unfulfilled is only there because we humans created and are perpetuating the system that results in such inequities, then we all will have lost some of our humanity. Not one of us truly prospers as long as others are forced to live below poverty level. But we all pay for it dearly! What will it take for us to learn that if one child fails in school, we all fail in some way?

5

Where Is My Paycheck?

America's organizations and their employees are mired in the mentality of entitlement, *the firmly embedded sense that what you get is a* right, *rather than something that has to be* earned.

—JUDITH M. BARDWICK

"Where is my paycheck?"

"Where is my paycheck?"

"Where is my paycheck?"

"Is that all people can think about these days?" Dave paced up and down the floor of his office.

"Here it is, only noon on payday, and six people have already come in to ask for their paychecks so they can take off early." Dave looked frustrated. "They always tell me they have to take their kids to the doctor or something like that. They must think I'm stupid!"

A knock on the door interrupted our conversation. It was another early request for a paycheck.

"Well, at least this one didn't want the afternoon off; he sent his wife instead!" he said, after she had collected the check and left the office.

Dave walked over to his desk and sat down in his chair. "I don't know how these people do it. They live paycheck-to-paycheck, and most of them are over their limits on every one of their credit cards. I know because the bank collection people call me quite often. All my employees have high school diplomas and most have college degrees. How can such educated people be so screwed up financially?"

Dave, a longtime friend, had invited me over to discuss some problems he was having with his company. Business had slowed down for his computer software company, and he was preparing to lay off about a third of his 30 employees. There was unrest throughout the company because the employees were expecting a raise that was not going to materialize. Now Dave would have to tell them there were going to be layoffs, too.

"I can't afford to give them a raise when there are no profits," he said. "But if I don't offer a raise, I'll lose my best people and only the ones who can't find a job elsewhere will stay." He stopped and thought for a moment. "I can't win. If my best people leave, I am out of business anyway!"

He stared at the floor. "I don't want to lose anyone. Most of us have been together for years and I consider them all a part of my family. It hurts me to hear about their money problems, but the fact remains that this company has money problems too."

Dave finally looked me in the eyes and asked, "How come you don't have employee problems when you have offices throughout the world? Your profits are up, aren't they?"

I nodded.

"Don't your employees want more money when you make more money? How often do you give raises?" Dave sighed and waited for my reply.

I began slowly. "First of all, we don't have employees in the traditional sense. We'd be broke and could not afford to do business today if we had employees. Most people we work with are independent. They work with our company, not for it."

"Are you a franchise or a multi-level marketing company?" Dave asked.

"No. Most people we work with are in business for themselves. They know how to create money, or are in the process of learning how to create money for themselves."

Dave looked puzzled. "What is the difference between working for money and creating money?" he asked, quick to pick up the subtle distinction I made between the two.

"Working for money is only a small part of the process of creating money." I used the analogy of riding a bicycle to explain the concept to him: "There are many parts involved in riding a bicycle. Working is like the pedaling part. It is an important part, but there is much more involved. If all you know is how to pedal, you're destined to fall on your face. Unfortunately, most people think pedaling is all there is to riding a bike, so they are pedaling harder and harder but getting nowhere. They aren't learning how to balance or steer. If they are staying upright at all, it is only because they've taken to riding one of those stationary exercise bikes, where you pedal like mad and stay firmly planted in one place."

Dave frowned, obviously confused. But it was obvious that he was interested. "Go on," he said. "I want to hear more."

"Everyone who works with our company," I continued, "is constantly refining their abilities to create money, not simply waiting for a paycheck. We are more than a business; we are also a school. The people who work with us are training to be generalists in business and can swap places with anyone throughout our organization. We are constantly training everyone associated with us to be generalists in business. And although we have a few strict rules and policies, everyone is encouraged to experiment, to make mistakes, correct them and report their findings at our meetings. Our business is always growing. All of us are continuously learning and changing. It is definitely not a boring place to work in, believe me! Here's something else I'd like to point out: there is no such thing as a crazy idea in our organization. In fact, if someone isn't experimenting with some crazy new idea and making mistakes, we encourage them to do so."

I turned to Dave and asked, "What do most of your people do to earn their paychecks?"

"They work hard at their assigned jobs."

"Do you involve them with the overall management of the business?"

Dave looked at me and asked, "Do you mean planning, making decisions, solving problems and things like that?"

"Yes."

"Well, not really," he answered, hesitantly. "Most people aren't interested or they simply don't know enough."

"So they just work and get paid. Right?"

Dave nodded, wrinkling his brow as he contemplated everything I was telling him.

"So how do you determine when a person should get a raise?" I asked.

"They get regular, incremental raises with seniority or they get a promotion that includes a raise," Dave replied.

"So the longer they work here the more they get paid?"

"That's right. And we have a good insurance package and a retirement plan. We used to have a bonus, but it seemed no matter how much the bonus was, they weren't happy. They always thought they deserved more." He stopped and shrugged, expressing his discouragement. "But none of that makes any difference now because we don't have the profits to pay anybody a bonus or a raise. In fact, a lot of people are not even going to have jobs."

"Let's look closely at all this," I said. "You are telling me that your people come to work, do their jobs, work hard, don't make mistakes, collect their paychecks and then go home. Is that about it?"

Dave got defensive. "Well, we enjoy working together. We have fun and they tell me I'm a good boss."

I got up from my chair and walked over to the flip chart. On it I wrote the words:

Where * Is * My * Paycheck

I turned to Dave, "Aren't you sick and tired of hearing these words?"

"You know I am!" Dave admitted.

I asked him to walk over to the flip chart and circle the first letter of each word.

Then I asked him to say the word spelled out by those circled letters.

Dave stood silently for a few seconds, then slowly read off the letters, one by one. "W, I, M, P. WIMP! It spells wimp," he exclaimed, surprised by his discovery.

"Dave, either you have a pack of wimps working for you or you are treating them like wimps. Which is it?"

Dave got angry. "I'm good to them. I take care of them. This is a nice place to work. I just can't afford to pay them more."

I let him calm down before I fired off another set of questions. "Why don't you teach them more about the business? Most of your employees are highly skilled computer people, right?"

Dave agreed that they were.

"Why not give them broader responsibilities and encourage them to participate in running the company?"

"Like you are doing," Dave fired back at me, still on the defensive.

I nodded.

"Well, first of all, most of my employees don't want to learn about business. They only want their paychecks. They only want to do the job they are qualified to do. Most of my employees think business people like you and me are crooks. They think we make too much money and exploit people. They don't want to be part of that; they only want their paychecks, their benefits, their vacations and their retirement. The last thing they want is more work and responsibility!"

His intensity grew as he aired his real concern. "If I teach them how to run this business, they'll leave and start their own companies and compete against me. They won't need me or my company anymore!"

"Now we're getting down to the real issues," I said, thanking Dave for expressing his real fear. Now we could get to work. We had reached the core of the problem. "Do you know what co-dependency is?" I asked Dave.

He shook his head, "No."

"Co-dependency," I said, "is a term psychologists use to describe a person who is attracted to people who are addicted to a substance or some kind of destructive behavior. To keep it simple, let's say that you are the co-dependent and you are always finding yourself attracted to alcoholics. You may complain a lot about your alcoholic partner's behavior. You may criticize them and even beg them to change. But the truth is that you are just as addicted to this kind of partner as your partner is addicted to their drinking. In fact, if you are a true co-dependent, you would probably lose interest in your alcoholic partner the moment he or she got help and stopped drinking. And pretty soon you'd go out looking for another alcoholic to hook up with.

"The co-dependents live in this closed circle of hating how they live but going back to the same pattern again and again. They believe that life is a constant struggle for survival, and of course it is as long as they keep going back to their stuck, self-destructive pattern.

"For most people, the employer-employee relationship is a co-dependent one. It is based on an addiction to survival thinking. The very thing employees and employers find most attractive is also the source of their downfall. In this case the paycheck is the addiction. Not that we don't need money. We do. Back when we had an agrarian society we might have been able to trade potatoes for rent. But can you imagine trying to send the utility company five bushels of potatoes to pay your electric bill, or sending the bank three pigs every month to pay your mortgage? Of course not.

"The point is that in the past 100 years, money has become almost as necessary for survival as air, water and food. In today's world, money is synonymous with survival, and when survival is at stake, people get desperate. Out of fear they get hooked up with the easiest and fastest and most secure way to get those dollars in their pockets. They stop taking risks and they stop learning and they stop developing their own potential.

"Despite the fact that money has taken such an important place in our society, our educational system still fails to address it directly. Like a stubborn co-dependent who won't look at what he could do to free himself of his addiction to alcoholic people, the educational system refuses to look at what it might do to teach the actual principles of money, the ethics of money, and how money really works.

"Sometimes it seems to me that our entire society is avoiding the subject. Even when we do talk about it, in school or on television programs, we discuss it in sterile and lofty theoretical terms not put it in everyday terms that ordinary people can understand. And our educational system, which should be taking responsibility for teaching about money, continues to treat it as corrupting and evil. Don't get me wrong. Money can corrupt. But the system seems to use that as an excuse to ignore the fact that money is a cultural necessity in today's world and can do a lot of good. To say that money is corrupting and evil in a world which runs on money makes about as much sense as saying that pigs or potatoes are corrupting in an agrarian society.

"Our social system continues to promote the ethic that everything will turn out okay if you just study hard and work hard, if you will just do as you are told, don't make waves, don't make mistakes and memorize what you are told. God forbid that you would somehow learn to think on your own or take any real initiative. Our system encourages us to specialize, and to then go out and find a good and secure job.

"Maybe a hundred years ago all this looked like a pretty good idea. But today there is no such thing as a secure job. In our rapidly changing world, the myth of job security is kept alive only by schools and businesses, both of whom know better, or should. Similarly, the idea of working your way to the top is obsolete. Too many times, we find ourselves climbing career ladders and getting almost to the top, before we discover that we've leaned them against the wrong walls and those walls are coming down.

"Let me put it as simply as I can. Security is possible but it can't be found in a particular job any more. The only way we can have security is through our own knowledge. We need to know how money works in our lives. We need to know how to be flexible and make changes when it is necessary. We need to know how to learn new skills and adapt quickly no matter what happens. In short, we need to learn how to be generalists first and specialists second, not the other way around as our present system teaches us.

"When I say let's learn about money, I'm not saying let's learn to manipulate and exploit each other for the sake of amassing bigger and bigger fortunes. That's just another form of addictive behavior that in the long run isn't going to help make any of us any happier or any more secure. Let me give you an example:

"In the mid-'70s, business schools began teaching MBA students to be take-over artists and so-called financial wizards. Instead of teaching them to be visionary business people who could create new goods and services to expand our economy, they were taught to exploit the system, which ended up actually shrinking our economy and creating problems for all of us. A lot of these take-over artists ended up in jail and the American people ended up with a multi-billion-dollar debt to pay off the damage that they did. This is co-dependency and addiction carried to its worst extreme!

"Business schools are still teaching MBA students to make money with money, thus creating money managers instead of courageous business leaders. Getting bigger salaries and bonuses has thus become more important than the idea I am most interested in promoting here, that we can actually make an important contribution to our world even as we are getting rich. We can get rich and make a contribution only if we get out of our co-dependent relationship with money and really learn how it works!

"Think of the kind of world we could have if instead of teaching people financial co-dependency we began showing them how to create new products and services that the world needs. Why, we would be breathing new life into the entrepreneurial spirit that once made our country great, a spirit which at the moment seems to be dying a slow death.

"Our greatest ally in all this could be our educational system. But, as everyone knows, that system is in deep trouble. Educators know it, parents know it and students know it. The system's failure to respond to change is causing a revolt. In every major city public education is sliding into a state of anarchy, where nobody is really in charge. Students know they are being trained to be obsolete. They know that information necessary for their own survival is not being taught in schools. Most of them realize that the idea of working for one company all your life is ludicrous. In spite of this we grow up having the idea drummed into our minds that we should decide on a job or career specialization in our teenage years. But just stop and think about it for a moment. How many of us have ended up training for jobs in companies or industries that weren't even around by the time we graduated? We're not talking about a handful of people here, we're talking about millions.

"Is it any wonder students often rebel not only against their schools but against society? They aren't stupid, they're bored. They look around them and they can see that what the society is offering through the schools really isn't all that relevant. So they cut classes, drop out or simply have little interest. Most students make their way through our educational system for one reason, to get a diploma. They view a diploma as a way to open the next door. Sadly, all too many of them eventually discover that the years spent getting the diploma were a waste of time, with little gained. The doors they thought were there never materialize, and when they do they don't necessarily open up just because you've got a diploma in your hand. And it's not just high schools that are suffering in this way. Statistics show that there are more unemployed college graduates than ever before in history.

"I meet all too many people who are sitting around wondering what happened to their lives. Their dreams aren't even beginning to come true. Their incomes have hit a plateau and they know that at the rate things are going they will soon find themselves in their retirement years, dependent upon government assistance just to make ends meet. They see just a handful of other people gaining financial well being. As for themselves, they continue to work harder and harder while falling farther and farther behind. What happened to the promise of the good life? they ask themselves. After all, they followed all the rules society taught them—being good, doing as they were told, studying hard, working hard. What could have gone wrong? Well, what went wrong is that they learned, all right, but they learned the wrong lessons.

"Unfortunately, most hard-working, promising students have been turned into co-dependent wimps by the time they graduate from high school or college. All they know is how to work hard and do as they are told, in spite of the fact that the job is no longer secure or doesn't pay enough to keep up with the wildly escalating cost of living.

"The only way to keep up with change is with knowledge. Our true wealth is found only in what we know. So many people I encounter in my work are still poor and struggling because they haven't made enough mistakes in their lives. They have continued to hang onto the co-dependent relationships they were taught in school and that you should avoid making mistakes at all costs. And that belief keeps them imprisoned in their own ignorance more than any other single thing we are ever taught.

"Instead of growing people who put their energy into avoiding mistakes, they become paycheck-addicts. Then reality strikes, usually around the age of 35. Suddenly they realize they either hate their jobs or are losing them because the skills they've developed have become obsolete. With the world crashing down around their ears, they simply don't know where to turn. They don't have any alternatives because they don't even understand their own co-dependence or what it is doing to their lives.

"But what about the boss? Unfortunately, this scenario also fits the heads of most companies. A company of co-dependent wimps never develops much real strength. In the end, the business loses profits and employees from the bottom to the top are left wondering why they were laid off or why they didn't get raises when, after all, they played by all the rules for success that they were ever taught. Employees, as well as business owners, are finding themselves in this position, too, asking why, wanting to break out of their self-destructive co-dependencies and addictions but not knowing how to do it. Indeed, most companies which are suffering in this way can't even imagine an alternative.

"Today, we're beginning to see a new kind of business coming onto the scene. These successful new companies are either employee-owned or the employees pay to work for the company. I know it sounds absurd for employees to pay to work for a company, but it is already happening and seems to be a trend of the future.

"The most successful new real estate companies are either employee-owned or the employees pay a fee every month to belong to the company. The old method of a real estate sales agent splitting a commission with the owner of the company, for example, is being phased out.

"Today, a real estate agent pays a fee to a company that advertises her or his services throughout the country, or at least through the area the person is working in. The individual salesperson is in business for him- or herself, however, getting the use of the company logo and benefitting from the widespread advertising. But the salespeople are responsible for renting an office, getting their own listings, working with their own customers, and processing their own papers. They pay their own phone bills, their own license fees, and even pay for their own for-sale signs.

"Do you see the point I'm getting at here, that they are not just paycheck junkies, they're not sitting on a stationary bike cranking away at the pedals? They are out there on the road, not just pedaling but steering, balancing and watching for traffic. They have responsibilities in every phase of the process that allows them to make a living.

"With these new business structures the less successful salespeople are being phased out. It is a business of perform or perish. No more will the realtor-in-charge provide a desk and services in hopes that the salesperson can sell. The result is that employees are carrying the company rather than the other way around. And it's working!

"This trend of employees paying to work for a company is an idea that every business needs to look at. People want to make their own decisions instead of being dependent on a boss who controls the amount of security they have or the amount of money they make. Our company does it. Not only do my profits grow along with my employees' earnings, but the people themselves bloom.

"Our educational system, however, is still teaching people to ask, 'Where is my paycheck?'

"Today, all of us are paying for an educational system geared to training people to be mindless robots who end up working themselves into a corner of economic co-dependence and obsolescence, with no personal wealth of any kind, neither viable skills and knowledge, nor money. They remain addicted to the steady paycheck because they don't know how money is generated."

I stopped. My friend Dave sat staring at me. He didn't look happy but I have to say that he had begun to look more interested than ever. "You're suggesting that my addiction to this system is as much a part of the problem as my employees' addiction to their paychecks," he said.

I nodded.

"But I'd have to argue that at least on some level the old system is working. People do continue to get paychecks. Companies do continue to make it one way or another. For every business that fails, another seems to take its place. People may shift from one job to another, one company to another. But I guess I don't feel the same as you. I just don't think it's all that bad."

"Let me show you something," I said. I reached into my briefcase and pulled out some transparencies I'd been working on for a presentation I was going to be giving in a couple of weeks. I handed them to Dave to read:

How We All Pay for Our Inadequate Educational System

1. **Business and government leaders who cannot think.** Our business schools create MBAs who are creative in accounting so that a business can look good on paper even when profits and growth are diminishing. They offer training in the art of finance and acquisition, which when put into actual practice causes stock prices to jump and then crash. An MBA degree is often a ticket to the top, allowing people to avoid essential work experience. These new leaders lose touch with employees as people, and business becomes an accounting job. The company's "bottom line" becomes the sole concern and people are treated as little more than troublesome but necessary resources.

2. **Exploitation of Resources.** Western business only believes in what it can see, touch, smell and taste. It thinks only in terms of tangible objects such as land, oil, gold, trees, crops, machinery, etc. Western society teaches only about the visible. It almost ignores the invisible, those less tangible aspects of our lives such as morale, motivation,

self-esteem, trust, the spirit of a group when they are working well together. It has yet to develop a way to teach people how to make use of the invisible world, which is infinitely greater than the visible world. One of the main reasons Japan is strong financially is that they are able to harness the invisible while we continue to ignore it.

Japan has no native raw materials with which to build their products. Their "secret weapon," with which they are able to beat the Western world, is found in their use of the invisible. They beat the Western world with information and technology, importing whatever visible or tangible resources they lack. They design better, more efficient production technologies to produce high quality products (the invisible) which they sell to the West. The irony is that with all the money they make from the effective use of their invisible resources, they are buying up businesses and real estate in many countries outside their own. Our business leaders, and those of other western countries, cannot comprehend what the Japanese are doing because our societies only teach us how to use what is visible and tangible.

3. **A nation of co-dependent wimps.** More and more people blame the government for their problems. And increasing numbers of people spend all their spare time submitting their resumes to other companies, always in search of a better job and benefit package. I overheard a woman in a restaurant gloating to her friend that she had quit her job with a company that was going broke and had gotten a job with the state government for more pay, a better benefits package and less work. On top of that, she was happy because she said it was almost impossible to get fired from the government, so she could just coast along and still have greater job security. And we wonder why our tax burden goes up while less and less gets done! Everyone seems to be looking for a job with more pay and less work.

4. **An education that fails those who need it most.** Since we punish those who don't do well in school, they often drop through the cracks and are ignored by the system. When you tell them to get a job that will only keep them at or below the poverty level, the sense of self-worth diminishes. And when a person's sense of self-worth goes down, the desire and ability to work decreases too. Through

this system we literally create hundreds of thousands of welfare-dependent families and people who have no hope for a better life. Under these circumstances, crime increases. As Jesse Jackson commented during the Los Angeles riots in 1992, in an environment of terrible poverty and hopelessness, going to jail is actually an improvement over the life they know. They've got nothing to lose and everything to gain by committing a crime.

"You see," I told Dave as he finished reading these paragraphs, "when you start looking at all the factors, you begin to see that everyone would have a lot to gain if we were to teach everybody about money and how it works."

"I think I'm beginning to see what you're driving at," he said.

"You know," I said. "There's a little story about Henry Ford that I like to relate when I'm telling people about money and the value of the invisible. As you know, Ford was a multi-millionaire at a time when a million dollars was still a lot of money. Someone once asked him what he would do if he lost everything. Without a pause, he replied, 'I'd have it all back in less than five years.' How could he do that? He could do it because he knew that his real wealth wasn't counted in how many dollars he had in the bank, or even in the number of factories or the amount of real estate he owned. His real wealth was in what he had between his ears: the intangible, the invisible, the knowledge he had about what money is really all about. For all their emphasis on knowledge, our schools most neglect this kind of resource.

"Until our educational system stops punishing people for making mistakes, and until the creation of money is made a part of the school curriculum, people will continue to live lives as co-dependent wimps. They stop growing and stop thinking until the only question they know how to ask is..."

"Let me fill in the blanks," Dave interrupted, finishing my point for me: "Where is my paycheck?"

"Right," I said. "Where is my paycheck?"

6

If I Have All the Right Answers, Why Can't I Think?

Human beings were given a left foot and a right foot to make a mistake first to the left, then to the right, left again and repeat.

— R. Buckminster Fuller

When I was ten years old, I had a run-in with a substitute teacher which I have never forgotten. As she handed back the results of a pop quiz, I was surprised to find that I had received an F. I had missed 10 out of 10. Now I don't remember all the questions on the quiz, but I do remember one of them. It read, "Johnny went to the store to buy flour for his mother. At the store he found a one-pound sack of flour for \$.35 and a five-pound sack of flour for \$1.50. Which sack is a better buy?"

Well, I had answered that they both were given the limited amount of information provided. I remember saying something about variables such as the consumption rate of the family, the storage available (my mother had thrown out a bag of flour full of bugs only a few days earlier), and how much money Johnny had available to him at the time. I even remember feeling pretty proud of myself after taking the test because I felt I had really thought my answers through quite thoroughly.

The teacher didn't see it that way. Although she was trying to be polite by listening to my explanation, her impatience was obvious. She stood pointing to her open teacher's manual, which clearly dictated that the "right" answer was the five-pound sack, no ifs, ands or buts about it!

Knowing I had absolutely no chance, I asked her if I could see the answer book. As expected, she looked stunned and said, "Don't be silly, then you would know all the answers."

"No, I wouldn't," I replied, "because my answers aren't in there. If I had your book I might know all your so-called 'right' answers, but I wouldn't really know anything. I'd be just like you!"

That last remark quickly put an end to our discussion. As I was being escorted to the principal's office, I was surprised that the majority of my classmates were razzing and heckling me. What was wrong with them, I wondered. Couldn't they see my side? But it wasn't until later, years later in fact, that I understood that they were just conforming to the rules of our education system—don't make waves, accept the "right" answer the teacher gives you, memorize and regurgitate to receive a good grade. Meanwhile, I was labeled a "disciplinary problem" for constantly questioning the answers, a label that followed me throughout my school years.

When I got home, knowing the school had called and "ratted" on me, I cautiously looked around for my dad. To my surprise, he just looked at me and began to laugh.

"Son," he said, "I heard about your argument. You have a good head on your shoulders. I'm glad you're using it for something more than a hat rack."

This came as quite a surprise. I thought I'd get a horrible scolding. Why wouldn't the man who would eventually head the educational system for the state of Hawaii be upset at his son for being a discipline problem? But just as I was about to open my mouth to say something, my dad's eyes saddened and I could hear the frustration in his tone.

"Unfortunately, son," he said, "teachers must follow the rules of our educational system. Requiring students to know one 'right' answer to each question is the basis of that system. It makes it a lot easier to test and grade students. The teachers are not at fault; they're just doing what our system requires."

Looking back, I guess I should have thanked that substitute teacher. That confrontation had a tremendous impact on my life. I never actually went to battle with any of my teachers again but I continued to question the "right" answers they gave me. Perhaps it was all part of my stubbornness about not wanting anyone to tell me what to do, but I am thankful I never quit questioning the answers because I have learned a lot. That controversy with the substitute teacher even taught me to be a little more polite. The teachers, however, still dreaded me.

A few years ago, I was discussing the value of asking precise questions with a group of businesspeople. A gentleman in the audience told me the reason I was fixated on questions was because I was Oriental. It was a predominantly Caucasian audience. Diplomatically, I suggested he might be watching too many David Carradine *Kung Fu* shows on television, where the wise old master of Kung Fu asks his student questions like, "Grasshopper, what does it mean when a blue heron scratches its beak?"

After the laughter died down, I added that children of all races and backgrounds have an innate desire to ask questions—sometimes to the point of exasperating their parents. Questions stem from a natural curiosity to learn. Parents are often the first to crush this curiosity. It is further diminished with formal education because of the system's determination to tell a child what to think and believe. And, in the end, it is the child's natural spirit and creativity which is crushed. This is why I've always felt that watching a child go through our educational system is like watching reverse metamorphosis—in flies a beautiful butterfly, out crawls a clumsy caterpillar.

Throughout our society, but particularly in our educational system, we are taught that there is only one "right" answer, ultimately making students believe that all other answers are wrong. This has a way of encouraging students to stop thinking after they've discovered what the system says is the "right" answer. By the time we reach the sixth or seventh grade we've been pretty well indoctrinated into believing that memorizing is the same as learning. It is not, of course. Memorization is a poor substitute for thinking. Many times over I have asked audiences to tell me how much they remember of all that they memorized during their school years. A raise of hands reveals that most people remember less than five percent of what they have "learned" in this way. One educational psychologist stood up in an audience one day and told me that if we took everything the average person has retained from all his years of school and put it into one series of lessons, we could teach it all in about three weeks.

When a teacher asks, "When did Christopher Columbus sail the ocean blue?" all students reply, "1492." The teacher is happy because the students' answers match the one in her manual and the students are happy because they are right and know they will not be punished for making a mistake. But was anything of value actually learned? And did anyone have to think? No. And that's the problem!

Instead of asking a one-right-answer kind of question, let's imagine that the teacher asked, "How did Columbus motivate a crew to sail with him when most people at that time believed the earth was flat and you could sail off the edge of it?" Granted, this open-ended question doesn't adhere to the standardized right-or-wrong format that educators prefer, but it does challenge the student to think.

Limiting students to right-wrong thinking cripples them, crushing their curiosity, dampening their enthusiasm and stunting their creativity. The long-term utilization of this process not only causes boredom, it also teaches them to be dependent on an outside authority figure to tell them the "right" answers. Ultimately, this deprives students of their full potential to succeed in life.

It is important to remember that teachers are not only spokespeople for our society, they are products of it as well. When I hear teachers complain about working conditions and low pay I ask them one question, "Why do you put up with it?" The usual answer is, "Because I love teaching." My next question is, "How could you teach and make more money?" And most of the time the answer is, "Get a part-time job," "Sell real estate on the side" or "Marry money." Many jokingly add, "Win the lottery." These are all answers I have heard all too many times before. Rarely are there any original ideas.

When I ask, "What could you do besides those things to make more money?" they reply: "It can't be done," or, "It's not possible."

As these conversations progress, we finally begin to see that the real problem has little to do with options that are or are not available to teachers; rather, the real problem is the inability to think creatively.

When I speak with teachers I am reluctant to inform them that I have become wealthy and financially independent through teaching—a profession that I, too, love very much. When I do mention this, I usually receive glassy-eyed stares in return. Most people with whom I talk simply can't believe it possible to become rich in the profession of teaching. I imagine the kind of blank stares I get from them are comparable to the vacuous looks they often get from their own bored students.

I had a college friend some years ago whose literature professor believed that only his own interpretations of the classics were correct.

As a result, he lectured and allowed no time for any discussion. When the class began reading *Moby Dick,* a book that even the author admits has multiple interpretations, the professor still insisted that his interpretations were the best, the only correct ones that he would accept. He insisted that anything less than a perfect mirroring of his lectures on the final essay would receive a bad grade. Finding this class boring and frustrating, my friend went to the professor and explained that by demanding that she memorize his interpretations he wasn't allowing her to think for herself. The professor replied, "I didn't study literature for eighteen years so I could have students tell me what they think it means!"

There is no doubt in my mind that some people like having only one "right" answer. It makes life easier—at least on the surface. But let's face it. Most of us find memorizing a lot easier than thinking. It's too bad that few answers in life aren't that simple. Take, for example, the question, "What do you want to be when you grow up?" The memorized answer: "A teacher." Now ask, "How can you be a teacher who earns a million dollars teaching?" That question requires thinking, not simply a memorized answer. The problem is that if you have followed the doctrine of the educational system too closely most of your life, you won't know the difference between thinking and memorizing.

Until we can make a clear distinction between the two, we live our lives running around looking for the "right" answers to questions that can never be answered that way. Of course, we all know people who convince themselves that they have the right answers. Their paradigm is "I'm right," which ultimately prevents them from looking beyond their "right" answer for other answers. The face they present to the world is usually seen by others as "narrow-minded" and "self-righteous."

There's a real danger in believing that we are thinking when in actuality we are only regurgitating memorized answers. I think Henry Ford summed this subject up best when he stated, "Thinking is the hardest work there is—that's why so few people engage in it."

One of the saddest things about people who have to be right is that they cannot see how more than one "right" answer might exist. This shouldn't surprise us, since it is what our system teaches us. The problem is that the one-right-answer way of life clearly limits the degree of success people are able to experience in later life. They are the ones who end up chanting "Where is my paycheck," as the end of the week approaches.

One very serious problem that we're facing today is that all too many of our businesses, social organizations, schools and governments are run by laypeople who were successful in academia. They fit the system's mold perfectly. They are often the ones who were labeled intelligent primarily because they agreed to go along with our system of the single right answer. But the world is changing and memorized right answers are no longer adequate in most cases. Still, most keep using those same obsolete answers and formulae. These smart leaders are running our businesses, governments and even our families straight into the ground because they cannot think creatively in changing times. They are proud, but tragically failing examples of our present system.

What makes matters even worse is that too many of these paragons of education believe they can think. Most are only repeating ideas someone else gave them. They are not much more than robots who record and play back everything they are told. They are secure in only one thing—that they are pedaling away madly on stationary bikes that are solidly anchored into a concrete foundation that hasn't budged an inch since it was set in place.

Highly successful people have learned, usually outside school, that most things worth doing have multiple solutions. They have found that accepting only one right answer limits their potential. Many unsuccessful people are stuck in jobs wondering why they don't succeed when every day of their lives, all the way back to their first years in school, they have been doing exactly what the system asked them to do.

Because students are often asked to blindly accept right answers, the idea of challenging the system is equated with rebellion. Once this lesson of blind acceptance is learned, people become terribly inhibited, particularly as employees, fearful of questioning their superiors.

The bottom line is that our educational system dictates to students rather than encouraging them to think for themselves. It demands that they memorize what the system wants them to know, instead of teaching them to learn how to solve their own problems or develop their own inherent creativity. In other words—to borrow the moral of an ancient fable—they are supplying the fish instead of fishing poles. Ultimately, this means that there are millions of intelligent people walking around who have all the right answers but who don't know how to think. As a result, they are emotionally, professionally and financially trapped. The system has robbed them of their ability to think.

The good news is that each and every one of us has the power to turn that around in our own lives. And this turnaround begins by having the courage to un-learn the lessons of the past, a process that begins by letting go of the lie that there are only single right answers to anything. The best inspiration I can offer for accomplishing this is found in the words of Buckminster Fuller, which I quote at the beginning of this chapter: "Human beings were given a left foot and a right foot to make a mistake first to the left, then to the right, left again and repeat."

7

Money Is Evil

You have to make up your mind if you want to make money or make sense, because they are mutually exclusive.

—R. Buckminster Fuller

"Money is dirty."
"People with money are greedy."
"Businesspeople are crooks."
"The love of money is the root of all evil."

• • •

While growing up I heard many comments like those above, and I still hear them today. No doubt about it, money is definitely a hot subject. And because this subject is such a controversial and emotionally-charged one, I held off writing this book for many years. As an educator, I could already imagine the outcry, "How dare you pollute the hallowed halls of knowledge with this filthy subject!" But it finally dawned on me that our ignorance about money is the root of much more evil than our knowledge of it could ever be. So I decided to go ahead with writing this book and worry about what my critics might say after it was published.

As a child, it did not take me very long to recognize the lure of money. At the age of about two years, I was spanked for putting a penny in my mouth. I did not know what the words "dirty" and "choke" meant, but I soon found out. I could feel the emotion in my mother's voice as she lectured me about this thing in my mouth she called a penny. From that day on I knew there must be something special or magical about money, since my mom didn't throw the penny away like she did most other things I put in my mouth. She carefully placed it in a safe spot.

The power of money continued to be reinforced every time one of my grandparents gave me a piece of paper with green printing on it. I learned that such pieces of paper had a special power because everyone around me would "Ooooh" and "Aaaah" and exclaim how lucky I was to receive them. I do not remember my first purchase but I must have enjoyed it because before the age of five I was hooked on money and its apparently magical power to get me the things I wanted.

But this was also when the confusion set in. I really didn't understand money. There truly seemed to be a mystery surrounding it. I only knew I wanted it.

I remember being scolded for asking my granny for money. That's when I first heard the words "ungrateful" and "greedy." I didn't exactly know what these words meant, either. But I could sense I had done something bad, and it frightened me. I didn't want to be a "bad" boy and have my parents angry at me. I just wanted the toys and other things that I knew money could buy. None of this made much sense. How could something that seemed to make so many people happy and excited be so bad?

The confusion increased the first time I encountered a checkbook. I was about eight when I realized my parents could write a check for any amount instead of paying with cash. I thought I had hit the mother lode. People didn't need cash; they just needed checks. One day I remember asking my mother to buy me something. She responded, "I don't have any money."

"That's okay," I replied, "just write a check."

This time I got more than I bargained for. My parents sat me down and attempted to explain how checks and the banking system worked. My confusion only increased. But I was determined to someday figure all this out.

Not long ago I was reminded of this early lesson in the meaning of money when I saw a plaque in a gift shop which read, "How can I be broke? I still have checks left." I chuckled as I recalled my mom and dad attempting to explain the banking system to me.

At the age of nine I decided to take matters into my own hands. I got my first job. Every Saturday, for ten cents an hour, I stacked and dusted off canned goods in a grocery store. I figured that the only way to learn about money was to get first hand experience earning some.

Since that first job, I have spent much of my life "unconfusing" myself about money. And in my years of study, I have come to see that I am not alone in my effort to demystify the mighty dollar. A great many people in this world are confused about money—even those who have lots of it. In fact, I am convinced that confusion about money causes the majority of our world's problems.

What is most frightening and disheartening is that many of the people who handle large sums of money—bankers, stock-brokers, administrators and politicians—are often the most confused, yet pretend not to be. If you doubt this, just look at the fiscal condition of our banks, savings and loan associations, governments and businesses. It is hard to deny that where you find a lot of money you will also find a lot of confusion, greed, and—unfortunately—evil.

The first lesson we absolutely must learn is that money itself is not evil. It is simply a tool, just as a pencil is a tool. A pencil can be used to write a beautiful love letter or a memo firing someone from a job. While a pencil is designed to write with, it can also be used as a lethal weapon to stab a person in the eye. The thing that makes the difference isn't the object, but the motives of the person holding the pencil—or handling the money.

I like what Reverend Ike, my Southern Baptist preacher friend, says: "It is the lack of money that is the root of all evil."

We cannot afford to keep people ignorant about this subject any longer. Money is a tool of business—and what activity is not associated with business in some way or another? Churches, charities, computer companies, governments, music stores, museums, schools, weapons manufacturers, sports teams, family homes...the list goes on and on...are all businesses. Money comes in and money goes out; whenever that occurs, we're talking about business. I know many people who hate business and everything it stands for. But these feelings are nothing more than the byproduct of our confusion and ignorance about money—certainly not our knowledge of it.

We need to probe a little. Why does our educational system do such a poor job of teaching us about money? Why did our teachers resist teaching about it, and why are our children's teachers still resisting? Why do people who should know better continue to support the old myths that there is something inherently dirty about money? Could it be that the people running the schools have never learned about it themselves? If that's true, we desperately need to make some changes. Directly or indirectly, our continued ignorance about money is causing long-term damage to generations of people.

Can Success Buy Money?

Let's say that 20 percent of students who graduate from high school learn about money and go on to do very well for themselves. That's undoubtedly a generous estimate, but let's assume it's somewhere in the ballpark. Some would say that this 20 percent success rate was pretty good. But how good is it if it means that the remaining 80 percent will continue to be confused about money, and go on to lead less-than-fulfilling lives?

The really serious side effects of neglecting the subject of money in our schools seldom appear until nearly 20 years following graduation. That's when most adults begin to notice that their careers are plateauing and the dreams they once had are not coming to fruition. The tension and the disappointment and the desperation continue to build up as the person nears retirement. For many people, especially those of the baby-boom generation, retirement will be a nightmare, not a dream, because they simply never learned the basic principles of money.

Are there any hard facts to back up my claims about how our ignorance of money affects our financial futures? Unfortunately, there are. According to the U.S. Department of Health and Human Services, publication #13-11871, 6/90, only four out of 100 people in the U.S. ever reach financial independence.

Moreover, for every 100 people who start careers, at age 65: 25% are dead; 20% have incomes below the poverty level; and 51% have incomes above the poverty level but below $35,000 annually. Of that 51%, most would be described as: (a) struggling financially but too embarrassed to ask for help; (b) receiving extra support from their families; (c) dependent on some form of government support. I have to say that if this is the best we can do during the boom years of the late 80s and early 90s, what is going to happen when we are downsizing for the late 90s? This illustrates how financially ill-prepared we are.

What will it take for us to fully realize that the success of our educational system cannot be measured in terms of our academic standing on the day of graduation, but that we must measure it according to how it serves us for our lifetimes?

The principles of making money are surprisingly simple. You don't have to be intelligent or well-educated to be rich. We need no verification of that. Most of us know at least one wealthy person who is neither educated nor smart. In fact, judging by the number of poor people with Ph.D.s, higher education must actually be a hindrance to financial success.

I have learned a lot about money over the years, and there is no doubt in my mind that financial success requires very little knowledge. If you got through the second grade you have enough education to become a millionaire. Truly rich people—not those who do it with mirrors—that is, with loans, leveraging and manipulating other people's money—simply have different habits.

Describing the basic principles of money is beyond the scope of this book. But for those who want to pursue this, I highly recommend the book *The Richest Man in Babylon*, by George S. Clason. It is a wonderful place to begin. For now, trust me when I say that the habits you need to learn in order to become a millionaire are no more complex than the rules for playing Monopoly. So, you may ask, if the principles really are that simple, why aren't they taught in school? Here are four possible explanations:

Possible Explanation # 1

If everyone knew the principles of money, education would be forced to let go of its biggest lie—that you have to go to school to be successful. That lie could be the most successful PR job in the history of advertising. People have continued to believe it in spite of overwhelming evidence to the contrary. Nobody has ever proved that there is any direct correlation between formal education and success. Quite to the contrary.

Many successful people were quite unsuccessful in school. Abraham Lincoln had less than a year's formal education. Harry Truman never went to college. George Bernard Shaw, Nobel prize winner in literature, left school at the age of 16, as did John Major, Prime Minister of England.

I have a college degree but it had little to do with my financial success. In fact, much of what I learned after second grade had to be unlearned along the way before I could enjoy the success I enjoy today.

Possible Explanation # 2

If people knew the principles of money, schools could no longer use fear tactics to motivate students to study and memorize irrelevant, boring subjects.

Possible Explanation # 3

Businesses of the world would lose their cheap labor. If everyone understood money they could easily make all they wanted or needed without ever becoming an employee. There would no longer be any paycheck slaves, and the companies that still depended on them would have to close their doors.

Possible Explanation # 4

The educational system honestly does not know about the principles of money.

Can I prove what I say? I am my own guinea pig. I am a professional teacher. My business is education. I was financially able to retire at the age of 43, solely through my earnings as a teacher. Yet, I am not sitting around, going on cruises or hanging out at the country club. Why? Because I love what I am doing, and I would never give it up. I hate being bored. By simply applying the principles of business and money to my profession of teaching, I often earn more in a week than many teachers earn in three years.

Poverty—The Real Root of All Evil

Just imagine what kind of world this would be if everybody understood money, if there was no longer any confusion and desperation about it. We'd have less crime—less street crime as well as less white collar crime in business and government. All crime, white collar or the street kind, diminishes everyone's well being, ultimately creating more desperate people, then filtering down, creating more street crime. We build more jails with our tax money. Jails mass-produce smarter criminals since prison is merely a "graduate school" for the advanced study of crime. Seventy percent of all inmates in federal penitentiaries fail on the outside, are arrested again and return to prison for "refresher courses." Are they successful in their quest for money? Recently, a criminologist told me that the average lifetime earnings of the total criminal population is about one third of the U.S. poverty level. Is it possible that if we started educating young children about money, we would have fewer criminals in jail and less crime and greed in business and government?

Who Guards the Hen House?

Up till now, education about money has been left up to the individual. The only people I see taking the time to educate the public about credit, credit cards and savings are banks and other financial institutions. But when we look at the track records of these institutions, it becomes quite obvious that these "teachers" have a lot to learn themselves, before they start advising other people. To let bankers educate the masses about credit is a little like having the fox protect the hen house.

If we got past the false belief that there is something basically dirty or evil about money, and we began educating children regarding its real meaning and purpose in all our lives, within 30 years we would have a more financially secure nation, better-run governments and businesses, fewer people dependent on government handouts and a much stronger national economy.

Let's never forget that the first priority of public education is to teach people to master the basic skills necessary for functioning well in society. If we fail to do that much, there's something seriously wrong with the system.

Where do we begin rebuilding our society so that our dreams of one day being rich and happy can come true? The answer is really quite simple. We begin by redefining money, not as the root of all evil but as a basic instrument that every schoolchild must thoroughly understand before he or she reaches the sixth grade. To keep our young people ignorant about money in today's society makes about as much sense as failing to teach young people in an agrarian society how to till the soil, plant their crops and bring in the harvest.

This single correction of our basic perceptions about money, can do wonders. Not that our responsibility ends there—far from it! But with this change of mind we open doors to a whole new world of possibilities, a world no longer divided between the haves and have-nots. We cannot call ourselves a responsible society until we can honestly say that we are doing our best to understand and teach the principles of money. And that education starts with this simple change of mind—that ignorance about money is the real evil we must fight, not money itself.

8

What Is Financial Security?

Money is the seed of money, and the first guinea is sometimes more difficult to acquire than the second million.

—JEAN JACQUES ROUSSEAU (1754)

What is Security?

- A high-paying job? (Having money to cover all your wants and needs.)
- Working for the government? (You'll probably never get fired.)
- Working for a large corporation? (The benefits are great and there's a lot of room for advancement.)
- Money in the bank? (Nice to have a cushion just in case anything goes wrong.)
- Investing in stocks and bonds? (Extra income without having to work a lot of extra hours.)
- A retirement plan? (Great to be able to look forward to that day when you won't have to work any more.)
- Medical and life insurance? (If you get sick or are injured, there won't be any financial worries for you or your loved ones.)
- Working for a small company? (Where everybody knows everybody else, and you all pull together, working cooperatively.)

- Working for yourself? (More control of your own financial life.)
- Marrying somebody rich? (You'll never again have to bother your own head about making money.)
- Having a gun in your house? (The police department is so overworked, self-protection is becoming a fact of life.)
- Owning real estate? (Legend has it that you can never lose there.)
- A burglar alarm system? (You need to protect what you have.)

These are the traditional things people feel will make them secure. The trouble is that none of them comes with an ironclad guarantee. What may constitute security today may fall apart in the future. And what may seem like security is often only an illusion. Regardless, people turn to those sources of security listed above because they don't know what else to do. In the long run, hooking up with one or more of these "security systems" can end up preventing you from ever finding any real source of security.

"Train now for a high-paying job with a secure future," the radio commercial for a medical technicians' school blared. Riding in a cab through downtown San Francisco during lunch hour, I saw streets that were crowded with men and women in dark suits, rushing around against a background of bums and beggars.

I wondered who felt more secure—the bums and beggars or the corporate warriors. As I looked into their faces, employed and unemployed, it was difficult to find even a single one who looked secure. Everyone looked at least a little frightened.

It was 1981 and I knew first-hand what insecurity was all about. I had lost everything, had jeopardized my father's property and was in the midst of digging myself out of a deep financial hole, desperately attempting to save a sinking company.

I had only one thing going for me after being humbled into realizing I did not know all the answers after all. I had made the decision to learn from my mistakes. I had quit pretending that I knew everything and had begun to discover what I did not know.

I had vowed to master the art of business. I realized that if I mastered that, I would no longer have to be a slave to a job or dependent on the stability of the economy. If I was truly a good businessperson, I could make money doing anything. And if I could make money doing anything, then I could do something that satisfied my heart, my soul and my spirit. If I was truly a good businessman, I could give my unique gift to this world. That would be the greatest joy of all.

It had been tough for me to commit to learning rather than going for the dollars, as most of my friends were doing during the booming '80s. But I had discovered the hard way that at this point in my life I had to put all my energy into learning rather than earning. For a while I would make knowledge my top priority, much more important than money. Even though I would have a lot less money than my friends for a few years, my true wealth (knowledge) would eventually pay off, and it would continue paying off for the rest of my life.

While growing up I learned about investing. I knew how to make money with money. When my mother told me to "study hard so I could get a good job," I didn't listen to her. I was convinced that I already knew it all. I would get rich through investing. However, investing failed to give me a sense of being a productive, contributing member of society. By 1977 I was feeling incompetent and unfulfilled. So I decided to become a businessman. I set out to build a business. Well, the business did very well for a while, then failed. It would be easy to say that it failed because of a crooked partner who literally ran off with the profits. But that wasn't the real reason. It failed because I continued to act as if I knew all the answers. Whatever other factors may have contributed to my downfall, the bottom line is that I lost all my money because I would not admit to myself that I had a lot to learn about business. My arrogance turned out to be very expensive.

After losing my own company, I had several lucrative job offers. I looked at them all very carefully. Although the money was tempting, especially with banks and creditors hounding me, I turned down every offer. Instead, I continued my educational process, putting everything I could into learning how to be a complete businessperson.

But that isn't all I was learning. Part of my discovery was that in order to be a good businessperson I was going to have to learn how to be a kinder, more open human being. After four years in a military academy and six years as a Marine Corps Officer, I had become tough. I had treated the people in my company as if they were members of a combat squad. Not only did I alienate my partners, but also my wife, who left me.

By 1984, I had become a little more civilized, in both my business and personal life. It was then that I met my wife, Kim, whom I married in 1986. In 1987 we celebrated the most important financial event in our lives since the day I lost my company. At last my net worth was down to zero. We cheered wildly. This was a brand new beginning for us. Why, you may ask, were we celebrating a net worth of zero? Because for years we had been looking up from a net worth that was so far down in the red, that even a glimpse of a zero looked pretty damn good. At last my assets equaled what I owed.

Just five years later, having mastered the foundation principles of business and put them into practice, Kim and I actually found ourselves in a position to retire. Our primary reason for working shifted at this point, from working just to earn more money to working because it truly nourishes us. The money continues to pour in, that is true. But now we have the invaluable luxury of viewing our work as a way to make a contribution to society.

My definition of security has radically changed from the day I first dreamed of having my own business. Today, security means:

1. Working when I want, where I want and with whom I want.
2. Knowing how to enjoy prosperity whether the general economy is up or down.
3. Being willing to lose everything and knowing I'll be wiser for it when I get it back.
4. Not having to work at anything I don't want to.
5. Not spending hours each week stuck in commuter traffic.
6. Achieving everything I want without damaging myself, my family, the environment or anyone else.
7. The ability to increase or decrease my income at will.
8. Freedom from all money worries.
9. Freedom to live wherever I choose.
10. Traveling with pay and enjoying frequent vacations.

When I think about our society's misconceptions about security, I am often reminded of something that happened when I was a fighter pilot in Vietnam. During a combat mission, every pilot, "for his own security," was fitted with a bullet-proof vest, or "bullet bouncer," as we called them.

One day I saw what happened to a pilot when a large caliber bullet hit his "bullet bouncer." The bullet didn't bounce. On the contrary, when the bullet hit, the vest acted more like a net, catching the bullet and spreading its impact over a wider area, virtually crushing the pilot's entire body. Some security! I thought. The next day, as I prepared for my mission over a particularly hot combat zone, I realized the vest provided nothing more than a false sense of security. What's worse, it hindered my arm movements, interfering with my ability to fly. I knew that day that my only real security was knowledge—what I knew about combat and flying—knowledge I had acquired through hours of trial and error, through making mistakes, correcting them and learning from them. I jettisoned the vest that day and never wore it again.

Security in the real world is just like that vest. Our security has to come from trust in ourselves, not from externals like the bullet bouncers of modern life—the right college degree, working for a company that offers good benefits, or even working in the government where nobody gets fired. Each time I take a risk, make a mistake, learn what went wrong and correct it, my security increases because my wealth (knowledge) increases.

Security will forever elude those of us who follow the rules we learned in school—be good, do as you are told, don't make mistakes, etc. All these rules do little more than stop the learning and personal development process. In today's rapidly changing world true security can only be found in ourselves and in our ability to admit what we don't know, learn, and thus grow from any situation.

Most of us are so enamored by the idea of security that even when unhappy with our jobs we will stay with them, day after day and year after year. The truth is that staying in situations which are unsatisfying only increases our sense of insecurity. We begin to feel there is no other choice but to sell our souls in the name of security. When we've committed ourselves to a life like that, it becomes very difficult to see that we're sacrificing ourselves every moment of every day to a false sense of security provided by a "bullet bouncer" that really doesn't work.

None of us is alone in creating our illusions of security. Our society, starting way back with the first years of school, indoctrinates us with the belief that if we just keep wearing our "bullet bouncers" we'll be okay.

By the time we're adults we become so wedded to these beliefs that even when we've seen evidence proving that the safety vests don't work, that they even seriously restrict our movements, we continue to cling to them.

Our social system creates fearful, specialized drones who believe that their lifetime security (the safety vest) means getting a good job with plenty of benefits. We have a prime example of this in the Northwest United States. Long dependent on a single product, timber, that industry has lately come under attack by the environmental movement, automation and exports. What was once an industry with a fairly high degree of job security is now undergoing tremendous change. People who once believed they had a job for life are finding themselves starting all over, looking for work in a new specialty. Those who had seniority are having to start all over again at the bottom of a new industry for which they have little or no training.

If they were generalists, thinking for themselves, they could profit from the change. Change brings new opportunities. Granted, such opportunities are not always clearly apparent. Often they have to be created, and this takes the skills of a generalist. But as long as we have been trained to just do as we're told and not ask any questions, we can never be much more than robots, totally dependent on others to provide us with a place to work and a paycheck at the end of the week.

But let's not pick on the Northwest. This same scenario exists in many other industries worldwide. It's happening in the auto industry, the steel industry, and in dozens of other industries that for two or three generations have supported whole cities throughout the world. Change is now so rapid, owing in part to the fastest-changing technology in the history of humanity, that job security itself has become obsolete, a dinosaur that is dying out. That is why one must be a generalist first, a specialist second.

Becoming a generalist allows a person to benefit from change instead of denying or fighting it every inch of the way. The generalist has the skills to build a new way of life, to create alternatives instead of being trapped in co-dependent relationships with companies which themselves are addicted to false security and resistance to change. And for my money, that's a personal goal worth fighting for.

Believe me, I've known what it is to lose everything and be like a bum on the street—or even worse, a bum with debts amounting to far more than most people will ever build in assets! I know what it is to be buried under debt and wake up in the middle of the night in a sweat, wondering if I'll ever be able to work my way out.

It's a terrible temptation just to quit at such times, and many people do. But it is often in the face of seemingly overwhelming challenges like these that our real education begins. It is often only when we've hit bottom that we are able to look honestly at our mistakes and begin learning, really learning, for the first time. It is then and only then that we begin to find the path to real security, based on knowing ourselves, our gifts and our shortcomings, and knowing how to create the opportunities that other people or the world can't provide for us. It is then we discover that our first lesson is often to un-learn everything that has been taught to us up to that moment, and to start learning to be a generalist.

Meeting these challenges in my own life proved to be a path to security and profitability that I could have previously only imagined or dreamed about. And today I can honestly say that this is the single most rewarding decision I have ever made. Though I do not regret those years, I am convinced that a personal crisis of the magnitude that I confronted would not be necessary if we had an educational system that taught us to be generalists first, specialists second.

What does it mean to be a generalist? This subject is one that we will be exploring throughout this book, but there are a couple of observations I'd like to share with you that will at least get us pointed in the direction of understanding this concept. For example, John W. Gardner, the founder of Common Cause and former president of the Carnegie Foundation for the Advancement of Teaching, once wrote that, "What we must reach for is a conception of perpetual self-discovery, perpetual reshaping to realize one's best self, to be the person one could be." That's the essence of the generalist, to be constantly moving toward a horizon which can never be reached.

Cavett Robert pointed out in his book *Success With People Through Human Engineering and Motivation,* that preparation for the future can no longer mean preparation for a specific job. The world is changing so quickly that even in a specialized field such as medicine, law, or economics, a person must expect to be retrained at least four times during his or her lifetime. He states, "In our approach to knowledge we must realize that preparation is a constant process of change with no ending.

It must be forever moving, never static. School is never out for the person who wants to succeed."

To be a generalist, then, means always to stay open and alert to change. It is found in our constant and continuous preparation of ourselves to meet the constant and continuous changes in the world around us. The generalist's motto, which is more important today than ever before in history, continues to be that success is a journey, not a destination. Above all, the generalist is one who never ceases to grow.

9

Who Says Women Are the Weaker Sex?

More than five million women-owned businesses, the Fortune 500 firms of the 21st century, generate more jobs than the big corporations on that over-esteemed list.

—PATRICIA ABURDENE & JOHN NAISBITT

"We were happily married for 14 years. One night, he didn't come home."

I was having dinner with one of my classmates from high school. Sandra and I had always been good friends, though we had never been romantic. She was telling me about her divorce and what happened to her 14-year marriage.

"After high school, I was really happy to leave for college to get away from my parents," she said. "It was my time to grow and find out who I was.

"I had been away at college for only a few months when I met Dan. He was a senior. The attraction was immediate and sparks flew. I never felt so alive, beautiful and in love. He used to escort me from classes to my dorm. The walk was lined with ancient oaks and, in the autumn, the rust-colored leaves would swirl around our feet. The air was crisp, and I remember the first time he put his arm around my shoulders to pull me closer so I wouldn't get cold. That moment was just perfect. I'll always cherish the memory."

Sandra's story was one I'd heard many times. Dan graduated and went to law school and they moved in together. Life was bliss, and they knew they were the perfect couple. After Dan finished law school they were engaged and married. To help with living expenses, Sandra took a job and quit school, six months short of her degree. She vowed to finish, someday. That day never came. Dan's career came first. Then they were buying a house, then the children started coming.

Sandra was the perfect wife, a caring mother and the emotional pillar of the family during the years that Dan was struggling to work his way to the corner office at the firm. After ten years he was a full partner in a thriving law practice. He also had a girlfriend.

Dan's new love was fresh out of law school and worked for the same firm. Sandra knew something was wrong but did her best to push her fears out of her mind. One night Dan didn't come home. His excuses were flimsy. Over the next few weeks hardly a day went by that they weren't either fighting or ignoring each other. The children were ordered to their rooms while the "war" was on.

For a few months they attempted to save their marriage, but Dan never quit seeing his new lover. Eventually he moved out of the house, and a short time later Sandra filed for divorce.

Sandra looked at me across our restaurant table and said, "Do you know what destroyed our marriage?"

I shook my head.

"We had nothing in common." After a long pause, she added, "There was a lot of love. I know he loves me and I will always love him. Love wasn't the issue. When we had no money we had that in common. We worked together to get through college, to build his practice, to buy the house and provide for the kids. But once the money came in and life got easier we had nothing in common."

Sandra stared off into the distance. After another long silence she said, "You know, he did warn me in a strange sort of way a couple of years before his affair. He used to say it might be a good idea if I went back to school or got a job, or did something other than sit at home with the kids. But in almost the same breath he would say he didn't want me working and that he was the provider. That it was his duty or something."

She drifted off. I let a few minutes pass, then asked, "So what did you do during the days?"

"Well, I had my friends. We would go to aerobics classes together and do things with our children. I worked part-time at my children's preschool..." Sandra was obviously thinking faster than she was talking.

"You know, when Dan came home at the end of the day, we didn't really have anything to talk about. His career was exciting and interesting, but all I ever talked about was the kids. I guess I knew our paths were diverging. I just didn't know what to do about it."

Sandra's face was carved deep with worry lines as she relived the past. "I wanted to re-connect with him. I desperately wanted to feel the joy again that we had felt in college walking down the long oak-lined paths. In my heart I knew I was losing the most precious and dear person in my entire life, but what can you say to the person you love when all you do is cry? I felt so hurt, so betrayed and so helpless. But I also felt bitter. I just kept thinking, after all I've done for him, how could he do this to me?"

She ended her story by telling me about her plans to go back to college and complete her degree. Meanwhile, she was working for a large accounting firm, supervising the clerical staff. The pay wasn't great, but she needed the benefit package while she raised her children. She dated occasionally, but nothing serious. Dan was remarried, but not to the young attorney in the law firm. Company policy had prevented them from seeing each other, and having been delivered an ultimatum, Dan had stopped seeing her and she had left the firm.

I suspect most people reading this book have heard stories similar to Sandra's. Job placement counselors work with women in similar situations almost daily. These women often have greater financial needs than the market will pay for their marketable job skills and/or experience level. And if the woman has children, there are additional needs such as childcare, the need to take time off work when the kids are ill...the demands on the single mother go on 24 hours per day.

The question I hear asked again and again in these situations is: "How and why does it happen?" Occasionally, I hear women blame their husbands or men in general. But most of them actually know that they have somehow set themselves up. They know how they got there. They just don't know what to do now or what they might have done so that things could have turned out differently.

The purpose of this chapter is to offer some insights on women, money, success and self-fulfillment. But before we do that I must warn you that all this is from the limited vantage point of an admittedly only partially reformed male-chauvinist.

Who Is the Weaker Sex?

I was with a friend in a used-book store one day when he found an old book on etiquette, written by a woman for women. It discussed all the "right" things to do around men. My initial response was to laugh at some of the absurdities in the book. It said women should pretend not to be as smart or as able as men. Specifically it said, "Do not contradict a man's opinion. Make him feel his ideas are brilliant." As we read further it said, "In sports, do not be too talented or athletic, and always let the man win." In another section of the book, it said, "Never carry a cigarette lighter or matches, so the man can help you in lighting your cigarette."

Putting the book back, we walked away chuckling. My friend said, "Why would a woman want to live her life pretending to be less than she is?"

We both agreed that we were glad times have changed.

But have they?

The idea that women are the weaker sex has been one of the biggest con jobs in the history of humanity. If we are measuring strength in terms of muscle and potential violence, I might agree. But it is also clear that if our civilization is to evolve to a higher state we need to change the yardstick by which we measure "strength."

I do not remember when I first became aware of the women's movement, but I do know my initial response was one of mild shock and indignation. "What do you mean men don't treat women fairly? What do you mean 'equal opportunity'? My company hires lots of them. Sure they're low-paid. It's not my fault they don't have business skills. I know there are some men who are real barbarians with women, but they aren't my friends. They must be talking about other men, not me. Besides, what are they grumbling about? We take care of them and make life easier for them. I wish I had life as easy as women do. They aren't expected to be the bread-winners and protectors."

It took me a while to realize that men like me were the prime targets of the women's movement. As shocking as this realization was, I now thank the movement for the education. In 1985 I formed my first company with two women as equal partners. Until then, I only had men as partners. Had I known how much better, easier and more profitable business would be with women as partners, I would have done it years ago. While it took me some time to adjust to a woman's way of doing business, and although there were some heated arguments on handling certain problems along the way, I discovered some very interesting things not only about women, but about myself and other men.

In my life, women partners produced two outcomes I did not always have with men—peace and profitability. And once we had peace and profitability, I did not care about getting credit for my great business mind or who was which sex. Believe me, peace and profitability are much more satisfying that having my ego salved or being deep in debt. Maybe my experience is limited, and maybe I was just lucky. But today I would venture to say that based on what I've seen so far, women are better at business than men. Men are like moose with antlers. Too often decisions get made on the size of the antlers rather than on good sense or true knowledge.

The book *Barbarians at the Gate,* by Bryan Burrough and John Helyar, tells about the takeover of RJR Nabisco. It is a great story about what happens in the real world when you put big antlers over brains and good sense. In this story of mindless power struggles an entire empire fell. Take that story and extend it to a global economy and you may come to understand why our economy is in such debt. In this male-dominated milieau, big antlers and pea brains battle it out every day, driven by the single-minded goal of maintaining power over others rather than building a world economy that makes a genuine contribution to all.

Why aren't women running the show? I suspect it's because most men, whether they think about it or not, want to hang onto the myth that "women are the weaker sex." History shows that it is a myth made by men, and enforced by violence, fear and brute force. And most men know it is only a myth. The myth began to lose power once we entered the industrial age, when muscle gave way to machinery and mental abilities. Now that we are in the information age, machinery has given way to electronic information—and muscle is almost obsolete, except as it is used for its cosmetic appeal, as evidenced by the millions of men and women who work out in gyms and health spas developing "hard bods."

Even with all the technological changes we've seen over the years, the myth about women being the weaker sex continues, once again proving the power of ideas and thoughts. But I have to add this: Men aren't the only ones who are promoting and supporting the myth of woman as the weaker sex. Just as there continue to be male chauvinists, there continue to be dependent, wimpy women who play their counterparts, giving women a bad name. The cliché I hear these women use is, "I gave my power away."

As I have begun to look at the various ways I still cling to the old myth, and as I continue to let go of my need to feel superior to women, I find it easier to recognize when I need to get out of women's way and stop blocking their power and strength. I think the thing that gives me the most trouble is knowing what to do when I find women who, for whatever reasons, continued to play the game of helpless woman, dominating man. I'm know I'm not alone in this since other men also find this difficult. It's a reminder to us all that changing the status quo requires a joint effort of major proportions.

What Happened to the Women?

Even when I was in high school I knew women were smarter than men. They seemed to study more diligently and often had better grades. I wondered what happened to women along the way. What were the pressures that brainwashed them to continue to accept their terribly restricted roles in the male-dominated society? If they were as smart as they appeared to be in school, why weren't they running the show after graduating?

I asked women about the world of business. Some of the answers I received were interesting.

Although most women my age understand that having job skills is important, many continue to think of business as a man's domain. That may be true today, but that was not the way things started. Much of what we call business originally belonged to women. When humans lived in caves, and even today in some nomadic cultures, what we know as business was really tasks assigned to women. Early on, men had only two primary work functions: fighting (protecting their communities and families from other men) and hunting. The rest of the jobs were the woman's domain: they built and maintained the shelters, they produced clothing, they prepared food, they made utensils, cared for the sick, tilled the soil and educated the children.

As time passed, men were needed less for hunting and fighting. So they returned to camp and took over the women's tasks. Over hundreds of years, they turned these activities into businesses. Eventually they opened up trade routes with other countries, exchanging goods they had in abundance for goods that were rare or nonexistent in their society.

Today men dominate the business of housing, clothing, food preparation products, food distribution, medicine and education. While men have done much to advance technology in most of these areas, they have also brought the same energy they used in hunting and fighting. They have brought a "big fish eat the little fish" mentality into business. They have brought heroic, violence-oriented tactics into politics. They have even brought heroic tactics into medicine—where they "attack" epidemics, "destroy" bacteria, and "fight the war against cancer" with knives (scalpels), poisons (chemotherapy) and high-tech weaponry (radiation). One cannot help but reflect how our entire society would have evolved given the direction of more feminine principles, stereotyped or otherwise.

When I talk to men and women about business I hear the same complaints. Neither sex enjoys the violence, dog-eat-dog competitiveness, and outright hostility and warfare that we find in business.

When contemplating moving up the corporate ladder I encountered the same "kill or be killed" mentality I saw in combat in Vietnam. It saddens me to see men and women choosing to play this game and to see the kind of people they become in the process. I decided not to play the corporate game and so I leaped from the safety the corporate world offered into being in my own business. I quickly found how vicious and "dog-eat-dog" the real business world can be. I swam with sharks in blood-laden waters. My blood. After a while the bleeding stopped, and I learned to swim with some of the best. It became a fun game and, once I learned the rules, a fairly safe one. Sharks generally prey on the weak. You do not have to be a shark to survive; you just can't be weak or uneducated when it comes to the game of money, investments and business.

I sometimes talk to women's groups and when I do I give the same advice I give everyone—male, female, minority or majority: "Don't specialize too early in your working life. First become a generalist in business. Instead of choosing employment primarily for what it can offer in pay, benefits or security, work at jobs in which you can learn. A person's real wealth is their knowledge, not their bucks."

If a person has to work, full- or part-time, why not take jobs that develop experience in sales, marketing, production, accounting and finance? Within 10 to 15 years you're well-rounded in business and less prone to shark bites, rather than a burned-out dental hygienist, executive secretary or computer programmer.

As valuable as these skills can be for running a business, that's not the primary reason I recommend pursuing them. I recommend them because they are the fastest way I know for most people to enhance their self-confidence, knowledge and income. Further, as labor becomes more expensive and the cost of goods continues to come down, anyone who has multiple skills and who can perform many tasks will command more money on the job market. It leads to fewer dead ends and more long-term freedom. Remember, there are few jobs in this world that aren't in some way connected with business.

The more women know about business, money and finance, the greater freedom they will enjoy, and the more likely they will be to discover their own power. I have known women who climbed the corporate ladder and played right into the male domain. Too many of them either surrendered their power or became masculinized instead of bringing their own powers and talents into the business world. Some cut and ran, getting out of the game as quickly as they could.

I know there is a glass ceiling and I'm glad women are finally making it to the top, yet I often wonder at what price. I found the mental and emotional pain of corporate life much more destructive than being in combat. War was open, violent aggression, not silent, insidious backstabbing by fellow workers.

We are seeing the male-dominated worlds of politics and business both giving way to women. But unless women have the courage to bring their own unique perspectives into the workplace, instead of trying to adopt ways of behavior that men find acceptable, nothing is going to change. We'll simply end up with women who are making the same mistakes men have been making for the past few hundred years. The bottom line is that to improve upon what we've already got, there will have to be a balance between what both sexes can uniquely offer.

Women who specialize play right into the dominating ways of men. My doctor has female nurses, highly specialized technicians doing most of the physical work while he gets the lion's share of the pay. I wonder if these women see the long-term trap and income plateau they are working into. Many find themselves bored or burned out. They make too much money to quit, yet many of them complain that they are not making enough money, nor do they have the status within the health-care community, to go out on their own and develop their abilities to the fullest.

In recent years, more and more women have been learning about the world of finances and investment, either as a full-time career or as a way of richly augmenting income from a more traditional job. I highly recommend this route, not only for women but for men as well.

There are many simple, well-written books on these subjects available in any good store that handles business books. There are also many consultants and teachers peddling their knowledge either through private consultation or seminars. Throughout my life I've attended many workshops and lectures, some of them free, some of them costing several hundred dollars. And I have to say that I've always learned something, no matter how good or bad the course.

The reason I recommend learning about investments is because investments do not care about your age, sex, color, religion or educational background. Investment requires little muscle or brawn, which makes it a fair arena for men or women. Interestingly, while men may control the investment world, women control most of the money. Apparently, women are better money managers because they often wind up with control of the purse-strings.

Nearly everyone who works directly with our company is required to know general business skills as well as have their own professional speciality. We find this creates a stronger, more secure organization.

My wife is one of my business partners. Before we married we had a heart-to-heart talk about her willingness to learn about business. I wanted to be sure that if we should part (which we have no intention of doing) she would be very able to do well on her own. I am happy to report that after five years of marriage she has become a far better businessperson than I will ever be. Now when our accountant, attorney, consultants or brokers call, they ask to talk to her, not me. If we ever did part, she would not experience any financial loss because she is able to generate her own income. Her standard of living would not even go down since she is well-rounded in business and not limited to any one product, industry, location, income level or husband.

The best part is that our marriage is stronger because of my wife's participation in the business. We have a lot in common in many areas of interest. Her self-confidence continues to grow along with mine, which adds to her inner and outer beauty. And in our mutual growth we inspire each other to continue to learn and grow. The more she grows, the more my respect increases for who she is. And vice-versa, I believe. Along with respect, our love for each other also grows. The more we learn and grow together, the happier our marriage becomes—and a happy marriage is priceless.

What Men Are Learning From Women

At the risk of generalizing, I have found that the women in our company often work more diligently than men. They handle problems and people with greater patience and compassion, are more thoughtful in financial decisions, and tend to think more in terms of the big picture than do most men I've known.

When I finally let go of my prejudices and began to trust women as equals I found I was better able to channel my often volatile male tendencies toward more productive ends. Thanks to the influence of the women in my life I have learned both the value of and the skills for speaking with kindness and compassion, even to people with whom I am angry. These newfound abilities have brought everyone in our company closer instead of blowing the business apart.

Not only have my relationships with women improved, my relationships with men are now kinder and much less filled with ego-driven superficiality. Today, I can see that where peace, trust and love exist, profit often follows. This is a far cry from the way I thought when I first started out in business, when I believed you had to be tough, competitive and unyielding to get ahead in business.

As more men and women come to recognize that strength is more than muscle and brute force, our humanity evolves on this planet. Many of today's economic problems and imbalances are primarily the result of male ego and greed. Production in most companies could be vastly improved if we could get rid of the subliminal aggression that smolders in work arenas. In education our children would learn more if less male "survival of the fittest" energy was incorporated into the way we teach and evaluate our students. There would be fewer casualties if we focused on instilling the love of learning in our children rather than being hell-bent on supplying fresh troops for our businesses to sacrifice to their wars with the competition.

I often ask women to step back and take a good look at the overall system of education. I ask them to use their God-given intuition to decide if the current system is the most beneficial way to teach. When women tune in to their feminine strengths, and when men get in touch with their feminine sides, it is not long before we begin to sense the extent to which we've blindly adopted male ego-driven teaching methods in our schools. The next question is, what would our educational system look like if we reorganized it according to more feminine principles. When I ask people to do this in workshops and lectures, discussions definitely start to get quite exciting and heated.

One of the most successful, non-traditional, private education businesses I know of is run by a woman named Bobbi DePorter. Her courses for teens are called SuperCamp. I attended the first camp in 1982 and was stunned to see the quantum leaps that became possible in learning when love, fun and compassion were combined with high-speed teaching methods. There are off-shoots of SuperCamp springing up in other areas; Discovery is making tremendous advances in education throughout Australia. It, too, is run by a woman. For education to evolve it is obvious that the strengths of women need to be brought in.

Occasionally when asked, "Is there anything the West can do to wrestle back business and economic supremacy from Japan and other upcoming Asian nations?" I say, "Encourage women to bring their strengths and influence into every arena, whether business, government, religion, medicine, law or education."

The Orient is still in the dark ages when it comes to equality for women. The women's movement is the West's secret weapon and most men are not yet aware of its power. Men need to let down their guard and become more human while women need to value their unique strengths and brilliance. If the West can evolve in this area before the Orient, it can regain its lead. If we continue rigid, "moose-antler" thinking, we will continue to decline. I predict the first country or culture which truly blends men's and women's strengths will be the next world power.

10

Teaching People to Be Mindless Parrots

I learned a lot of things in school that bothered me. But I also learned quickly that because the teachers who were telling me these disturbing things were also the same people giving me my grades, if I were going to get by in school, I would have to give their answers, regardless of what I felt to be true. Even though I gave their answers, I didn't stop thinking.

—R. BUCKMINSTER FULLER

Perhaps the single most important lesson for the generalist to learn is that memorization and knowledge aren't the same. Whenever I make this statement in one of my lectures a rumble goes through the crowd, telling me that I've struck a chord. People know that it's true, and that there is something important about making this distinction. They also know that our educational system puts a great deal of emphasis on rote learning, or memorization. Indeed, diplomas and advanced degrees are awarded on the basis of how good we are at memorizing. To clarify, let me tell you a story that illustrates my point in a slightly different way:

Before leaving for Vietnam to be a fighter pilot, I undertook advanced "gunship" training in California. Having completed flight school, I felt pretty cocky. After all, I had good grades in flying and academics. I could hardly wait to go to Vietnam and show off what I could do.

After I introduced myself to Lt. Johnson, the veteran pilot assigned to help me through the transition from ordinary pilot to gunship pilot, he asked me if I knew emergency procedures.

"Sure, I know them," I said. "I have them so memorized I recite them in my sleep."

The lieutenant wasn't too impressed but he said "good," then proceeded to quiz me. I thought this strange. Didn't he know I had learned all that stuff in flight school? I'd passed all the tests. I knew how to fly. I even had several hundred hours in this model aircraft. Didn't he know that I was a hot pilot? I just wanted to shoot!

A very long half-hour later I had passed his little quiz on emergency procedures. "You certainly have your procedures well memorized," he said. "Now we can go practice guns and rockets."

I grinned.

Soon I was low off the ground shooting like a maniac. Seeing that I was having too much fun for my own good, Lt. Johnson killed the engine. I stared at him in disbelief, but he continued to look out the front of the aircraft as if nothing had happened. Meanwhile, we were plunging earthward, out of control. I froze. My mind went blank. Had I been in charge at that moment I know that the lieutenant and I would now be laying atomized all over the desert floor.

"I've got the aircraft," the lieutenant said firmly, about 100 feet before impact. In silence he flew to an open area and set the aircraft down.

"You won't need any Viet Cong to kill you. Your incompetence will do it for you," he said dryly.

I didn't laugh.

"Almost anyone can memorize something, but if you have to think before you can do it, you don't really know it," he said.

"But I..."

"School days are over," he said. "It's time you learned how to fly. Right now you're no more than an idiot with a pilot's license."

The lesson was only too clear.

I learned the difference between real knowledge and memorization when Lt. Johnson killed my engine that day. After that experience, he drilled me and my friend, Lt. Ted Greene, the only other new pilot who had accepted the opportunity for more experience with emergency procedures. We pushed our learning beyond the limits of safety. It was intense. The frustration took Ted and me to a greater level of perfection. Then, one day we were calm. Emergencies became as routine as flying. Ted would almost yawn when I killed his engine. We flew as well with the engine off as we did with it on. Fear had been replaced with competence and competence led to quiet confidence, not ego.

A year later Ted and I were over the South China Sea. At 5:45 A.M. our aircraft carrier was slipping through the dark waters approximately 25 miles off the coast of Vietnam.

As I began pre-flight checks, Ted remarked that he was feeling uneasy about our assignment that morning. I admitted that I was feeling nervous about it, too, though neither of us could say exactly why.

Soon Ted, three crew members and I were airborne in our Huey gunship, cracking jokes and watching our carrier fade in the distance as we flew away. Within a few minutes the laughter subsided and we settled into the flying routine we had performed many times before.

Less than a half-hour later our engine died. We were flying at low altitude, so we had time to get out only a single emergency call before hitting the ocean. The next thing I remember was swimming out and away from the exploding helicopter.

Looking back at the events that happened as our engine sputtered to a stop that morning, I know only that we reacted quickly and instinctively. I have not a grain of doubt that had we stopped to think about our memorized procedures we never would have survived. Lt. Johnson's teachings literally saved the lives of five men that day.

Making Education Real

First and foremost, every educational system of every society should be successful in teaching the basic skills needed for survival in that society, be they physical, emotional or financial. If we were to establish only one educational goal, it certainly should be that. Above all, every student should come through the system knowing the most basic of all skills: how to learn, how to respond to what needs to be done right now. Anything else we might teach would be frosting on the cake, but if our educational system is failing at teaching the basic skills for living, we can hardly claim that it is serving us well.

If we are to be successful, not only in our own lives but as a society that our children and their children can enjoy, we must face the fact that most of the skills we really need for living successful lives have been pretty well trained out of us by the time we've graduated. In most cases, our natural responses for learning and responding appropriately to the world are deadened, or at least temporarily anesthetized, so that they are of little or no use to us.

The educational system rarely supports and builds upon our natural learning abilities. At the very least these abilities have been ignored; at the worst, they have been abused, thoroughly undermining our self-confidence and sense of self-determination. No matter how you look at it, we are robbed of the joy of learning that is our birthright, leaving us crippled as we go out into the world in search of success.

How do we even begin to regain what we've lost? And how do we make certain our children don't grow up in a system that not only fails to teach them the value of their natural learning abilities, but may actually undermine them? Change begins with understanding.

The three kinds of learning are:

1. Mental learning: memorized facts, consisting of storing certain chosen data in our brains, much as we'd file away data in a computer.
2. Physical learning: hands-on experience, involving all the senses, engaging most of the nervous system.
3. Emotional and subconscious learning: involving the student through feelings of joy, fear, sorrow, love, compassion, and exultation.

For learning to occur, all three kinds must be employed; one must not be emphasized to the exclusion of the others.

Take a closer look at the learning process by recalling how you developed the skills for riding a bicycle. You can divide the process into four stages:

The Four Stages of Learning

1. **Unconscious Incompetence:** You are excited about learning how to ride a bicycle, but having never done it before you are unaware of what you need to learn.
2. **Conscious Incompetence:** You get on the bicycle and start pedaling but quickly fall, making you aware that there are things you don't know.

3. **Conscious Competence:** Through trial and error, you correct your mistakes. You have observed, usually on an unconscious level, what you have been doing that causes you to fall and by trying different movements finally become a competent rider.
4. **Unconscious Competence:** You no longer think about what you are doing. You hold the knowledge you need within you, and you automatically draw upon that knowledge as you ride.

Consciously or unconsciously, you are probably aware of this process of learning. It is what you went through when you learned to drive, touch-type or play different sports. Perhaps you watched children go through this process when they learned to walk. First you saw the excitement as they discovered the possibility; then you saw their frustration as they tried, made mistakes and fell; next came the corrections and sense of self-determination; and finally you saw the exhilaration and joy in the child's face as she/he gained the ability to walk alone.

Regardless of what a person wants to learn, the Four Stages of Learning make it possible. The length of time it takes will differ, however, depending on the person and the subject being learned. Prior to school, this is how we all learned. And we loved it. It was exciting. It made us curious, so we wanted to learn more. Each time we learned something new we felt exhilarated; this special kind of exhilaration comes from a deep, mostly unconscious awareness that we each have within us the ability not only to learn about the world, but to master its challenges and even make an impact on it. As young children, most of us had a sense of our own potential and took great pleasure in its unfolding. But then something happened. School put an end to our fun.

Around age eight, our educational system cuts out physical and emotional learning and begins focusing almost exclusively on type one, that is, mental learning, primarily by overemphasizing facts and memorization. We progress from grade to grade only after "learning" certain facts mapped out by "educational experts" who have decided what children need to learn and when they should learn it.

If bicycle riding were taught according to the system of learning that is followed in most schools, students would not be allowed to even touch a bike until they had first memorized the facts about them. After a test on the facts, the number of right answers the student got would be tallied up and the student would receive a grade. Too many wrong answers and the student would not be allowed to progress to the next step, that is, to be assigned an actual bicycle so that he or she could begin riding. Those who couldn't do the memorizing would never get to ride. Never mind that these people might be the ones who would excel in physical learning and be able to master hands-on bicycle riding in an instant! Ironically, they might well be the ones who have the greatest potential for becoming Olympic champions in bicycling.

Imagine what might have happened had you learned to ride a bicycle this way. Here are just a few sample questions from an imaginary lesson plan, with comments about how they might play out:

1. ***When was the first bicycle invented?***

   Real Answer: In 1790 a Frenchman, M. de Sivrav invented the *velocifere,* a two-wheeled contraption with a wooden frame resembling a horse. The inventor sat astride it and propelled it forward by pushing against the ground with his feet. It was not until 1860 that a Scotsman by the name of Kirkpatrick Macmillan constructed a practical machine that could be steered with handlebars and propelled through a system of levers operated by the rider's legs.

   Student's real answer: Who cares? I just want to get on and start riding! If I flunk this test, they'll never let me even sit on the thing. How many more years do I have to put up with this? ...I wonder who's having a party this weekend.

2. ***A bicycle's frame is made of: a. Rubber b. Toothpaste c. Steel d. Aluminum***

   Student's thought process: In this magazine I read in the library last week, there was an article about the latest experimental bikes being made of an alloy of titanium and carbon fiber. Those won't be out until next year, but it's not an option on the test anyway. Some cheaper bikes are made of steel. Some expensive, ultra-lightweight racing bikes are made of aluminum. No telling what they're going to come up with for making even lighter, stronger bicycle frames ten years from now. How old is my teacher? If he's over 45 he'll only know about steel. I think he's 50, so I'll put steel.

3. ***Write a 250-word essay on the joys of riding a bicycle. You will be graded on creativity, originality and your use of conjugate verbs.***

Student's thought process: How would I know the joys of riding since they haven't let me do that yet? And, what the hell is a conjugate verb?

These sample questions should give you an idea of why mental learning alone will never help a person ride a bicycle, how mental learning only teaches about the subject, while emotional and physical learning is what happens when we actually do it. We can see from this that no matter how much information about bicycles a person memorizes, without physical learning and emotional responses, all that is accomplished is short-term knowledge of facts which, at best, might prepare the student for a spot on the TV quiz show *Jeopardy.*

To better understand this, let's look at Figure 1. We see here that each component of learning—mental, physical and emotional —plays an important role in any genuine learning process. This relates to the Four Stages of Learning: (1) Unconscious Incompetence; (2) Conscious Incompetence; (3) Conscious Competence; and (4) Unconscious Competence.

We can see learning's journey of hills and valleys, mistakes and corrections, which culminates in making knowledge part of us. And it shows that learning at its best ends up with a feeling of exhilaration derived from a sense of accomplishment and an inner recognition of one's own competence.

Looking at Figure 2, we see nature's true learning curve. We see a bird leaving its nest for the first time. At first, it loses altitude before being able to fly away. If the bird were afraid of falling, it would never leave its nest.

Too often in education, the over-emphasis on mental learning, particularly for those who don't normally learn best that way, plants the seeds of self-doubt in our minds. Indeed, the doubt can become so great that we never even leave the nest, convinced that we'll never learn to fly even before we've had a chance to try our wings. Our self-doubts can literally turn us against learning and growing; we turn into the kind of person who belittles education and personal growth in any form. When this happens to a person an important part of them dies. The inner drive that lights the spirit within us is gone, and we go through life in lockstep, running on automatic pilot instead of responding to the uniqueness of each new moment.

Fig. 1. Mental, Physical & Emotional Learning Curves

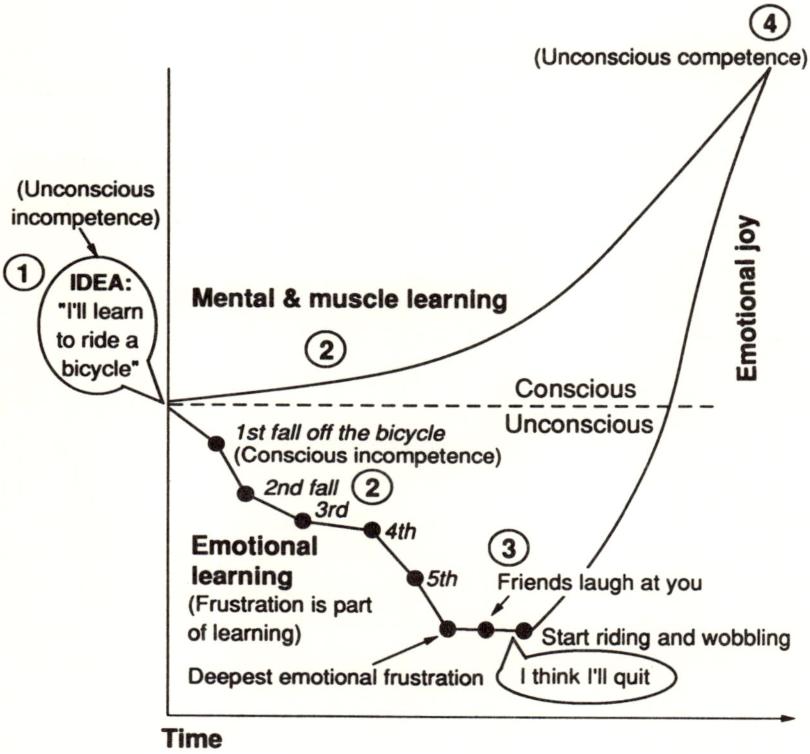

(Education only concerned about mental learning, retarding physical and emotional development)

(1) **Unconscious incompetence:** person has great idea, "I'd like to ride a bicycle." Person has no idea of what they do not know.

(2) **Conscious incompetence:** trial and error. Mentally learning and physical falling – emotionally upset.

(3) **Conscious competence:** riding bicycle – wobbly – mentally giving commands to body – emotional frustration at lowest ebb.

(4) **Unconscious competence:** learning is in muscles – never has to think about activity again.

Fig. 2. Nature's True Learning Curve (Young bird's first flight)

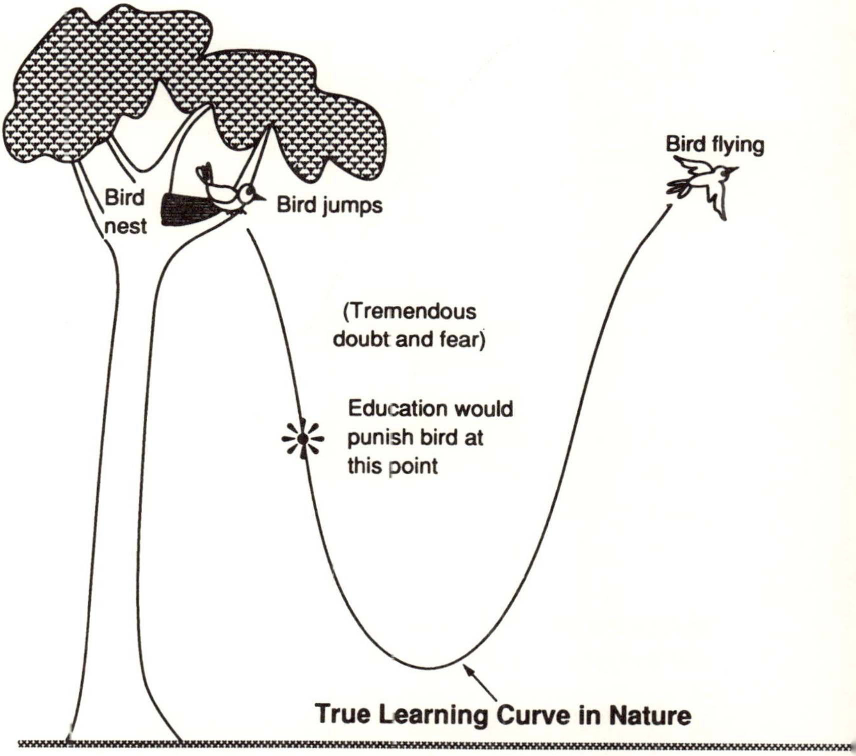

In Vietnam we had a nickname for pilots like this, men who were breathing but no longer seemed to have any spirit. "Corpse-people," we called them. They were on automatic pilot, simply putting in their time and hoping to survive long enough to get back home. They went through the motions of being alive but they really weren't. The rest of us knew these people were already dead and only a miracle would save them. Naturally, no one wanted to fly with them. All too many of them never made it home on their own two feet. Some came back in body bags.

Today I still see corpse-people out there in the world. They often work for large "corpse-orations." They stay in their nests grasping for what little security they can find, living paycheck-to-paycheck, finding little pleasure in their jobs, merely putting in time, waiting for the day they can retire and hoping against hope that nothing disastrous happens in the meantime.

These corpse-oration people lie awake nights worrying about not fulfilling their dreams. They eventually get to the point of searching desperately for anything that will alleviate the inner pain they are feeling, such as drinking, overeating or smoking. The saddest part is that they not only don't understand how to get out of this situation, they often don't even recognize where they are, and they certainly don't know how they got there. Many blame their own inadequacies. Others blame innocent third parties, such as their boss or the economy. Few realize that the anger and frustration, which have been intensifying over the years, are the result of those early seeds of failure planted in them as schoolchildren.

Teaching only by memorization leaves people walking one of two roads, both of them dead ends. If they were good at memorization and did well on tests, they left school believing they were educated and smart, even though the only thing their good grades really measured was their ability to memorize. What's more, they never left the nest because they learned that if they were to be rewarded at all it would be for not making mistakes. Even so, I am convinced that somewhere deep inside these people, a little voice tells them that this treadmill style of life isn't quite right. It isn't enough.

Yet, in spite of it all, they will do anything necessary to hold onto the belief that they still have all the right answers. They sadly go through life totally missing the experience of exhilaration that comes with the upward flight that follows the correction of mistakes. Never venturing out for fear of making those mistakes, they never discover the world beyond the nest. And they never quite discover the power of their own inner capacities for responding to the world and learning.

People with these kinds of beliefs never progress very far in life. Fearful of making a mistake, they constantly seek out environments where they are not asked to take risks. Often they hold the same job for their entire lifetimes, all the while suffering unfulfilled dreams, insufficient salaries and boredom. They become N.E.R.D.s, which stands for Never Ever Realizing Dreams. They know something magical should happen in their lives, yet many never get to experience it firsthand.

The other road is the one taken by people who don't memorize very well and are categorized as "not-so-smart." School diminished their self-esteem early on. They believed the labels that were put on them. They deem themselves stupid and accept that they are incapable of going very far. These people hate making mistakes because each mistake only reinforces their belief that they are stupid. Many give up because they are unaware that the inability to memorize has no bearing on their potential for success. This group doesn't attempt to leave the nest because they are certain they could never make it. Some on this road feel lucky to have a job of any kind, even if they are just as unhappy as their "smart" counterparts. The only hope they have of attaining their dreams is through the lottery or inheriting a fortune.

If we go through our early lives never quite feeling the exhilaration of learning, the primary motivation for going to school is limited to earning rewards such as grades, better than others that are in the class or diplomas that "prove" we are educated. Our educational system has convinced many of us that school is the only place a person can learn. Can a diploma ever be proof of our knowledge? Not under the systems of education we find in most schools! If you have any doubts about the lack of correlation between memorization and knowledge, just look around you at the number of people with higher degrees who are completely incompetent.

Of all the methods of learning that are available to us, memorization is the most monotonous, the least challenging, and the most boring. Many people who have experienced the four stages of the natural learning process are often very impatient with memorizing, finding it a difficult, painful procedure that has little relevance in their lives. In light of this, it should come as no surprise to us that so many young people drop out of school, cut classes or keep going only because of the extracurricular activities that school offers: partying, sports and sex.

How tragic that the message so many students receive, the good students along with the poor ones, is that learning is painful, boring and irrelevant! What's even worse to contemplate is that this feeling often lasts a lifetime, robbing all of us of the real potential of human achievement.

Is it possible that our greatest success in the educational system is teaching people to hate learning? If this is true, then we need look no further to answer why so many never succeed in life. How could it possibly be that the system we rely on to open doors for us also hurts our chances for success in the long term? Only when we come to accept this strange contradiction can we begin to correct it.

Our educational system has become little more than an initiation process, a way of earning what the Beatles long ago described as "a ticket to ride" in the employment process. Over the years, speaking to groups from all over the world, I often ask the audience to tell me why a person should go to school. The answers people volunteer are nearly always the same: the main reason for going to school is to get a job.

School produces employees by teaching them what employers want. By being taught how to memorize instead of how to learn, we eventually forget how to make use of the natural learning process with which each of us is born. Robbed of any sense of our own inner resources, we gain a sense of insecurity, not security. Is there a hidden agenda here that we haven't quite grasped? Perhaps. As long as we train people in this way, employees aren't as likely to leave their jobs or start companies of their own, which might create competition.

Our insecurity about what has happened to us ferments within us over the years, breeding dissatisfaction and more insecurity. The system responds by offering us palliatives, like more or better medical insurance, a bigger weekly paycheck and paid vacations. These become anemic trade-offs for the heartbreaking inner losses that we are suffering as a result of what we have been taught by our educational system.

Above all, our educational system teaches dependence on sources outside ourselves. Why do people feel trapped when they reach the age of 35? Some call it mid-life crisis. But mid-life crisis is not a natural process. It is another by-product of our educational system, coming when,

20 years out of high school, we realize that we stopped learning and changing and responding in any lively way to our lives a long, long time ago. It comes when we can no longer deny the fact that we've become corpse-people.

Mid-life crisis comes upon us when we notice that the world has changed all around us but we have stagnated. If we are working our way up the corporate ladder we begin to see younger competitors bypassing us. We feel cheated, yet it is only our knowledge that is outdated. Avoiding mid-life crisis requires that we know how to leave the nest, that we don't fear taking that risk because we have experienced the process of leaving and learning before, and we are confident that our lives will improve in the process. It requires un-learning the fallacies of our educational system and reconnecting with the gifts of learning that we received at birth.

Beyond the System of Winners and Losers

What are some of the ways we might begin to change the system, so that we stay connected with our natural gifts of healing instead of losing them? One thing we must change immediately is the social atmosphere of the classroom.

Most educational systems depend on the creation of an adversarial environment in the classroom: students versus teachers. I remember going to class and on the first day having teachers tell us we shouldn't expect to get an A because she or he was a "tough" teacher. So often I felt that teachers didn't want us to learn. Perhaps they wanted to motivate us to try harder, but there are better ways to accomplish this. For example, teamwork encourages both participation and cooperation. Learning becomes driven by excitement instead of fear.

The problem with having teamwork in our system right now is that teachers cannot be team players as long as they are required to give tests. Even though testing is known to be an inaccurate way of accounting for knowledge, it remains in place because administrators find it an easy way to rate their teachers, and parents have been brainwashed into believing it is a way of evaluating how their children are doing. The sad thing about grades is that they are virtually useless. In a system that teaches by rote, the only thing a grade can measure is how well the person can memorize.

Over the years I have heard many stories about teachers who have gotten fed up with the grading system and have tried to change it. A friend recently told me about a young teacher he had in high school who, at the end of her first semester of teaching, gave every one of her students an A. By the end of the week an emergency meeting had been called and she was up in front of the Board of Education trying to explain herself. She had to endure the humiliation of being scolded and told that she was part of a system that believes in a certain proportion of each grade being given.

One board member actually stated that there were "winners and losers" in every system, whether in the classroom or real life, and unless she was willing to acknowledge this "truth" she should look for another teaching job. She argued that this was an arbitrary system and that it had nothing to do with the way people really learned. She argued that it instilled unhealthy competition between students and was the basis for emotional stigma that usually resulted only in a further reduction of a child's self-esteem and potential. Although this teacher's "eccentricities" were tolerated for the remainder of the year, her contract was not renewed and she ended up seeking employment elsewhere.

Education is an inner process. It depends on a series of complex experiences: the four stages of learning that go on inside each student. For this reason, there should be a high level of participation on the part of the student. Instead of teaching through memorization and testing, teachers need to encourage students to "go for it"—to take risks, leave their nests of false security—and then to coach them as they discover their own wings and take to flight.

Whenever I think about education and what we need to do to revive our own ability to learn in our adulthood, I am reminded again of the training I received from Lt. Johnson, the man who taught me emergency procedures prior to my going to Vietnam. In contrast to the training I received from the educational system of my youth, I felt that Lt. Johnson was on my side. He was like a coach. I felt he wanted me to excel and that we were a team, learning together. For him, my success was a life and death matter, and above all, I was convinced that he wanted me to live, to not only survive the challenge ahead of me but to do the very best I was capable of doing.

Our educational system would benefit greatly from this kind of teaching. Lt. Johnson taught by actually offering us an opportunity to face the toughest challenges we'd be facing and work our way through any mistakes we made in the process. It was like saying to us, "Here's a place where it's okay to make mistakes, to find out exactly what it is you know." Knowing what you don't know, and knowing that you have the power to learn, you can quickly make corrections. On graduation day, you'll go away filled with confidence, not just because you got good grades and pleased the teachers, but because you have already experienced what your knowledge can do for you. You've not only left the nest, you've flown!

The main lesson we should teach is that the more mistakes the students are encouraged to make in the safety of the classroom, the more they will learn. Give students encouragement and emotional support during those frustrating periods when they are making mistakes. Let them feel what it's like to leave the nest. Let them know it's okay to experience the first moments of fear when they discover they're plunging into new territory. And above all, teach them to delight in the satisfaction of discovering their own power to correct their mistakes and fly. Let them soak up the exhilaration of fully making use of their own capacities.

Our system of education needs to teach that lifelong learning depends on our feeling confident about "leaving the nest" because to stay alive, truly alive, we must be comfortable with doing this again and again. We must, like my friend Ted in our flight-training days, become confident that when the engine loses power we have the power to handle the situation and not only survive but thrive. When we finally feel comfortable about leaving our false security behind, there is nothing to stand in the way of our success, be it financial, emotional or professional.

It wasn't until Ted and I crashed our helicopter and found ourselves floating in the shark-infested waters of the China Sea that I realized the depth of what Lt. Johnson had taught me. Silently, I thanked him. I thanked him not only for teaching me how to survive a crash, but also for freeing me from being just an idiot with a diploma.

Unfortunately, governments, cultural institutions and many businesses are run by people who memorized answers, yet still don't know how to fly. Changing all that isn't easy, but that change begins the moment we each become aware of the problems that we are facing in education. Armed with this awareness, we can change our own way of learning and begin influencing those educational systems with which we come in contact. Those of us who have children can encourage and support them as they experience these exciting natural processes for themselves. And we can share our knowledge with teachers and administrators, suggesting ways to bring this knowledge into the system.

11

When Being Wrong Is Right

There is the greatest practical benefit in making a few failures early in life.

—THOMAS HENRY HUXLEY (1870)

The school year had begun. Students and their teacher were still checking each other out in eighth-grade math.

"I give tough tests and I have no mercy," our teacher, Mr. Barber, began. "Either you know the answers or you fail."

I could feel the fear building inside me. I glanced around the room, seeing some of my friends rolling their eyes as if to say "not again." I sat confused. As much as I enjoyed learning mathematics, I hated the pain and pressure from the way it was taught and the stress presented by the teacher. The course was tough enough without him acting so macho. Why didn't he motivate us by making it fun instead of driving us by fear?

Despite these methods, we all passed and proceeded to high school. What we studied that year I don't really remember, but by the time I finished high school I had been through calculus, plane trigonometry, and spherical trigonometry. How much of that math do I use today? None. Today, could I solve those same problems for which I had studied so hard and had gotten the correct answers? No, I have to admit that I couldn't.

Today I don't use much of what I learned after the fifth grade. But that's not to say school didn't leave its permanent mark on me. The fact is, I left school with several behavioral traits I hadn't walked in with. Engraved in my mind was the belief that making a mistake, or "screwing up," got me ridiculed by my peers and often my teacher. School brainwashed me into believing that if a person wanted to be successful in life, he or she had to always be right. In other words, never be wrong. School taught me to avoid being wrong (making mistakes) at all costs. And if you did happen to make a mistake, at least be smart enough to cover it up.

This is where all too many people are today—not allowing themselves to make mistakes and thus blocking their own progress. The symptoms of this "disease" are feelings of boredom, failure and dissatisfaction, although most of us never come to understand why we feel this way. After having it drilled into us for so many years, it's hard to imagine that being "right" could cause such unhappiness.

In 1981, I had the opportunity to study with Dr. R. Buckminster Fuller. Although I can't quote him exactly, the first lesson I learned from him still sticks in my mind. He told us that humans were given a right foot and a left foot...not a right foot and a wrong foot. We make progress through our lives by advancing first with the right foot, then with the left. With each new step we both move forward and correct the prior step so that we come closer and closer to our destination. Most people, however, are still trying to walk the straight and narrow, avoiding mistakes and thus getting nowhere. What's wrong with the straight and narrow path? Perhaps nothing, except the fact that straight and narrow paths simply don't exist in the real world. Not even physicists have ever found anything that is absolutely straight. Only curves have been found. Straight lines exist only in human minds.

In *The Abilene Paradox,* Jerry B. Harvey writes about the "paradox of paradoxes." He explains the universal principle that "unity is plural." Just as "up" cannot exist without "down," or "man" without "woman," a "right" cannot exist without a "wrong." Similarly, people who can only be right eventually wind up being wrong. And people who are willing to risk making mistakes in order to discover what is "wrong" eventually end up knowing what is "right."

In maturing as a businessperson, I have learned to be cautious of people who act as if they have all the right answers. At the same time, I have had to acknowledge my own over-zealous desire to be right. I had to learn that a person who stayed on his right foot too long would eventually end up on the wrong foot—or worse yet, with that foot in his mouth.

Allowing ourselves to be wrong, to make mistakes, isn't easy. Think about how you feel when you hear the words "you're wrong." If you're anything like me, you become defensive and try to think of ways to prove you are right. In my own struggles, as well as in working with thousands of other people on this issue, I continue to be amazed at how terrified we humans can become at the thought of being punished for being wrong. Our efforts to prove ourselves right are often carried to the extreme, destroying marriages, businesses and friendships.

To finally discover that knowing the wrong answer can be the most powerful beacon we could ever hope to have, shining a brilliant light for us on the right answer, is greatly liberating. But to be able to enjoy the vast benefits of this insight we need to re-think how we handle mistakes; rather than punishing us for them, education should teach us the art of learning.

Our fear of making mistakes is so ingrained in us that we habitually react to our errors in ways that blind us to the real learning in them. Here are four of the most common and destructive "skills" that we have learned for handling those times when we make mistakes. These are the key reactions that stop the learning process:

1. **Pretending we did not make a mistake.**

The last U.S. President I recall accepting full responsibility for his actions was President John F. Kennedy for his part in the Bay of Pigs incident. Since then there have been such classic statements as "I am not a crook" (Nixon during Watergate) and "I don't remember" (Reagan during the Iran-Contra hearings). These men's avoidance of any responsibility has kept the issues alive and smoldering—as jokes, if nothing else.

It has been shown through other examples that the public demonstrates understanding and compassion for people who commit errors and then acknowledge responsibility for their actions. This seems odd in a world where we are taught to avoid making mistakes. Yet, it seems that each of us continues to be responsive to the wisdom that still lies buried deep within us that, as the poet says, "To err is human; to forgive is divine." Perhaps there is something in the act of forgiveness that makes us remember how we are meant to learn.

Comedian-actor Richard Pryor, after making the "mistake" of free-basing and badly burning his face and upper body, went on national television to come clean about drug use. TV evangelist Jimmy Swaggart admitted to visiting "women of the red-light districts." As a result, both their careers continued and their "wrongs" were put behind them. I cannot say whether they truly learned from their mistakes, but at least they didn't pretend they were not responsible.

2. Blaming something or someone else for the "mistake."

Immediately after the failure of my business in 1979, I blamed my two partners for the money loss. I was very stubborn, refusing to look at the role I had played in my downfall. I continued to dig in my heels and deny my own part in it for two years. I was angry, hurt and broke. It was not until I calmed down that I realized the experience was probably one of the best things that ever happened to me. I am not saying I would want to lose everything again, but I am grateful for the valuable lesson. Had I not lost my money in 1979, I am certain I would have lost it later because of my ignorance. There is the saying that "A fool and his money are soon parted." My mistake allowed me to better understand how I had been a fool, and how to avoid making similar mistakes again.

I know many people who are not successful because they are still consciously or subconsciously blaming other people for things that happened to them. I hear many horror stories about money or romance and how someone "did them wrong." The problem with that point of view is that the source of the mistake continues to lie dormant, just waiting to come to the surface again. One example of this is found with people who divorce and then marry a "different-same" person again and again, because they didn't learn the lesson from the previous marriage. They continue to blame the previous spouse for the failure of their relationship. Had I continued to blame my partners for what I did not know, I am certain I would have made the same mistake again and again, with different partners, until I either got the lesson, gave up or died broke, frustrated and bitter.

American society has become "blame-happy," and the term "victim" has become a part of everyday conversation. Courts are jammed up with lawsuits brought on by "victims" wanting compensation for being "wronged." No one can deny that there are legitimate claims, but we also know that the practice of suing has gone to extremes. Doctors have become fearful of delegating any of their duties to other clinicians with whom they work for fear of malpractice suits. This single factor has caused an increase in medical costs and a decrease in insurance benefits.

Similarly, the highest single cost of producing a car in North America is not steel, but insurance. Insurance of all kinds is a hidden cost of every car produced—for a commodity that benefits the consumer in no way.

We could do with fewer victims and with more people willing to learn instead of wanting to blame.

3. Rationalizing the "mistake" instead of learning from it. (Also known as the "Sour Grapes Syndrome.")

"Oh, well, I really didn't want that anyway."

The world is filled with people who are always ready with perfect rationalizations about why they are unsuccessful. For a short time after I lost my business, I used the rationalization that I failed because I didn't have an MBA. By clinging to this rationalization I only prolonged my mental poverty and slowed down my comeback.

One of the most prevalent justifications today is, "Oh, the money doesn't matter to me." I often hear it from people who are not winning at the game of financial well-being. Does money really not matter? Let's ask the question another way: is it a mistake to put yourself and your family in the position of not having enough money? At the very least, not having enough money should be interpreted as a "tap on the shoulder," a signal to change something in our lives.

4. Punishing oneself.

Possibly the most destructive behavior of all is the emotional torment people inflict on themselves as retribution for making a mistake.

When asked who is hardest on them, most people will point to themselves. They often do this with an apparent sense of pride and humility. And yet, punishment is one of the most destructive aspects of human behavior there is, whether it is self-inflicted or inflicted by a third party. One reason people are not successful is that they are consciously or subconsciously punishing themselves for something they did in the past. They cannot allow themselves to be successful because deep down inside they do not feel they deserve it. They are punishing themselves by withholding the opportunity to enjoy a successful life.

Truly successful people learn to take full responsibility for their actions; they apologize and do whatever is appropriate to correct their errors. They acknowledge the mistake, seek the lesson, make whatever corrections are required and then move on to become more successful.

Unsuccessful people harbor the emotional pain of self-blame and fail to get the valuable lessons made available to them through their mistakes. Not acknowledging mistakes makes for narrow-minded, self-righteous people who ultimately hinder their own ability to be happy and find financial success.

Always Having to be Right

Along with denying that we've made a mistake, there are several problems associated with having to be right:

1. Inability to see the future.

The person who has to be right often clings to old information, information which might have been right in the past but is no longer appropriate or true in the present. Most people confuse facts with truths. Prior to Orville and Wilbur Wright's successful flight in a heavier-than-air machine, the "fact" was that humans could not fly and never would fly. While it was a fact at that moment, it was not a "truth." Similarly, prior to the day Roger Bannister broke the four-minute mile barrier, sports physiologists presented dozens of very convincing articles "proving" that such a feat was "humanly impossible."

Most of what we call human knowledge is only information we that we have jointly agreed is "true." Another word for it is "consensual reality," meaning simply that it is knowledge that most people recognize as "true." History is filled with stories of great new ideas or inventions that were ridiculed because society adamantly refused to look beyond consensual reality. Businesses have been destroyed by failing to recognize a new reality that was staring them in the face. Today, changes are coming at a pace never experienced before, making it more hazardous than ever to cling to the notion that "what worked today will work tomorrow."

To learn from mistakes, we need to learn never to say, "That's a crazy idea. It will never work," no matter how crazy it may seem. We need to learn how to at least suspend our belief in consensual reality long enough to listen openly to new ideas and new possibilities. Rigid thinkers cannot hear new ideas as long as they cling to what they believe is "right."

2. No increase in wealth (knowledge).

People who have to be right rarely learn anything new because they are too busy having to be right. It is only when they are willing to be wrong that learning comes alive. Wealth only increases when people learn how to learn from their mistakes. After all, there is very little knowledge in the world that won't be obsolete tomorrow, or next year, or in the next decade. Facts change—and so must our minds.

3. More conflicts.

I remember, as a child, going to our family's Methodist Church. I remember asking my Sunday school teacher what the difference was between our church and the Catholic Church. She told me, "The Methodists are following the right teachings of Jesus and the Catholics are wrong." I was only ten, yet something about that statement struck me as ridiculous. But how ridiculous is it? People cause pain, grief and bloodshed in the name of needing to prove that they are "right."

Remember the slogan that was so prevalent in the years of the Cold War between the United States and Russia? The saying was "Better dead than Red," and indeed there were many times when our two nations stood on the brink of an atomic holocaust in the name of defending their beliefs.

Again, what most people and most nations insist is "right" or "wrong" is often only their point of view or opinion. Each of us has our own hidden agenda, an opinion that we are right and that anything to the contrary is wrong. We need to learn to think more broadly and to accept that there are probably infinite numbers of answers for every question.

Change in these matters can begin with our educational system, letting go of the belief that students should strive for the ideal of always being "right." It is the need to be "right" and the subsequent neglect of any real understanding that causes conflict between individuals as well as nations. As our planet shrinks, becoming increasingly crowded, "right-wrong" thinking will need to be reevaluated or the world is going to become uncrowded very quickly through global war.

As an ex-Marine and a person who grew up fighting, I've noticed much more peace in my life since I have allowed that other people also have "right" answers. I have greatly lessened my use of the words "right" and "wrong," as well as "good" and "bad." Instead, I try to comprehend different points of view and acknowledge that people differ. I have learned the hard way that opposing points of view don't mean that someone is right and someone else is wrong.

In our schools, however, I am afraid that we are still teaching our children to be narrow-thinkers. We are planting the seeds of war, not peace.

4. Stagnating income.

In most businesses, people are paid for what they know. People who have to be right all the time, as we've already seen, tend to stagnate, sticking tenaciously to the "nests" of what they know instead of taking the risks that would provide them with new knowledge. Since their knowledge never changes, neither does their income. In the worst-case scenario, they are discharged from the company because it has gone on to new technologies or is making a new line of products for which this person's knowledge is no longer useful. We see this every year in the hundreds of thousands of people who are let go or offered early retirement because the knowledge they have no longer serves the company.

5. Dimming futures.

A person who holds onto old ideas finds that his path becomes increasingly narrow. Often frustration and justification increase and opportunities decrease. The world is changing, but the person clings to the ways of the past or waits for the "good old days" to return.

6. Progressive inner blindness.

Growing up in Hawaii, I learned to love diving in the ocean for fish and lobsters. I used to see other divers coming home with octopi caught in the same area. I had never seen one.

One day, I asked a seasoned diver to take me out and show me where the octopus lives. He soon had me looking into a pile of dead coral. He pointed into a hole. I looked and stared as long as I could hold my breath but saw nothing. Then I pushed my spear into the hole. Immediately, an enraged octopus leaped out, scurried along the bottom and disappeared right in front of me. I realized the octopi had always been there, right in front of me, except I could not see them.

It is the same with business and investing. I find it amusing when a person tells me there are no more opportunities out there or that all the good investments are taken. Opportunities are always out there. Over the years, I have noticed that the more calculated risks, mistakes and corrections I made, the better my "eyesight" became. However, I would have to say too that people who are afraid of making mistakes frequently never see the opportunities, even the ones staring them in the face. The people who can't see call the people who can "sharks" because they are able to take advantage of opportunities that nobody else could see. The real problem is that the person who always needs to be right stops looking in new places.

7. Inability to reap the benefits of "doing poorly."

All too many people become so fixated on doing things right that they spend their entire lives doing nothing at all. This is the typical pattern of "perfectionists;" their own fears of making mistakes literally paralyze them. Progress is made by following the path with "both feet," as Bucky Fuller pointed out. We discover new paths and move forward by taking a new step, looking around to see where it has taken us, then taking another step with which we can both correct our course, if necessary, and move further along our path. Progress is always made by improving upon what you or someone else has done. Could we ever have built a 747 jet had the Wright Brothers not risked their financial resources and reputations, to say nothing of life and limb, to build and fly their crude heavier-than-air machine? What the history books often fail to tell us is the number of times they failed to get their machine off the ground and the number of times they crashed. Through this seemingly endless series of "mistakes" they made they became the brunt of journalists' jokes. Only their willingness to take these risks carried them forward to success and eventually won them a permanent place in the history books.

8. Personal potential turning to frustration.

I frequently meet people who have great potential but no cash or professional success. The same people seethe with envy and frustration. Much of their frustration stems from being too hard on themselves. They know they have what it takes to get ahead but they won't let themselves make the necessary mistakes and go through the learning curve which leads to personal satisfaction.

"Your son has so much potential," was the statement on the report card I took home. I remember going to school conferences with my parents and every time the teacher said the same old thing: "Robert has lots of potential, but he doesn't apply himself."

Now I understand my teachers' frustrations and my own. How could they expect me to manifest my full potential when I was always being punished for making mistakes? I went through those years knowing there were things I wanted to do and could do; however, I was living my life in the straightjacket of feeling that it was bad to make mistakes, that above all I had to be right. I didn't begin to grow and learn until I threw off that straightjacket and dared to make mistakes.

9. Being increasingly out of pace with the moment.

People who fear making mistakes are slow because they are too cautious; as the world speeds up, such people tend to slow down. This doesn't mean we should be reckless. But once free of the fear of making mistakes, we are much more likely to stay in the race. Asking a person who is afraid of making mistakes to keep up in the modern world is a little like putting a Volvo driver in a high performance Indianapolis 500 race car. The car has all the speed and power necessary to win the race but the driver is conditioned to a slower, more sedate pace. He can't get past his own habits and his cautious outlook on life long enough even to test the car's full potential. Thus, it's the driver and not the car that loses the race.

Successful race car drivers are conditioned to respond with swift but very small incremental corrections, which is the only thing that works at high speed. They know what happens when they don't recognize and acknowledge their mistakes and correct their course accordingly; they end up in the pits—or worse, on the wall.

As much as we may dislike it, our fast pace is a fact of modern life. Whether he's aware of it or not, the person who fears mistakes is constantly resisting this pace. And this resistance only compounds his stress and actually increases his chances of making mistakes. Unable to acknowledge or perhaps even recognize that he is straying off course, he cannot correct his actions and so ends up crashing.

A Major Turnaround Needed

The long-term effect of our grossly inadequate educational system is all too often the erosion of our ability to function well in the real world. All too many of us come away from the system with a lack of self-confidence, drummed into our hearts and minds by what we've failed to learn about the positive side of making mistakes.

We can no longer afford to tolerate an educational program that punishes honest mistakes and fails to design programs that make full use of our natural learning abilities. We must change the course of this antiquated behemoth that is degrading our society, eroding our children's desire for knowledge while causing pain and frustration. True learning can be frustrating enough without a system that makes it worse.

We must find a way to teach through love and kindness so that the "right/wrong" systems of education can be exposed for what they really are: filter systems for rejecting those who won't buckle under and conform to the system. We must have the courage to create new learning environments, where mistakes are applauded and seen as the invaluable source of wisdom that they are. We would prosper both in terms of tapping the full potential of our human resources and in terms of bringing greater happiness into all our lives. We must take this next step in our evolution so that we can finally see that we all benefit exponentially when we reach for the very best in ourselves and support others to do the same.

12

God Doesn't Create Stupid People—Our Educational System Does

Where there is charity and wisdom, there is neither fear nor ignorance.

—ST. FRANCIS OF ASSISI

I was in fourth grade when I first realized how painful school could be. I had already discovered how boring and slow paced it was, but I hadn't quite comprehended the depth of its insensitivity.

As I watched the teacher post math grades on the chalkboard I could feel butterflies in my stomach. When I saw that I wasn't one of the "victims" whose name would appear there in the column of failures, I sighed in relief. Once again, I felt I had "beat the system." I had passed without studying. When I looked around the room I could see that some of my friends hadn't fared as well as I. One girl, Martha, tried to hide her paper so that no one could see her score. But it didn't help. Starting with the best scores at the top and ending with the worst at the bottom, our teacher had just finished what she called "stack ranking" our class. Poor Martha was at the bottom—again.

A shy, sweet girl, Martha was gifted at music and she loved animals. But she was lost when it came to math. I leaned over to say something to cheer her up, but the teacher yelled at me. "I'll make you stay after school if I catch you talking again!"

Martha began to cry. I didn't know what to do. When class let out, some of the kids walked by Martha pointing, giggling and whispering "stupid" and "dummy." Judging from the expression on my friend's face, Martha died a little that day. It was a look I'll never forget.

I don't know what ever became of Martha. I do know she didn't graduate with the rest of us in 1965. Rumor had it that she quit school. If that was true, it was a great loss to all of us because in her own areas of interest she was truly gifted.

Is this example an extreme? Most people reading this book will know it is not. On the contrary, in many schools throughout the country it is much more the rule than the exception. Every day in our schools children are humiliated in front of their classmates. Every day sensitive children like Martha die a little. Schools have carelessly adopted programs which stigmatize our kids according to their level of learning, causing "slower" children to be cruelly teased by classmates who have learned, from this same system, that being the best and the brightest is more important than friendship.

Who knows how many Marthas there are in the world who have fallen victim to this inhumane treatment. Even one is one too many. Whether this kind of labeling occurs by "stack ranking" or "grouping," children believe these labels, causing emotional trauma which can lead to long-term scarring. Ultimately, it prevents children from reaching their full potential. I seriously doubt that labeling children has any value, except perhaps to make life easier on teachers and provide a way of eliminating "slow" students who don't automatically conform to teaching methods that have been "standardized" by the educational system. To continue the practice of labeling in any form, knowing it is capable of damaging the self-esteem of innocent children, is unforgivable.

My professional educator friends prefer to call their method of elimination they employ the law of averages (bell curve). It sounds so scientific! My military friends call it "survival of the fittest"—dividing the population up between winners and losers. Whatever label you wish to put on it, our educational system is playing this barbaric game with our children's lives at a time when their hearts and minds are open and vulnerable.

Today we have the wisdom of world famous researchers, physicians and psychologists, such as Dr. Bruno Bettleheim, Dr. Erik Erikson and others, who tell us that children progress and learn at different rates and that one child will excel at one subject while other children excel at another. One child may be ready to read at four, for example, another at seven, and still another at twelve. And yet, our educational system continues to weed out the best and the brightest in the areas it judges are important—math, science and English.

In spite of our knowledge about how young, vulnerable minds can be damaged by such tactics, our children are tested, branded and shunted through the system like robots which have exactly the same "hard wiring plan." As a result, the "strongest" are labeled "above average" and pushed to a higher level such as TAG (Talented and Gifted); the "weakest" are labeled "below average" and are mostly abandoned, allowed to "fall between the cracks" of the system, as it is often so colorfully expressed.

Recently a friend's ten-year-old daughter came home from school and tearfully announced that she couldn't be a veterinarian when she grew up, a profession she had dreamed of entering since she was seven years old. Her mother asked her why and the girl replied, "My teacher told me I am only in the average group at school. I'm just not smart enough to make it." This was happening to a girl who up to that moment had had a passionate vision of her future. While sensitive and easily hurt, she was also highly intelligent and gifted in her own way. She had never doubted that somehow she would make her dreams come true—at least not until that moment when she was told she was "only average."

Knowing the girl as well as I do, there is no doubt in my mind that the power of her dream would itself eventually propel her toward success. She would find a way to do what she wanted so much to do. But now there was a real danger that her self-confidence had been so undermined by the educational system's labeling that she would stop nurturing that dream. It is often this kind of not-so-subtle undermining that is responsible for people not living out their dreams. How far will people go to fulfill their dreams when they are immersed in a system that erodes their self-esteem? Not far enough.

Too often education turns into a game of attrition designed along the "bell curve." The quest for knowledge and self-development is replaced by the race to earn a winning place on that curve, preferably among that top 10 percent of students who excel rather than among the bottom 10 percent who will fail. Based on a law of averages, this system divides the world between winners and losers, insiders and outsiders, those who are accepted and those who are rejected by the system. It is a system of exclusion, not inclusion.

The trouble is that the students who find themselves "excluded" by the grading system aren't like widgets being constructed on the assembly line in a factory. They aren't simply discarded or melted down to be used as raw material for a new batch. The excluded students continue to attend school—at least many of them do. Emotionally, however, these students know that they have been excluded because the system has determined that they are inferior. They continue on their way feeling that they are "stupid" or "below average." Their self-esteem plummets and if they stay in school they tend to become behavioral problems, distracting other students and driving teachers half crazy.

When individuals are treated in this way, the cost in terms of behavioral problems and wasted human talent rises exponentially. What we do to our children is nothing short of criminal—especially when we know there is an alternative. The alternative is what I call "holistic education," which takes the child as a whole person and finds a way to teach every young person to the best of his or her abilities. Everyone has a gift, a talent, which can be developed if given half a chance, and if it is nurtured along not just to conform to a grading system, but up to the level where that person is able to make a contribution and gain self-esteem through whatever means he or she is capable.

Educational psychologists know that children progress according to how they see themselves and how the teacher perceives their abilities. This is the principle of the "self-fulfilling prophecy"—that particularly in our early lives we will rise no higher than what others expect of us. If we have been labeled as being below average, we will know that, even though never told directly, because of the way our teachers treat us. We then integrate that "prophecy" into our own thinking and allow it to determine how hard we try, how weak or strong we are in self-motivational skills, and where we place ourselves in the hierarchy of our peers.

The younger and more impressionable the child, the more he or she is likely to believe the labels placed on them. Even intelligent and talented children will begin to act below average if they are so labeled, and eventually people will treat them that way.

In one Harvard study, children were chosen at random, that is, without the benefit of tests, to be labeled according to current systems. Teachers were then told that certain children were "above average," certain others were "average," and certain others "below average." In spite of the fact that there were students of a variety of capabilities in each group, they all tended to perform according to the labels placed upon them, not according to their actual abilities. The study revealed that the children's test results were dependent upon the teacher's point of view rather than the child's ability.

Most of the testing that places students on the bell curve tests only for the so-called Three "Rs": Reading, 'Riting and 'Rithmatic. Unfortunately, it sorely neglects other talents or gifts the child might have—such as music, athletics, drama or handcrafts. Thus, a budding young Chopin, Michelangelo or Meryl Streep could easily end up on the "academic hit list," eliminated from the system only because he or she didn't do well in the basic subjects. How many young geniuses are made to feel stupid because of this system is anybody's guess, though we do know that even people such as Albert Einstein were among this group in their early years.

This game of winners and losers produces countless millions of people who lack self-esteem, who are terrified of making mistakes and who lead lives of mediocrity because they were conditioned to believe that they weren't as smart as their classmates. Only a few fortunate "losers" ever figure out they aren't as "stupid" as the education system led them to believe they were.

How sad all this is, and how unnecessary! It is not the responsibility of our educational system to be judge and jury, to determine who will be nurtured and encouraged to grow and who will be either ignored or neglected. It is the job of our educational system to nurture and to encourage learning, no matter what the child's gifts or limitations.

Today in education there is talk of right and left brain learning. It is based on the research that seems to indicate that the two hemispheres of the brain (right and left) divide tasks between those which are linear, like math, language and basic science, and those that are more intuitive, like music, poetry, athletics and art. There is a growing effort to recognize that some students are stronger in right brain processes while traditional education has been based on the more linear processes.

While it is encouraging to discover that our educators are paying attention to current brain research, and are attempting to respond accordingly, we might hope that they also give some attention to another part of the brain that we've known about for centuries—the subconscious.

This is the part of the brain that responds to the subtlest of messages, the teacher's words of encouragement and support as well as the often silent messages that both teachers and peers project, telling a young person he is not good enough. If we were to pay as much attention to how our teaching methods are affecting the unconscious as we do to how they are affecting the right or left hemisphere of the brain, we might start turning out far more winners than we presently do.

If a teacher is unable to make "slow learners" learn, perhaps it is because these children have been labeled slow one time too many. I wonder how different these children would feel if they were told they were smart, encouraged with praise and taught with kindness and love rather than being classified and judged according to bell curves and grading systems.

Once again, in his book *The Abilene Paradox,* Harvey asks, "Does it strike you as odd—that virtually all educational institutions in our culture, from kindergarten through graduate school, define cheating as 'giving aid to others or receiving aid from them?'"

Tragically, our system of education not only mass-produces "stupid" people; it also produces people who are cruel and inhumane, people who do not even know they behave in that manner. This particular "hidden curriculum" is fostered by our defining cheating as "giving aid to others or receiving aid from them." This leads to competition rather than cooperation, widening the gap between "smart" and "stupid," rich and poor, winners and losers. The belief that there is something inherently wrong with helping others or receiving help ripples throughout our lives, producing lonely people who don't understand why they can't get along with other people.

We see examples of this every day. People believe throwing money at a problem is enough instead of giving of themselves mentally, physically and spiritually. In order to solve our massive social problems, human compassion must become more important than money. School teaches people not to get involved with those weaker than themselves. Year after year, children are taught that being the strongest, the best and the smartest is the way to succeed. To feel empathy for the "stupid," or to help them is "against the rules," a form of cheating. Money becomes a way to protect us from "undesirables" such as the homeless people, the hungry and the poor, while at the same time relieving any guilt we might be feeling.

Not long ago I spoke to a young mother who was in the process of moving to another state. Her primary concern was to find a house in the "right" neighborhood so her children wouldn't be exposed to undesirables. She even considered sending her children to a private school. While it is valid for parents to want the best education for their children, children can learn more from diversified surroundings than from the so-called "best" environments. Real education takes place between a parent and a child. Children will learn from a situation what a parent teaches them. If a child is sent to a private school, ignoring the fact that poor people exist, then the child will never learn the true meaning of poverty. It only expands the distance between the haves and have-nots and results in a step backwards on the road of humanity.

If you doubt that this cruel system of "survival of the fittest" is alive and well, just observe who gets laid off first in any company. It's the weakest, the ones with the least power, and with the least ability to get back on their feet; it's the people with the least self-confidence. They did not run the company into the ground, yet they are the first to be removed from the payrolls.

In all the business classes my organization teaches, participants are required to study and take tests cooperatively. If our educational methods were to be evaluated by traditional teachers, they would say we encourage and promote "cheating." We know it by a different name—cooperation.

It is a well-known fact that "two heads are better than one." The Japanese know it, and that is why Japanese students study in cooperative groups. They realize that while one student may be strong in math, he or she may need help in another area, say language or music. When two or more students cooperate, everyone benefits, since each person not only learns but gains a sense of their self-worth through helping others. This sense of cooperation, contribution and self-fulfillment teaches far more than how to get a good grade—though the truth is that it does a very good job of doing that as well.

Western education tends to favor the John Wayne approach to learning, emphasizing the rugged individualist, completely omnipotent, self-contained and alone. These supermen and superwomen know all the right answers at a given moment and are rarely, if ever, wrong. No one can tell these people anything. They are tough on the outside, weak on the inside. If you have an organization filled with these ego-driven individuals, you will have so much internal competition and chaos you won't need outside competitors. Western businesses are riddled with back- stabbing, melodrama and gossip, as well as management fighting labor, stockholders demanding bigger returns and people climbing over each other to get to the top—everybody acting as if the only thing that mattered was getting his or her own selfish needs satisfied. With all this internal strife, it is no wonder that we are falling behind in the global economic race.

The reason Japan has been so successful in business is because they have little internal competition. In Japanese culture, drama and upset are considered disgraceful. In contrast, perhaps the worst that I have witnessed is in Australia where if you are not fighting internally, you are not considered a "real businessperson," and it is thought to be "unmanly" if labor and management cooperate. Fighting is part of the Australian business culture. Their economy is reflecting it and the people are paying for it. And it all begins with the schools!

A few educators are making strides in the area of cooperative study and more enlightened test taking. The only problem is that parents oppose them because they continue to want some way to find out how well little Johnny is doing in relation to the rest of the kids in his class.

As I come to the end of this chapter I find that I have a sick feeling in my stomach as I picture my friend Martha, of long ago, sitting at her desk crying over a math test. How sad and upset she must have been, thinking she was the "dumbest" person in the class.

It is this needless suffering by innocent children, which so many of us felt in school, that makes me wonder why parents continue to allow their children to be subjected to the same heartache.

Until we are all willing to put a halt to the kind of harm that was done to us, insisting that it no longer be done to others, our educational system will continue to be an emotionally destructive game in which even the youngest children are pitted against each other. We must stop this system where children are driven by the fear that there are only two categories of people here—winners and losers—and they would do anything to be the former. We've got to start turning things around so that each student's gifts and self-esteem are nurtured as the treasures they truly are.

13

Why Most People Die Poor

The more is given, the less the people will work for themselves, and the less they work, the more their poverty will increase.

—Leo Tolstoi (1892)

"I don't have to worry, I'm still young."

How many times have you heard people say this? For that matter, how many times have you said it yourself? Each time I hear it, I wonder at what age that person will begin to view the aging process as a reality.

As I settle into my own middle years, I see clearly how the lives of my classmates, friends and peers have been unfolding. While some are doing exceptionally well financially, the majority are running on treadmills, never quite able to catch their breaths. They get up in the morning, go to work, enjoy the coffee breaks, return home, eat, put the kids to bed, watch TV, sleep—and spend weekends dreading Monday mornings and worrying about how to pay the bills.

What I'm describing are educated, middle-class people beginning to experience the professional, financial and social plateau. They no longer say, "I don't have to worry, I'm still young." They feel themselves falling behind even though they work harder and harder. Worst of all, they don't know what to do to stop the vicious cycle that is consuming their lives.

In the last few years I have spent many hours with people ranging in age from 60 to mid-90s. Viewing life through their eyes, I have gained priceless lessons which can be applied in my own life. When I was younger and had more energy and vitality than I knew what to do with, I had no idea what effects the aging process would have on my life, nor did I really care. To me, life was one big, exciting party.

A short while ago I had a gathering at my home for 30 senior adults with whom I had been taking an art class. I was surprised to hear many of them talking about the difficulty of getting up my rather steep walkway. I felt like an inconsiderate buffoon for not having thought about this before. My ignorance again stemmed from taking my youth for granted; what seemed a slight grade to me was a mountain for them.

If I summarized all I learned from my experiences with these senior friends, it would be: health and finances need to be cared for when we're young, not when we're old. Too many of the senior adults I talked with that day had not planned adequately for their old age. They had thought about it, yet had no real concept of how age would affect them, just as I had no concept about how my walkway would affect them. In fact, most said something like: "The years went by so quickly…before I knew it my working years were over and I found my retirement income wasn't enough."

All too many of us live on the hope that tomorrow will be better. But just as a person's health is a result of habits, so is a person's financial position. Too many of us treat our health the same way—until we begin to lose it. After all, one pack of cigarettes might not kill a person. But one pack a day for thirty years might! Similarly "just making ends meet" for one month can't do us a lot of harm. But thirty years of "just breaking even" can.

Unfortunately, when we're young it's not always obvious to us that the quality of our lives in our retirement years will depend on how we prepare for it in our youth. A man I know who is in his early 70s represents one of the more touching examples. Ken spent his working life as a government employee. Just before he retired he and his wife both became very ill. Ken's insurance did not cover his wife's illness adequately, so he borrowed against his house. The good news is that she survived, although she will be bedridden for the rest of her life. The bad news is that the ordeal of two illnesses and a diminished income left them with huge debts. Less than a year after he retired, Ken was forced to sell his house in order to pay even his more pressing bills. But it wasn't enough. Soon they began living on credit cards. Eventually the court had to step in.

In the two years I have known Ken, he and his wife have had to move out of two desirable retirement complexes because they could not afford to live there. They found refuge in a charitable organization's retirement home. But just as they settled in there, Ken's vision deteriorated and he lost his driver's license. Now, just getting his wife across town to see her specialist is an ordeal. He told me he hates being a burden to his children, who are not in good financial shape themselves. Ken said it best one afternoon: "I spent 47 years working hard so I could enjoy retirement, but now I'm working harder just to survive."

Ever since President Kennedy emphasized the importance of physical fitness, that craze has boomed. Most of my friends are fitness zealots. They are often pains-in-the-you-know-what because they are always on my case about my less-than-healthy eating habits. As much as I hate their prodding I also appreciate it, for they keep me thinking about my health, something I might otherwise not do until it became a crisis. Their concern prompts me to take steps to improve my health rather than allowing it to deteriorate.

However, when I ask those same zealous friends about their financial fitness, they clam up. The walls of their minds slam shut. They act as if they have been personally attacked. I am beginning to wonder if the subject of money isn't even more taboo than fat! People don't like to talk about it, or think about it, especially if they are in trouble. Most of these people earn substantial salaries, so why don't they want to talk about it? Because even though their incomes are high, so are their debts. And to add to it, their savings are minimal; the only investment they have is their home, which may not be as secure as they think. Like too many others, they barely break even every month because so much of their income goes to paying debts from excesses of the past.

Often people say they are buying a home as an investment. That statement is a misuse of the word "investment." It would be more accurate to call a home a "necessity" and say that "investments" are tools to support your "necessity." Or, as one saying goes, "Never be your own tenant." A person should buy four houses—one to live in and three for support in retirement years. Excessive? Just think about it. If you still say it can't be done, go to the chapter on paradigms.

If your home is your largest "investment," you should consider reading some books on investing soon. Then talk to older retired people—some who planned well and others who didn't. Too many middle-aged baby boomers still think as their parents did that their home and their retirement income will be adequate for the future. It may be, but I wouldn't count on it.

If you are between the ages of 35 and 55, and living month-to-month with no investments, your senior adult years will most likely be painful ones.

After talking to many senior adults, I found five broad categories of wealth and health that we all need to be think about and discuss:

1. Health and no financial wealth
2. Financial wealth and no health
3. Financial wealth and robust health
4. No financial wealth and no health
5. Eroding financial wealth and health

When I lost my financial wealth, my physical health also rapidly deteriorated. In the ten years it took me to rebuild my self-esteem and financial wealth, my physical health took a beating. I know if I do not change direction I will wind up in category 2, "financial wealth and no health." Today, having learned from my experiences with senior adults, I pay close attention to my health.

Where are you?

Think about it.

Continue on the course you are on today, and where will you be when your working days are over?

Will you have the health and financial resources you desire? Will you be able to do all the things you want to do? Will you be able to travel and see all the places you want to see? Or will old age be little more than a struggle for survival? Will you spend your later years worrying about catastrophic medical expenses and inadequate insurance coverage? Will you spend them in regret, wishing you had done something about your future earlier?

Will you become a burden to your children?

Part of the problem we all have with thinking ahead and planning for the future is that we live in an "instant society." We all want things right now, and there is an expectation that everything should be available at our time of need. We have fast food restaurants, mini-marts, drive-thru dry-cleaners and instant teller machines. It seems that we don't really have to think ahead for anything anymore. In the past, people had to plan their banking on weekdays according to bank hours. Now withdrawals and deposits can be made with the help of a machine 24 hours a day.

This drive for immediate satisfaction of all our wants and needs has led to a very destructive "get-rich-quick" way of thinking. Who wouldn't love to get rich overnight! But, as with my health, I have learned it doesn't work that way. I can't lose 30 pounds overnight. And I know I'd have to run more than a couple of miles to strengthen my heart. Success rarely comes to anyone instantly. As the years pass, we begin to feel more discomfort about our financial situations. The result is that either we start taking more risks or we retreat into ourselves and take no risks whatsoever, clinging desperately to whatever we have. Some of us play the lottery, hoping to find salvation from our financial woes. Others fall prey to con-men who lure us into attractive "get-rich-quick" investments that are doomed to fail.

We all know we should do something, but what? We're bewildered. Products of our educational system, we were told, "Be good. Do as you're told and don't make any mistakes." We were taught in school to look for a secure job with good benefits. We should be taught instead that there is no such thing as a secure job. Over 66 percent of America's workforce is employed by small companies. Most of these companies have no adequate retirement plans. Many employees wonder how in the world they can plan for tomorrow when they can't even make ends meet today. As rap music star M.C. Hammer so aptly sings, "We pray just to make it today."

Our financial short-sightedness prevents us from enjoying financially secure futures. Instead of thinking creatively, we wait to be told what to do or we continue to use old answers which no longer work. The result? Financial paralysis.

It harkens back to the old 80-20 rule; 20 percent of the people will be well off financially, the other 80 percent will lead lives of financial purgatory—or worse. It does not have to be this way. Though it can require years of schooling and a higher than average intelligence to become a doctor or a rocket scientist, it only takes a second-grade education to become financially successful.

If our children are taught the principles of money and business, which could be easily done with games as simple and fun as the old standby Monopoly, everyone could learn how financial well-being can be theirs, regardless of race, color, birthright, family background or educational degrees.

Why can't our educational system teach these basic skills for survival? At the very least, we should insist on that much. Could it be that by doing so education would lose its last big threat, no longer able to say, "If you don't study hard, you won't get a good job." We would have to abandon fear as our main motivator and start motivating students through the sheer love of learning.

There is a saying: "If you do not change the direction you are heading, you may wind up where you're going." So, what might this mean in today's society where most young people look upon education as a prison sentence? It's a frightening prospect to say the least. It is time we took a long, hard look at that and charted a new course where young minds can become the very best they can be. It is time for all of us to look long and hard at our educational priorities, accepting the reality that unless we are succeeding in teaching virtually every citizen the rudiments of how to achieve economic well being in our society we are failing ourselves and our children.

14

How Rich People Can Be Poor

Better is bread with a happy heart
Than wealth with vexation.

—AMENEMOPE (11TH CENTURY)

"Money can't buy you happiness."

Mom was lecturing again. It seemed the older I got, the more frequent her lectures. I stood in silence, knowing what was coming next....

"There's more to life than money...why, when I was your age, I was too busy doing my chores to think about such things...it's not good for you to be so obsessed with money."

I tuned her out. All I heard was "blah, blah, blah." When she sighed I knew she was running out of gas; it meant the ending was near. Her last sentence was predictable: "You know, son, I'm only scolding you for your own good."

Then she would calm down as I promised to do whatever it was she wanted me to do. Meanwhile I was crossing my fingers and telling myself, "She doesn't know what she's talking about!"

This lecture was all too familiar. My brother and sisters never got such lectures, but they didn't feel as I did about money. I loved money. Everything about it fascinated me. My brother loved cars. We nicknamed him the "broke-chanic" because he was more interested in taking things apart than in making them work. My sisters were interested in the arts and spirituality. My mother was proud of their hobbies. But when I suggested to her that money was my hobby, she just thought I was greedy. While my brother and sisters were encouraged to explore their interests, Mom often expressed her concern about my turning into Donald Duck's rich greedy uncle, Scrooge McDuck.

Her objections went unheeded. By the time I was nine, I had my first job for ten cents an hour. I went on to manufacture my own money, both paper and metal, until dad explained that this was known as "counterfeiting"—which was against the law. I had to stop just as I was getting good at it. At ten I joined the country club and began playing golf. Dad found this amusing since he had never belonged to a country club and wondered how in the world a boy my age had ever managed to get accepted. (I negotiated!)

As I grew, so did my obsession with money—and so did the vehemence of mom's lectures.

"Money can't buy you love," she said.

To argue my position, I pointed out how many rich men in town had young, good-looking wives or girl-friends. That day she almost slapped my face.

In spite of my mother's efforts to change me, I spent most of my first 34 years pursuing my first love, money. Then one day I asked myself, "Is there more to life than money, pretty toys, fast cars, wine, women and song?"

At this point in my life I started to gain a little more appreciation for my mother's opinions about money. She associated money with greedy, evil, manipulative, immoral and valueless people. Granted, this world is full of them. I was one of them for several years. I had absolutely no sympathy for people who were poor and, in fact, did my best to stay away from them. But as I sat thinking that I had what most people could only dream of, I began to feel confused about my life.

My parents had worked primarily for the fulfillment of their minds and their souls. My mother was a registered nurse who worked for her love of people. My father was a teacher and worked for that same love. For two years they worked with President Kennedy's Peace Corps. My mother stressed that I should find work I enjoyed. I couldn't understand why she was unhappy with what I did. I loved driving ships and piloting planes throughout the world. As I matured, however, I noticed a fine distinction between what my parents did and what I was doing. Yes, I was doing what I loved. The difference was that part of what gave my parents pleasure was the realization that what they did not only gave them pleasure but also benefitted others. I did what I loved for only one person, me. The work they did to make the world a better place was a form of wealth that I must admit I didn't have. With all my dollars, I was living in a kind of poverty.

David Suzuki, a great Canadian of Japanese descent, provides a story that best summarizes my way of thinking. He is noted, among other things, for his research on fruit flies. I shall paraphrase the story from his book, *Metamorphosis.*

He begins with the parallels between the lives of humans and fruit flies. After birth, humans and fruit flies begin responding to their environments. They grow, learn and become more mobile. A fly or maggot goes through a series of molts. A child experiences various stages of maturation, learning to walk and talk, then entering puberty, and so on. Early in life both are in the gathering, or "me" stage.

On cue, the maggot enters a phase called pupation. In butterflies, pupation happens when the caterpillar spins a cocoon, to emerge some time later as a butterfly. At pupation the fruit fly maggot digests what it has accumulated (as adults digest accumulated experiences, information and knowledge), goes through metamorphosis, and then flies about the planet performing the mission for which it was genetically designed. This is where humans and fruit flies differ.

David Suzuki says that the difference between humans and fruit flies is that, "Many people remain maggots, growing larger, richer and more powerful, without an accompanying evolution in wisdom, sensitivity or compassion."

Before I lost everything, I did my best to become a very big, rich maggot. It wasn't until I became a flat-broke maggot that I began to evolve. At 32, my thinking changed dramatically. I found that I had a deep need to give back instead of just gathering and taking. I began to search for a different kind of wealth. Money was no longer the main motivator in my life. With the help of dear friends and teachers, I began to see things I had never seen before. I began to enjoy the kind of wealth that eludes all too many rich men and women.

For the very first time in my life I began to appreciate how it might feel to be a poor person—that poverty of any kind had a direct impact on self-esteem. Most people think of poverty as something experienced only by the homeless or by people living in ghettos. But there are many different kinds of poverty. In the final analysis, it may best be defined as "a need without the wherewithal." If a family, for example, needs a larger home and does not have the knowledge or the wherewithal to acquire it, that can constitute their poverty. But if a person feels unfulfilled emotionally or spiritually and doesn't know what to do about that, this is a form of poverty, too.

My own poverty was of this latter kind. It had less to do with money than with fulfillment of my self. Though I had all the money I had ever wanted, I was still living in poverty because I did not know how to be happy. I remember how shocked I was to discover that poverty wasn't limited to money—that all the material wealth in the world would never heal the ache I was feeling.

I discovered two other categories of poverty during this period: emotional poverty and professional poverty. The "need without the wherewithal" in people is alarmingly high. There are people who suffer in abusive relationships, not knowing how to get out; there are couples whose marriages were dead years ago, but who are clinging to little more than a now-vague memory of happiness. And there are lonely people who, in a world of over five billion people, can't find that special someone with whom to share mutual loving and caring.

Emotional poverty does not discriminate. And one of the worst wastes of all is the financially wealthy person who is emotionally bankrupt.

The other category of "need without wherewithal" is professional poverty. I am amazed at the number of people I talk with every year who are either bored with their jobs or simply hate their work. How anyone can get up day after day to go to a job he or she feels is empty and ungratifying? If we must spend most of our waking hours at work, why not figure out a way to spend it doing something that is nourishing to our minds or our souls? When we start looking at the afternoon coffee break as the high point of our day, we're in trouble.

Increasing numbers of people are expressing the desire to do something meaningful with their lives. They want to make a contribution rather than merely working for a living. So many people end up feeling that their lives make little or no difference. While there are a great many people who think a raise is compensation enough for the emptiness they feel in their work, there are also people who find their work so satisfying that they don't care that they take home a small paycheck. They work because they are satisfied that they are making an important contribution to society. This sense of making a contribution is why most teachers stay in a profession that offers less money than most.

Without a sense of self-worth and personal satisfaction, we live in poverty, in a void where there is little or no real happiness—regardless of how many dollars we have in the bank. And whether this poverty is derived from a miserable relationship or an unfulfilling job, it will not magically disappear just because we increase the amounts in our bank accounts.

Must we choose between happiness and money? On the contrary, there is no reason in the world not to have both. One of my greatest teachers, R. Buckminster Fuller, awoke me to the fact that poverty has nothing to do with money and that money does not produce wealth. Fuller said that wealth is what a person knows, and that the more people know, the richer they will feel. In its present condition, our educational system diminishes a person's knowledge by punishing mistakes; in the end this produces people who enjoy the wealth of neither knowledge nor money.

Mother was right. It is one of my greatest regrets that she died before she saw her son metamorphose—hopefully, a few stages beyond his identity as a maggot.

15

When 1 + 1 Doesn't Always Make 2

Every man is fully satisfied that there is such a thing as truth, or he would not ask any question.

—CHARLES SANDERS PEIRCE (1951)

Why are so many people and organizations terrified of change? Why do they run from the unknown? Why would people resist trying something new even when the old way obviously isn't working? Why do people cling to simplistic answers of "right and wrong" or "good and bad," even when it can be demonstrated that there are multiple answers, each one with its own unique benefits? Put in even more personal terms, why are our own first responses so often to go along with the crowd rather than to think for ourselves?

The answer to all these questions begins with our schools. Whether the result of tradition or habit, we have been taught to believe that every question has only a single "right" answer. When you were in second grade and you were asked "What is 1 + 1?" you were undoubtedly told you were wrong unless you replied, "The answer is 2." If you answered 6, the chances are pretty good that you were told that you were wrong. Only a single answer would suffice—2, and only 2.

Well, you may ask, is 2 the wrong answer? Of course it's not, at least not in the particular math system being taught in most schools. But there are other systems where the answer can be a little different. For example, what's 1+1 if we are talking about sets of objects? If you had 2 teams of 3 people each, the "right" answer could be 6.

While a few schools are now using more progressive systems for teaching math, the one-right-answer principle continues to be the rule in all too many cases.

We may not have been taught the wrong answers, but we have been taught to think that there's a single set of right answers which, if we work hard and get good grades, will be our prize upon graduation day. To go on with our lives, living as if this was true, is to greatly limit our thinking, making it difficult to accept new ideas or to tolerate the differences that are a normal part of life.

One can't help but wonder how Christopher Columbus would have done turned out if he'd grown up in the kinds of schools that most of us did. On his student evaluation I can imagine words like "inattentive," and "daydreamer," or possibly even "discipline problem." When told that "the earth is flat," he would have challenged his teachers, insisting it was round, and later, on the playground, his peers would have laughed at him and called him "stupid" for even suggesting such a thing.

Our rigid adherence to one-right-answer thinking forces us to filter out or distort information that doesn't exactly fit what we've been taught. This intolerance to ideas outside the accepted system crushes today's budding Columbuses. It discourages independent thinking and seriously underplays creativity in our lives. What a paradox it is to have a system of education that praises Christopher Columbus as a hero on one hand, yet punishes students for having the same kind of original ideas that made him so.

The educational system, with its obsession for right answers teaches rigidity. Those who "get it right," who do the memorizing correctly, are rewarded with good grades and praise. If we question the system, however, or think for ourselves, we are often chastised or punished with poor grades. What a shame that we weed out inquisitive minds while rewarding those whose only gift is rigid conformity.

Many governments, businesses and families are headed by people who continue to cling to rigid one-right-answer thinking—people who believe that their own point of view is the only point of view that's possible. Our business history is filled with rigid-minded individuals who clung to one-right-answer thinking and went bankrupt or limited their company's growth because they were unable to look at alternatives.

Near the turn of the 20th century, this kind of rigid thinking found expression in none less than the head of the U.S. Patent Office, which announced that "There are no new ideas to be discovered." Those who were in charge of registering applications for new patents, as well as many manufacturers, were so overwhelmed by the sheer mass of new ideas, and so awed by new products, that they became convinced that humanity had completely fulfilled its creative potential. Humanity finally had all the answers, had done it all. This announcement came at the dawn of the biggest technology boom in history, during a period when the Patent Office was literally flooded with applications for new inventions. All of that day's problems seemed to have been solved. For a moment in time it was believed that we had found all the right answers.

Of course, closing the Patent Office seems absurd to us today, with technology still expanding at a rate no one could have even imagined a hundred years ago. And yet, our one-right-answer thinking persists, permeating our society.

"My way or the highway!"

"That is a crazy idea!"

"It will never work!"

"It may work for him, but it won't work for me!"

These are all statements expressed by people who have been blinded by one-right-answer thinking, clinging to their own sets of rigid rules, their fixed points of view. While being single-minded can be an admirable trait, it is possible to be single-minded yet open. It is possible to choose one way of thinking and use it consistently while accepting the fact that it is only one way, meanwhile leaving room for other entertaining possibilities.

One of the chief reasons our educational system is in chaos is that it is still closed-minded, archaic and slow to respond to new ideas, new styles, and new ways of being. The worst part is that laws force kids to attend school and to conform to one-right-answer thinking. Often the only choice kids have is to rebel. Out of this rebellion our young people have formed societies of peers, which cut them off from the benefits of learning from people who are older. The rigidities of elders make it impossible to develop mutual respect, and so we are creating an adversarial society which divides young people and their elders.

There is a saying coined by author-lecturer Wayne Dyer that "we will see it when we believe it." This phrase describes the role our own belief systems play in our lives—that we tend to see only the reality we hold in our own minds. If we believe that every question has only one right answer we will tend to see only that single answer—and judge ourselves and others according to our knowledge and acceptance of that answer. Anyone who doesn't know or accept the single answer is deemed an idiot.

During the late 1700s many sailors on whaling ships reported meeting South Sea islanders who had never seen a white man before, nor had they ever seen a three-masted whaling ship. And yet, ships' logs proved that both the ships and the white sailors had entered their waters many times. It was finally found that the natives were actually blind to those huge ships, even when they were right in front of them. It was not a lack of intelligence that caused this blindness. The natives became aware of the interlopers only when the mother ship let down the smaller boats that the natives were accustomed to seeing. Until the boats touched the water the natives saw nothing—the large ships anchored in the bay right in front of their noses simply weren't realities they could recognize.

Oh, you may say, it is easy to see how this could happen with primitive peoples, but surely it can't still be happening today. On the contrary, every day there are businesses that fail and personal relationships that degenerate into hopeless conflict because the limits of our belief systems don't allow us to see alternatives that should be obvious.

The sad thing is that this kind of blindness can be easily prevented—by teaching from the first day of school that virtually every system of thought is a creative endeavor, not an absolute truth that can never be challenged. Sure, we must teach the fundamentals, but we must never forget that those fundamentals are only one-right-answer thinking—not the only way.

We must begin teaching that our greatest power as human beings is not the belief systems that lie outside us, but our own thoughts—both positive and negative. Once a person says, even silently, "I'll never be rich," we create a filter as powerful as the filter that prevented the South Sea islanders from seeing the tall ships. And the resulting blindness, limiting our lives, remains in place until the thought is changed.

When a young child is called "stupid" and does not know how to repel that powerful thought, the thought becomes a belief that will play itself out in that child's life until he or she discovers how to change it. And that single thought can blind the person to her own potential. Even worse, that child will tend to pass the same belief system onto her child. We humans have a terrible habit of doing unto others what we have hated being done to us.

How can we break out of this one-right-answer thinking? In recent years, science has begun to think in terms of "paradigms." What this means is that from moment to moment and day to day we hold in our minds a particular model of reality which consists of assumptions that our society, or the community in which we live, holds to be generally true. We take this inner model of reality so much for granted that most of the time we can't even see that this is indeed the way we "make sense" of our lives. The rule that says 1 + 1 = 2 belongs to one paradigm; it is not the only paradigm, however. If we are to learn how to manage change, if we are to learn how to improve our own lives, we need to know that we do not have to be limited to a single paradigm—no matter how "real" it seems to us or how long we have clung to it as the only reality there is.

While the word paradigm is usually reserved for whole systems, such as communities or cultures, it is also useful in terms of talking about our personal beliefs. I say making money is easy. That's my paradigm. To a person whose paradigm is that you get rich only through sheer luck or because you were born under a certain star, I may seem like a liar.

Teaching people that there is only a single paradigm can be financially, professionally, emotionally and physically costly. Since most people have never had the opportunity to learn about paradigms, they tend to cling to the notion that our educational system puts forth—that there is only one paradigm. I see it all the time in my classes. I see it in my students' eyes. Just beyond their pupils I see the steel gates guarding their personal paradigms. As long as I say nothing that might challenge those paradigms, the steel gates stay open. The moment I say something outside their paradigms, the gates slam shut. They become glassy-eyed or squint in skepticism and distrust.

For our educational system to adequately serve our society, it needs to break out of the rigid notion that their paradigms—the ones they teach—are the only true or real ones. There are infinite numbers of possible paradigms either already existing or which are even now being created. And in most cases, the solutions to today's problems—whether personal or world-wide—are going to come out of paradigms that are yet to be created. This concept of limitless paradigms needs to become basic knowledge taught in our schools and throughout society.

Our educational system abhors this more open way of thinking. Yet there can be little doubt that our outmoded, one-right-answer method of teaching can severely cripple our children's ability to find success later in life. It is my belief that the goal of education should be to expand people's beliefs, not diminish them.

We all need to learn how to think, not what to think—and our educational system is going to have to do the same if we are ever to stop the exodus from our schools. None of us can any longer afford the dropouts and increasing number of discipline problems that one-right-answer thinking creates. Just as poor people can't be rich until they let go of their beliefs about "being poor," so our society cannot grow until we are all willing to let go of our need for one-right-answer thinking.

If the educational system could see its limitations, maybe the world would witness a whole fleet of Christopher Columbuses going off to explore the unknown, with no fear of being ridiculed for their challenge to the acceptable knowledge of their time. Maybe it is time to reevaluate our educational priorities. Could it be that memorizing the year Columbus' boats landed on the new continent might be less important than appreciating the fact that a dreamer named Columbus challenged his contemporaries' belief that the earth was flat and had the courage to sail to the edge of the earth? Isn't the courage and vision of which humans are capable at least as important as memorizing a date?

In this changing world, we need more Columbuses, new people in business, government and education who aren't limited to one-right-answer thinking. Where are the new ideas? Where are the visionary leaders? Where are the people with the courage to put everything on the line and lead us forward, through the tremendous chaos of our time? Where are our Columbuses?

As they are today, too many of our schools are systematically eliminating our young explorers, creating instead a world of people who are afraid of making mistakes and who don't have the courage or faith to pursue new visions, not even their own.

It is time to take a close look, not only at our own thoughts, but also at our own actions. It is time for each of us to ask ourselves, "Am I on the ship with the new Columbuses or am I standing safely on shore, clinging to the past, shouting doomsday warnings and heckling the youthful explorers?"

16

It Is Not the Teachers

And gladly would he learn, and gladly teach...

—GEOFFREY CHAUCER (1387)

"We need better teachers," a frustrated parent yells.

"If you were better parents, your kids would be better students," a teacher fires back, with just as much anger and frustration.

Parent-teacher meetings have changed since I was a kid. When I was in school the only person blamed for doing poorly was the student. Now the teachers are blaming the parents and the parents are blaming the teachers. And together they're both screaming at the politicians. To top it off, taxpayers are getting sick of the whole thing. Our educational system is in a chaotic state, with everyone pointing fingers at everyone else. It seems everyone has someone to blame.

Numerous "solutions" have been proposed by various people and organizations in an effort to improve education. Many you've heard—higher salaries for teachers, smaller class sizes, better educated teachers. All these concerns have merit, but each one is only a singular solution, addressing merely one fragment of a much larger system. My favorite proposal is the one that would keep kids in school longer. Now, that's enlightened thinking! Give students more of what isn't working. Bore them longer. Humiliate them more. Give them a larger dose of that medicine which drives out creativity and independent thinking.

This comical suggestion stems from Westerners' belief that problems can be solved with a single answer, without looking at the whole system. The sad part is that this "solution" is being seriously considered. A friend of mine recently read an article on this very topic. The researcher stated that since Japanese students go to school more days per year than students in the United States, and since Japan's scholastic test scores are higher than U.S. scores, one must conclude that U.S. students aren't doing as well because they don't go to school as many days as Japanese students. It is this kind of narrow-minded thinking that keeps our educational system back in the Dark Ages. Westerners see only what they want to see. This particular article also showed that other countries had their students go to school almost as many days as the Japanese students, and far more than U.S. students, yet their scholastic test scores were among the lowest in the world. Blindly looking at only one part of a system is a dangerous and unsuccessful way to try to solve a problem.

We saw a similar scenario in the business world when Japan began to dominate world markets. American business people looked at the Japanese and saw that they used something called "quality circles." Americans then began to use quality circles—and the experiment, for the most part, was a dismal failure. They did not know that quality circles are the last step of a larger system that included the whole history of the Japanese people.

As long as we continue ignorantly to pick and choose one "easy answer" at a time in an effort to cure our various social and economic problems, our society will continue to suffer. When will we stop seeking singular quick-fix solutions and start studying systems?

It is grossly unfair to blame one facet of the educational system, such as teachers, lack of money or short school hours. Each is merely a tiny piece of a monstrously complex structure. Outside influences also affect what happens inside school. Just look at the competition our schools have today: television, videos, Nintendo. No wonder our kids are bored by school!

Read the controversial books *Magical Child* and *Magical Child Matures*, by Joseph Chilton Pearce, on the subject of intelligence, learning and children and you'll get still another perspective on how influences outside school affect learning. Pearce writes about how delivering children Western-style actually destroys a child's intelligence before and during birth, with practices such as the mother lying down instead of squatting as she is biologically designed to do. Pearce believes this adds massive "negative programming" to the defenseless child's subconscious. What's more, drugging the mother drugs the child within 45 seconds, which may explain the large number of drug-dependent people in our society. Cutting the umbilical cord too early causes oxygen deprivation and brain damage. Taking the child away to an incubator instead of allowing bonding with the mother damages the child's future ability to have successful emotional relationships, as well as impeding the ability to learn.

Regardless of whether you agree with everything Pearce says or not, his point that a child's education begins long before he or she begins school is an important one to consider. It is just one more piece of a system that needs to be considered before we start blaming the teachers or any other single factor.

Successful systems produce successful results. Our educational system is not one of these. In the Western world, system-creation is rarely even considered, and most systems in place today were created in a vacuum. The effectiveness of the complete system was never a factor, so the end result is a whole society of dysfunctional systems, the educational system being only one.

I hear people screaming at professional educators to change the system! But is this not a little like asking a fish in the ocean to clean its water? They are so deeply immersed in it—literally and figuratively—that they can't see that it is part of a larger system. So their efforts to change it end up being exercises in futility. Just as the fish does not know how the water fits into the larger system, so most of those to whom we turn for solutions are unable to see the larger picture.

Most of us are tired of hearing about Japanese high-tech, innovative, quality products at excellent prices. Yet, let's not forget that there was a time, not so long ago, when "Made in Japan" meant inferior products. The person responsible for the change was an American named W. Edwards Deming. Very simply, what the Japanese did was change their systems of business and manufacturing.

Deming reports that 94 percent of all failures in business are system failures. Only 6 percent are people failures. So even if all our teachers were replaced and their replacements were given higher pay and smaller class sizes, nothing would change because the system would still remain intact. Japan, Deming points out, doesn't excel because it has better people but because it has better, more effective systems. Meanwhile, we blame our educational failures on inadequate teachers, or low pay, or class size, perhaps only because these are the most visible parts of a system whose other 90 percent is invisible.

We in the West have a hard time dealing with what we can't see. It may be right there in front of us but we can't see it. Instead of dealing with whole systems, we offer simplistic slogans or throw more money at the problem, hoping it will go away. One claim of the Bush administration was that by the year 2000 the U.S. would be rise to the top in math and science because more money was being allocated for these two subjects. Nobody questioned it. This was what most people wanted to hear, and so they were temporarily placated. That is perhaps always the purpose of a slogan—not to actually solve problems but to placate.

Teachers have become the scapegoats of parents, politicians and administrators who would rather invent new slogans and throw more money at the problem than learn something about systems and how they could effect lasting, worthwhile change. The evolution of our society will continue to be held back until we all start looking at it in this new way. Only then can we begin to reap the emotional, professional and financial benefits that all of us are capable of making a reality.

Let's wake up and stop making teachers our scapegoats!

17

The Courage to Change

Can success change the human mechanism so completely between one dawn and another? Can it make one feel taller, more alive, handsomer, uncommonly gifted and indomitably secure with the certainty that this is the way life will always be? It can and it does!

—Moss Hart (1959)

As a partner in a manufacturing company, I was constantly faced with problems of productivity. Our products were wallets, hats and handbags, and at one point we were constantly being undersold by competition from the Orient. It was very common for me to go to a buyer of a store and have them show me a product made in Korea or Taiwan that was similar to mine and ask me to beat the price. Very often, the price of the product from the Orient was half my cost. My workers needed and deserved raises, and yet the competition was destroying us. My partners and I knew that if we didn't come up with a solution we would soon be out of business.

That was in 1981. It was then that we began to study the systems of Edwards Deming, the quality guru from America who is credited with creating Japan's industrial might. Deming urges managers to change the system and demonstrates that if this is done the productivity of its people will change too. He makes the point that people are not the problem; the system is the problem. My partners and I eagerly began putting Deming's recipe for success to work in our factory. Nothing changed. Something was missing, but what? We kept experimenting. And then one day we struck upon the solution, one that surprised us all. It was a solution that required us to look at something that was quite invisible—our own cultural biases. Here's how that worked:

Being Japanese-American, I began to look at Deming's work from the point of view of the cultural differences between East and West. I began to ask myself, how did I think as a Westerner and how did I think as an Oriental? These are definitely two different ways of thinking and I noticed that I acted differently when my cultural point of reference shifted from one culture to the other. That's when I noticed that Deming's recipes for success worked best when I was in my Japanese mode. The same recipes appeared to fail when I was in my Yankee mode. This was one of those blinding revelations that literally change the way we see the world. The strange thing was that I had heard this before, how Deming's recipes were designed for the Japanese mode, yet I hadn't fully comprehended until that moment.

My discovery was that our system would not change until the thinking (assumptions) within that system changed first.

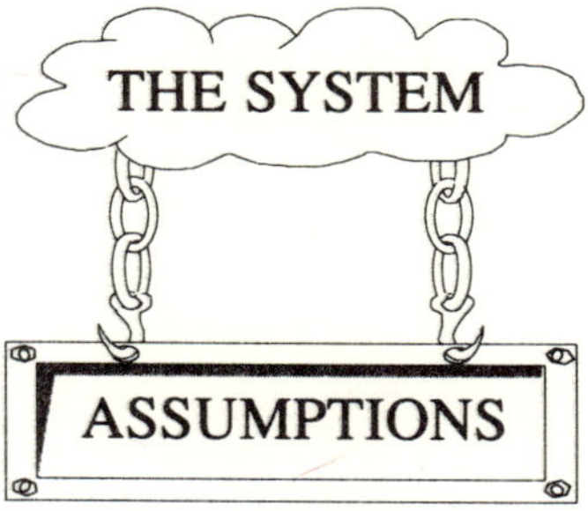

Before any system can change, first the assumptions holding it in place must change.

If I wanted to increase production in my factory, I first had to change the assumptions in the minds of my workers—as well as in my own mind!

Most of us held in our minds assumptions that work was tedious, boring and something one only did because of financial necessity. My talks of quality, pride in one's work and cooperative team work fell on deaf ears. However, these same words appealed to my Japanese side. It was my Yankee side that was deaf.

I began to explore the American side of my brain to find out what it wanted. I had a difficult time finding what I was looking for because my assumptions blinded my insights. Finally, a light went on. My assumption that work was boring and tedious blocked me from feeling any kind of real involvement with Deming's system. When I asked myself, "How can I make work fun?" the little voices in my head screamed in protest: "Work isn't fun. It's serious stuff. Blah, blah, blah."

Off I ran to the shop floor to call a meeting with the workers. "Lets have fun here!" I yelled.

They had the same initial reaction I did. Their faces scrunched up and they looked at me as if to say, "The idiot is being an idiot again!"

I could almost hear the voices in their heads saying, "Work isn't fun. It's serious stuff."

For weeks I continued to hold meetings about how we could make work fun. There would be much more open communication between employees during work hours. People would be encouraged to work together in teams where more socialization would be possible. Surprisingly, production went up when the work environment was humanized in this way.

More and more ideas began to flow and I could sense that our assumptions were changing. All of a sudden, the excitement began to rise. During the lunch break, workers engaged in friendly athletic competitions and games. People who had been working side by side as complete strangers for several months suddenly became friends, sharing their lives with each other. Slowly the factory was becoming an enjoyable place to be. People were actually looking forward to Monday rolling around again so they could get back to work.

What we learned from all this is that "quality and pride of workmanship" may be goals that work in Japan, but "fun" is what works with the American worker. That single revelation turned our business around. One day we looked at our production figures and discovered that productivity had jumped over 350 percent. We were back in business.

With Deming's recipe for success in place, hooked into the spirit of fun, production continued to rise. We had more than fun. We fell in love as a company, and that made all the difference. For the first time, whites, blacks, Japanese, Laotians, Vietnamese, Filipinos, Latinos, Cambodians, Hawaiians and all combinations, all with different languages and cultures, came together. Quality jumped and productivity soared—all simply by changing that basic assumption about work.

What I had learned spilled out into other parts of my life. I began teaching entrepreneurship as a hobby. I used SuperLearning educational techniques and added the element of fun. It was working, yet I found that something else was needed. Again, I was running into problems and I began to wonder why. I sat quietly and began looking at my assumptions about learning. If changing my assumptions about work had produced such astounding results, perhaps I'd get similar results by looking at my assumptions about learning.

It wasn't easy to identify those assumptions. It never is, because how do you question an assumption you do not know you have? So many of our assumptions are buried in our subconscious minds. If you were to ask most people, "Do you want to be rich?" most will reply "Yes, of course." This response comes from their conscious mind. Yet, from deep down in the caverns of the subconscious comes another silent assumption: "Your mother said you were stupid. You will never be rich." So no matter how hard this person works, no matter how hard he studies, this negative assumption sits there dictating the results of his life.

There are many methods to rid ourselves of these silent assumptions—everything from hypnosis to positive affirmations to psychotherapy, and if you suspect that you may be held back by such assumptions I encourage you to go out into the world and find the method or methods that work best for you. Many books, tapes, videos and counselors are available to support you in this quest. The most important thing is to begin the search.

How did I eventually find out about my assumptions concerning learning and education? The truth is that I at first became very frustrated. Then, one day while teaching a class, that light of revelation flickered in my mind. I began to notice my own thoughts as I was teaching. The first sneaky thought I caught running through my mind was, "I know more than these students."

I fell silent. My mouth dropped open. The adult class of businesspeople stared at me as if I had lost my mind. I told the class to take a break. I sat in the corner of the room reviewing what actions I had taken because of that thought. I realized that I had been lecturing like the ultimate authority instead of asking others in the class to share what they knew. All of a sudden, a whole string of assumptions came forth from that realization.

I began to see that I had already judged and categorized certain students in the class. I had begun to believe that there were students who were smart and others who weren't. I had predetermined how fast they would learn. I believed that I already knew those who would use my material and those who wouldn't.

I began to notice how my assumptions had been affecting how I talked to each student. If I thought one was able, I was willing to push harder. Likewise, if I thought a student was less able, I did not put my energy into teaching him or her.

I was judging, classifying, discriminating and determining who was going to succeed and who wasn't. I was imposing my limits on my students and subconsciously putting pressure on them to comply.

My assumptions about my students were working as self-fulfilling prophecies. The students who I thought were smart did well, and the students I classified as slow did poorly.

My conclusion is this: As long as the system makes the assumption that there are smart people and slow people, it will reward the smart ones and punish the slow ones. It is the equivalent of an educational witch hunt.

My own organization now teaches with the assumption that all people want to learn and are able to. Every time my judgments get in the way, I have trouble—and what's more important, so do my students. When I am able to suspend my judgments and treat everyone as fast and bright, that's what I get in return. Our instructors are constantly reminded to do their best to suspend any judgments. Our teaching methods are designed to encourage everyone to move forward into active learning. Our instructors learn how to accept and handle different behaviors and personality types, yet keep the constant thought that all people are able and bright.

If we are to evolve as a species, the first thing that must change is the negative assumptions we impose on ourselves and others. This needs to happen in our homes, our work places, in our communities and in our schools.

Other Assumptions We Might Be Making

As adults, we may still be unconsciously harboring assumptions that others—parents, teachers or peers—imposed on us. These may presently be holding us back or limiting us in one way or another. In addition, if those same negative assumptions are affecting us, it's a sure bet that we are projecting them out to others—our loved ones, our co-workers, our employees, our bosses, and our students if we are teachers. Here is a list of eight common assumptions:

1. Nobody really wants to learn so you have to use force or threat.
2. Learning must be boring and slow.
3. You can't have fun and learn.
4. You can't teach anyone anything unless you control them and force them to sit still.
5. Testing and grading are necessary.
6. Not everyone is smart.
7. Not everyone can pass.
8. Teachers are smarter than students.

My great grievance with education is the constant use of fear to motivate students. Tests are used as threats to force kids to study rather than to find out how effective the system is or to identify what a teacher might do to reach students who are having trouble. As it is, the system sacrifices a certain percentage of children for no other purpose than to frighten the others into working harder and complying with the system.

Perhaps using fear to motivate people has its time and place. The problem comes when it is used as the primary motivating tool for educating young minds. We all come to this planet with a unique gift. You can see it as a special glow in the eyes of the newborn. It is a curiosity, a desire to learn and an eagerness to give. It is a genius that resides in the heart. The true purpose of education is to marry this genius or gift with the mind so the person will be able to fulfill his or her purpose or destiny on this planet. Once we have identified this gift in ourselves, it will direct us to learn what we must. This is a lifetime process.

Einstein said that "Inspiration is more valuable than knowledge." Our educational system's unrelenting drive to force children to memorize questionable, often unprovable knowledge is crushing the gift that resides in each of our hearts. Each of us knows that the more we force people to do something, the harder they resist. The more we force students to study, the worse they will do. This merely illustrates Newton's law: for every action, there is an opposite and equal reaction.

If we continue to use fear to motivate learning, we will lose one of the most precious resources we are given in this lifetime—the gift of genius that each and every one of us receives at birth. Given that this is so, we all have a responsibility to get to know our assumptions and change those that fail to nurture these gifts in ourselves as well as others.

18

The Wapakununk Factor

The return from your work must be the satisfaction which that work brings you and the world's need of that work. With this, life is heaven, or as near heaven as you can get. Without this—with work you despise, which bores you, and which the world does not need—this life is hell.

—W.E.B. DuBois (1958)

I recently had the pleasure of talking with an American Indian leader of the Winnebago tribe. He was telling our class about what it was like to be an American Indian growing up in a predominantly white culture.

This tribal elder's family moved away from his tribe's reservation for several years when he was a young boy. Growing up in the days before television, he would rush home from school to listen to the radio. His favorite program was "The Lone Ranger." Being an Indian, he particularly loved it when the Lone Ranger got in trouble; to whom did the Lone Ranger turn when things got tough? His wise Indian partner, Tonto, of course. In these chaotic times, maybe it is time that we, like the Lone Ranger, look beyond the Western or Japanese systems for ideas to reform education. Perhaps it is time we listened to the Native Americans.

The Winnebago tribe holds that the purpose of education is to help their young people achieve what they call "Wapakununk." The approximate definition of that word is, "To be able to do everything to exist in this world." To achieve "Wapakununk," the elders take turns educating the children so they are able to fish, ride horses, comprehend medicine, grow food, be spiritual, hunt, tan hides, make pottery, arbitrate disputes and be responsible for the well-being of the whole tribe.

In the modern world "Wapakununk" might be interpreted as, "Becoming competent, confident and comfortable with life and its constant changes." Our current educational system, however, by requiring people to be memorizers instead creative thinkers, to become highly specialized before becoming generalized, and to be employees rather than entrepreneurs who fully comprehend money and business, is educating people to be inflexible rather than to be able to change with the times. Too many young people are coming out of the school being anything but "Wapakununk."

Recently, the *Wall Street Journal* had a long article about the employment picture in the U.S. The article said that the hardest person to find employment for is the 45-year-old college graduate who is a middle manager from a major corporation. Not only are such a person's financial needs extraordinarily high, but their specialities are often obsolete and they are not good candidates for retraining. Most of the time a company would rather hire two or three younger people with a fresh outlook and new information. Those two younger people usually come for the same price as one older, less flexible, middle-aged person who often proves difficult to retrain. While age discrimination is illegal, rest assured it is alive and well.

The long-term problem is that those fresh new faces being hired for less today will quite probably confront the same issues as the older person they replaced when they themselves turn 45. Failing to keep current with new ideas and new technologies, resisting change in the world around us, is a very risky career path during volatile economic times. It is definitely not Wapakununk.

While many people do very well for themselves during their peak years of employment, they are rarely prepared to to handle their uncertain futures. Entrusting one's future financial security to a company pension plan, for example, may have been the way things were done 50 years ago but in today's world it is unwise, to say the least. The pension plans of all too many major corporations are empty, pilfered by greedy, over-ambitious business leaders. One major U.S. airline was having trouble selling their assets because their employee pension fund was approximately $850 million in the red! Consider how the men and women who had spent their lives working for this company must have felt when they found out about this.

Who ends up with the money from pension funds when a company goes belly up? Do the employees get it or do the creditors? Unfortunately, it's usually the latter. People who have counted on that money, people who have contributed to the pension fund for years, end up with nothing.

Now, you may say, how could this happen to educated people, business leaders who presumably should know how to plan for a secure future? Well, it does happen, and all too frequently. The August 27, 1991 issue of the *Wall Street Journal* reported that over 70 percent of the 155 large law firms surveyed have unfunded retirement plans. This mismanagement could cripple these law firms in the future when today's 35- to 45-year-old attorneys are ready to retire. These baby-boomers' retirements may have to be paid for by future attorneys who are in elementary school today.

Not only are most people unprepared to make decisions concerning their retirement but vast numbers of people limp through life, crippled by a lack of competence, confidence and comfort. These are only minor reflections of our failing educational system. Instead of achieving a state of Wapakununk, most people will spend their productive years clinging to jobs they don't even like, probably for inadequate pay. And what will they do when they retire? That's anybody's guess because only a few are even aware of the choices—or the risks.

An Incomplete Education

Our Native American guest told us the story of a mis-educated student who through a series of oversights by his teachers failed to achieve Wapakununk. The story, a very old legend in his tribe, went something like this:

There was once a bright young brave who quickly achieved Wapakununk. Following tradition, this young brave had been educated by several elders. While each teacher was educating him in a specific skill necessary to achieve Wapakununk, nobody remembered to teach him humility, an essential human trait for young braves who might one day become leaders. Each elder thought that one of the others had taught this young brave humility.

It wasn't until the brave was older and had attained a position of power that the elders realized their oversight. While the brave was very skillful and competent, he used his power abusively instead of with compassion. Lacking humility, he became stubborn and inflexible, refusing to learn anything new.

The elders called a secret meeting. How could they handle this arrogant young leader? It was too late to teach him humility. He only knew arrogance, which ironically was being supported by the high level of skills they had taught him when he was very young. They could not kill him since this would be an act even worse than his arrogance. They dared not ask him to leave, for in his arrogance he would retaliate and use his power against them.

After several nights of secret meetings, the elders came up with a plan. One chilly autumn morning, they called the brave to their council. They had a task for him. It was a difficult task, for they knew his ego would respond to such a challenge. Their tribe had been pestered by a band of particularly smart wolves which were led by a large spotted male.

The elders told the brave that his tribe would be forever grateful to him if he agreed to go out and kill this lead wolf. They added that it would look even better if he did this alone because it would increase his status in the tribe. Naturally, the arrogant brave accepted the challenge. He spent that night bragging about his mission as he sat around the great fire with other members of the tribe. His arrogance blinded him to the hidden plan of the elders.

The next morning, just as the sun was peeking over the horizon, the entire tribe gathered to wave good-bye to the arrogant brave. As they did, the brave waved back, striding confidently across the frost-covered plain. As soon as the brave was out of sight, the entire tribe rallied together and quickly broke camp. They collected all their belongings. Families and friends said good-bye to each other and covered their tracks, erasing all evidence of their existence. Then they disappeared in every direction to join other tribes. Their tribe ceased to exist forever.

I sat stunned as my guest ended his story. The lesson seemed quite clear, if painful to accept. Here was a once-great community that had been literally destroyed, wiped off the face of the earth, because the elders had neglected to fully prepare its young leader for the position of power and responsibility he would one day assume. When I asked if this was what his tale was intended to teach, the storyteller nodded.

He smiled and began to explain to me the culture of the American Indian. He told me that the Indians did not hold that humans were any more important than anything else in the scheme of things that we call life.

"We are all equals in the eyes of 'The Great Spirit,'" he explained. "A tribe or a single human is not any more important than a tree or a squirrel. All of us here on Mother Earth contribute to each other's lives. The deer and the buffalo were given by Mother Earth to help support all life as one complete system. Each of us, every person, animal, plant and rock is important to the other and should be respected."

Even in modern times, my guest told me, his people look upon all things as gifts from Mother Earth, even cars and TV sets, since they too ultimately come from the earth. The Native Americans offer us all a great lesson in their view of Mother Earth as the provider and their treating all things with equal respect and reverence.

Unfortunately, for all of us, a great arrogance has spread over our land. It not only destroys our natural environment but also destroys our people. This arrogance provides no room for kindness or compassion. We have forgotten to care about the future. It is this arrogance that prevents us from learning, keeping us clinging to what we have been taught are "right" answers.

What is the source of this arrogance? What is the source of this plague that has spread over our land, robbing us of compassion and any concern for the world around us? It is a disease that began in our schools, where smart people with good grades are taught to avoid slow people with poor grades. It is here we learn to divide the world between good and bad, winner and loser, rich and poor. If your sister or brother is in trouble academically, you are not to help them. Ignore them. Good grades are proof that you are intelligent and ambitious; you should not associate with those who get poor grades and who are just too slow and lazy to be successful. Learn to discriminate quickly and hang out only with *your own kind*. Seek higher degrees. Shun the "losers." This is the intelligent way—the very epitome of arrogance gone wild.

America's virus of arrogance is like a plague, producing incomplete and ultimately infirm leaders. Like most viruses it is indifferent to the health of its host, bleeding the very community that supports it, exploiting everyone in it—exploiting Mother Earth, as my Winnebago friend would say. This virus of arrogance is the same one that prevents leaders of most Western countries from correcting their mistakes and learning new things. How can we expect leaders to recognize that their responsibility extends beyond their own selfish needs and ambitions? How can we expect them to open up to new ideas when they were taught that they must be *right* at all costs?

We all pay the price for this plague, this arrogance that deprives us all of new economic ideas, vision and leadership. The poor get poorer and poorer. And the middle class pays the price in a slowly eroding standard of living, with higher taxes and fewer benefits. We all pay the price as our once-thriving institutions such as libraries, community colleges, concert halls, and theaters close their doors due to financial cutbacks and the indifference of our leaders. The closing of community theaters, art galleries, museums and symphonies deprives us all of those activities that elevate the human spirit and cement the bonds of community.

It sometimes seems that the only thing growing in the Western world is poverty, the antithesis of Wapakununk. Only a short time ago, the homeless could only be found in the streets of Bombay and Calcutta. Now we find them lying on grates in the streets of Washington D.C.—the seat of government for the most powerful country in the world. And their numbers are increasing. The poverty rate of children went up over 20 percent between 1980 and 1990. That rate is also increasing. Today, one of every five children in the United States lives in poverty. Poverty does not discriminate. It hits men, women and children. It is no longer only a problem of ethnic minorities, though it continues to strike these groups the hardest. In the last 10 years, Hispanic children were the worst hit, with an increase of 33 percent in the number of children dipping below the poverty line. Meanwhile, poverty for white children has increased by almost 20 percent, and for blacks by about 6 percent.

The most arrogant of the arrogant turn their back on poverty. "It's not my problem," they say. But it is. Whether we believe it or not, we are one, just as the Native American elders teach. We see this reflected in the inner cities as "arrogance combined with poverty breeds crime." And we all pay for this with the rising costs for law enforcement, rising costs of insurance, and the rising cost of the anxiety that comes with living in a society where we cannot feel secure even in our own homes.

The inability of people to survive in our society is a consequence of a failing educational system. Like the elders in the story of the young brave we are failing to teach humility and other human values that would make this a stronger and more caring society. What's worse, much of what we do teach lays the groundwork for despair, hopelessness and lack of opportunity. In the face of all that, is it any wonder that so many people revert to crime, convinced that there is no future for them?

Money Can't Buy You Love, But...

I have had many heated discussions with teachers who say that there is something "morally unhealthy" associated with teaching young children about money. They say that teaching of this kind will create selfish, materialistic, money-greedy adults. I submit that not teaching kids about money will only increase the numbers of desperate, greedy people. And desperate people perform desperate acts—acts that often lead to crime.

We pretend that money isn't an issue, yet we have kids as young as 7 and 8 turning to crime, learning about money from street criminals instead of teachers. Poor and desperate, they learn to make hundreds, and sometimes thousands of dollars in a single day of selling drugs. In a neighborhood where desperate poverty is all they can see, this kind of money makes them feel like "winners;" in their minds, the "losers" are those who continue to go to school each day, looking forward, at best, to graduating and getting a job paying minimum wage.

Only the most arrogant of our people could claim that the problems of poverty don't affect us all. Only the most arrogant would insist that we are not one, but are separated by invisible boundaries that divide "them" from "us." To maintain those boundaries they are willing to use force—guns and violence if necessary. But what are the lessons we teach with such solutions?

Like millions of other Americans, I watched with interest the news coverage of the war against Saddam Hussein and the people of Iraq. The coverage was very different than the coverage of the Vietnam war. There were no gory pictures showing the bloodied bodies of women and children. The only footage allowed consisted of pictures of dead Iraqi soldiers or of Allied medical teams' humane treatment of Iraqi prisoners. The pictures were very "sanitized." Even the live bombing video pictures were sterile. Who does not remember seeing over and over again the direct hit of one of our laser bombs as it dove into an air-conditioning duct and blew apart the building from the inside? You can't get cleaner and more sterile than that! The U.S. cheered. We were proud of our troops. Yellow ribbons were displayed everywhere. Patriotism was back in style at last. Military soldiers were treated as heroes even though most saw no action. Our humiliation in Vietnam was finally vindicated. We were winners again. Millions of dollars were spent on parades. Euphoria abounded...while we all waited for economic recovery.

Meanwhile, problems at home continued: poverty, homelessness, crime, cultural decline, income decline and unemployment.

In the past, the U.S. and its allies have responded to world problems or troublemakers by bombing them. We attempted to handle Vietnam by bombing the country. We handled Noriega by bombing Panama. We handled Grenada by military intervention. If it worked there, why not extend the same policies to our internal strife? We begin to see why the Native American tribe dissolved rather than continue with its arrogant leader.

From the Taoist classic known as "The Masters of Huainan," comes an ancient lesson still applicable today. The story goes like this:

The supreme warlord who ruled a country asked one of his ministers what had caused the destruction of a certain nation-state.

The minister replied: "Repeated victories in repeated wars."

The warlord said, "A nation is fortunate to win repeated victories in repeated wars. Why would that cause its destruction?"

The minister said,"Where there are repeated wars, the people are weakened; when they score repeated victories, rulers become haughty (arrogant). Let haughty people command weakened people, and rare is the nation that will not perish as a result."

How long will it take us to learn the lesson that when you divide people into winners and losers, everybody ends up a loser.

In our schools, we play winners and losers with our children's minds, hearts and futures. Trapped in our own assumptions about winners and losers we continue to train our young people in the art of divisiveness rather than in the art of living as one. We educate without humility, without love, compassion or respect for the planet that supports us or for the web of life that ultimately is our only strength.

Perhaps war has its place, but that place is certainly not in our schools—and certainly not in those centers of desperate poverty and crime that crisscross our nation and our world.

While many of my peers rebelled against what they believed to be our government's unjust, undeclared war in Vietnam, I was one of the warriors whose actions they were protesting. As a pilot in that war, I also experienced the war as sterile. From the cockpit of my plane, I only saw what millions of children saw on TV during the Iraqi war—bombs going off and clean destruction. Every night I flew home to an aircraft carrier, got a hot shower, enjoyed an excellent meal, watched movies and retired to a comfortable bed. A great ending for a hard day at war.

Then one day I was on the ground, near the base exchange, when it came under rocket attack; suddenly I was immersed in the reality of war. As I picked myself up after the shock wave of a terrible explosion, I realized the building I had been about to enter, to buy some toothpaste and other personal items, was ablaze. The enemy rocket had scored a direct hit. I ran forward to see if I could be of assistance, but the intense heat kept me away. All I could do was stand back, away from the flames, trying to block out the screams of people caught inside, my stomach churning at the smell of their burning flesh.

Will it take sensory assaults of random killings, of fires consuming our inner cities, of more homeless people dying in the streets, of increased crime, of more jails and more children knowing only poverty, before we wake up and correct the arrogant educational system that continues to play cruel games of winners and losers with our children's hearts and minds? The violence of poverty becomes increasingly difficult to sanitize as it scores direct hits closer and closer to home. We cannot bomb it away. It needs to be addressed with kindness, love, compassion and education.

Money will not end poverty. Handouts only increase it. If you give a person a fish, you feed him or her only for a day. But if you teach that same person to fish, you feed them for lifetime. It is time our educational system began teaching everyone to survive financially. These are the "fishing skills" we must pass along in today's world. It is time to stop teaching our good students to be arrogant winners and our slow students to be the sacrificial lambs of the wealthy. We need to learn to give aid to those in need even though our educators define giving or receiving aid as "cheating." The future of our nation and our legacy as a civilization will be measured by the amount we, as individuals, "cheat." If we don't end our arrogance and learn how to teach "Wapakununk" to our people, we may also cease to exist as a tribe.

19

How to Become Wealthy On a Small Budget

If one advances confidently in the direction of his dreams, and endeavors to live the life which he has imagined, he will meet with a success unexpected in common hours.

—HENRY DAVID THOREAU (1854)

In 1989, I was walking through an apartment house that my wife and I were considering buying. The building consisted of 12 very nice two- and three-bedroom apartments. The complex was in an excellent neighborhood and, except for some minor repairs needed, the building was in great condition.

After going through eight of the twelve units, I noticed a trend. Every one of those eight apartments had a large-screen television set, one of the expensive brands. The least expensive set I saw in those eight apartments would have cost at least $650. In one apartment there was an ultra-large-screen TV with stereo, a CD player and all kinds of bells and whistles. I knew it had to cost over $8,000, not including the hundreds of CDs this family had.

As I stood there running a cash flow analysis of the building through my mind, I suddenly realized that my wife and I could afford to buy the apartment building but could not afford one of those expensive TV sets like our tenants-to-be had in their living rooms. Now, don't get me wrong. I enjoy the "good life" and spend money like everyone else. So why could I afford to buy the apartment building but not an expensive TV set? The answer is that TV sets are expensive, while an apartment building is affordable. Why can I afford the apartment house? It is because my renters are helping me buy it, whereas nobody is helping me buy the TV set.

It was at this moment that I fully recognized the difference between being rich and being wealthy—that you may be rich enough to buy a fancy TV set but using your money that way may be robbing you of someday being able to enjoy real wealth.

The first step toward creating wealth on a limited budget is a decision to use the money you have in a very specific way. Although there are many ways to create wealth the one thing they have in common is that you must build a corral. Let me explain with another story.

In the early days of North America, Indian hunters got up every morning, kissed their wives good-bye and set out into the forests to hunt for deer. It was the manly thing to do. Now, a male deer is called a buck and a female deer is called a doe. Today, hundreds of years later, nothing has changed. Modern men and women are still charging out the door, saying good-bye to their loved ones and running off to work to get a few "bucks" so they and their "dough" can live comfortably. However, instead of carrying a bow and arrow, they now carry briefcases full of important papers. The hunting instinct is still alive and well. Every morning you can almost hear the shouts from every business man and woman: "Let's get out there and get those bucks and dough before someone else beats us to it."

Chasing bucks, however, is not wealth, no matter what they taught you in school. To begin to grasp what it takes to get wealthy we'll have to go back to the story about the Indian hunter.

One day, our Indian friend got a bright idea and thought to himself, "Why waste my time running through the woods chasing the bucks? I have to do it every day and I'm getting tired of it. I'm getting older and it's just getting to be too much work to get up early in the morning and go out there. There must be a way to make life easier."

So he got the bright idea of building a fence that would form a holding pen. That took a few weeks, but he figured it would be worth it in the long run, even though he had to work doubly hard in order to both provide for his family and build the pen.

Finally the pen was finished. He went out into the woods and captured some deer. This time, instead of killing them he brought them back alive and put them in his pen. Then he and his wife fed them and cared for them. Because they were in a safe, bountiful environment, the deer slowly began to multiply. Soon the pen was too small, so he built other pens. But he still had to hunt for food because his herd was still growing and not ready for consumption.

His friends laughed at him for working so hard. They attempted to get him to go down to the trading post to do some shopping—to trade some of those bucks for a new Jet Ski, a few lottery tickets or a family vacation to Las Vegas and Disneyland, but he ignored them.

The years passed. Then, one day he and his wife noticed that they no longer had to go out into the woods to hunt. Their little operation was beginning to pay off. They would have plenty of deer for the rest of their lives, without ever having to go out to hunt again. They could even trade a few bucks to other people when the hunting was slow.

In today's financial world wealth means taking the time to build a corral for yourself and your family. Most people never achieve wealth because they spend all their time chasing bucks and spending dough on things that bring no returns.

Some people are born rich. Some get rich quick by winning the lottery. Others marry money or inherit it. If you have not achieved one of these options by the time you read this book, it's time for you to start building your corral.

Think of wealth as a tree. It takes time for it to grow and you need to nurture and care for it as it does. Most people either never take the time to plant a tree, plant it too late or cut it down before it bears fruit. If you want to retire in comfort, plant your tree now. Don't be like most people who wait until it is too late.

Corrals take many forms. Here are four of the most common ways people create them:

1. They build a business.
2. They save money (or collect objects that appreciate in value).
3. They buy real estate that other people rent from them, thus helping to pay the mortgage.
4. They invest in stocks, bonds, and securities.

You may be complaining that you don't have enough money to build your corral. But the chances are that if you are like most middle-class Americans you probably feel you can't afford to build the corral because you are already paying rent, buying a fancy car and purchasing the most up-to-date electronic gizmos. Remember, most of my tenants owned material goodies I felt I could not afford to buy. With a little planning, all that money could have gone toward the first down payment on an apartment house, or the first 500 shares in the latest technology. Any fool can make money. A wealthy person knows how to spend it.

Most people in the Western world have money but never acquire wealth. I had a friend who had lived paycheck-to-paycheck his entire life. One day, he received a check for $38,000, his share of an inheritance. He was elated. His ship had come in— and within three months it had sailed out again, the whole $38,000 had been spent. How many of you have ever noticed how quickly money flows out? If you never take the time to build your corral, there may come a day when your cash flow slows down to a mere trickle. Then you will wish you had taken the time to build the wealth instead of spending the dough. We all know people who are fifty or older who have little to nothing set aside for themselves. The problem is, many will live well into their eighties and nineties due to the advances in health care. The quality of their older years will depend on what they do now.

When I lost my business and my money in 1978, it was the worst thing that had ever happened to me—yet it was also the best because it was then that I learned three key ingredients for creating wealth:

1. **I learned humility.** Once I admitted to myself that I did not have all the answers, I committed myself to life-long learning.

2. **I found out what it feels like to lose my spirit.** When I lost my business and money, my knowledge remained, yet I lost the most valuable thing in the world to me—my spirit—my confidence in myself. It was my brush with the real meaning of poverty. One day, things got so bad that I went down and applied for government assistance. My spirit plummeted down so far I was afraid I would never get it back. Government assistance lasted three weeks. I simply couldn't accept any more.

   I learned at this time that spirit is more important than knowledge. Without spirit or self-confidence, no matter how smart I was, nothing worked. So I began rebuilding my self-confidence. It pains me to see so many people go back to school when what they are really in search of is some self-confidence. What is crucially important in life is the willingness to take action, to have the courage to take risks, to make a mistake, to stand up, dust yourself off, learn the lesson and take action again. Without confidence you can't do that. The trouble with poverty is that it robs most people of that confidence and spirit.

3. **I learned the value of wealth.** As long as money was easy and plentiful, I never thought much about it. I abused and squandered it. But when I suddenly found myself without money, I began to value it. I learned how it feels to have no "cash flow." I am so grateful that I learned this lesson when I did rather than when I was much older, and no longer had the time to do something about it. It was a horrible experience, but it made me commit to building wealth instead of merely chasing the buck and spending the dough.

My steps out of poverty were as follows:

1. **I began to invest my time and my money instead of spending it on consumer goods.** I also spent time unwisely. That's when I started following this rule of thumb:

   Wealthy people invest and poor people consume.

   Having a large screen TV set would have led me into violating this rule completely: The bucks I spent on it would have consumed money I could be investing, and I would have been tempted to waste my time sitting in front of it instead of studying.

2. **I began to build a business that I would love to be in for the rest of my life.** Usually it takes five to ten years to get most businesses off the ground. I looked at that fact and thought, "Well, that's going to be a bit of a struggle. And if I'm going to struggle, why do it with a business I don't love?" I might as well choose something I love and would be willing to do for free. In that way, the struggle might even turn into fun—and, of course, that's exactly what happened.

3. **My wife and I decided to live frugally for as long as it took our investments to fully support us.** Then we would allow ourselves more luxuries. We kept our expenses very low and our investment expenditures high. The process took ten years. In 1989, we allowed ourselves luxuries because our investments were paying for our living expenses as well as our luxuries.

Today we work as hard as ever, not because we have to, but because we still love our work and the business we've built. Most of our income goes back into investments since we already have all the goodies life has to offer.

The rich get richer because they invest and the poor get poorer because they consume.

Using Your Most Precious Gifts

Many people say that they can't be wealthy because they don't have money. Rest assured that if you share in that attitude you will definitely stay poor and keep struggling for the rest of your life. Remember, I created my wealth not just from zero, but from something worse than zero—a debt larger than most people's lifetime assets. As my Winnebago friend would say, I created wealth using the gifts from the Great Spirit. For me these are:

1. **Health.** While everyone knows how important our health is, I'd be foolish to leave it out of a list like this. Like money and time, health is an asset and a gift that we need to protect, living our lives wisely so that we can enjoy our old age as much as our youth—or hopefully more so.

2. **Relationships.** People are only as successful as the quality of their relationships. I was married once before, and I have to say that I was very unethical during my first marriage. It was only after my financial crash that I noticed that people I did business with were just as devious as I was.

   Often, when I find someone who is having trouble with money or with their relationships, there is an ethics problem somewhere. I was once asked to consult with a couple who was having financial problems and problems with their employees. When I asked them how their marriage was, I got these nice grins that said, "Oh, everything is wonderful." After three months of working with them, at a great expense to them, I resigned. I told them that I did not sense I was getting straight answers from them. Three years later, after the company folded, I met the foreman of their factory. He confided in me that both husband and wife had been cheating on each other. Their dealings with their employees were terrible, and the factory had been dumping toxic wastes down the city drains at night so they could save money on disposing of them legally.

In all too many instances where things aren't going well, where there is drama and crisis, there is often an ethics problem at the back of it. Dumping chemicals is unethical because it is destructive to the environment, which affects all of us. Cheating on your spouse is unethical because it is a betrayal of one of the most spiritual bonds on earth, the bond between husband and wife. Lying to friends, colleagues, lovers and consultants is usually a reflection of very low self-esteem which is bound to have a negative influence on one's potential for success.

I'm not claiming to be a saint, by any means. But I have found that if I want to be healthy, happy and wealthy, I have to nurture my relationships and keep them clean. As a friend of mine says, "I don't tell the truth necessarily because I am an honest person. I tell the truth because I'm tired of being pounded by the consequences of lying."

Success in life is only as satisfying as our relationships with ourselves, our families, our friends and our associates. When I have high-quality, honest, hard-working friends and relationships, my life works better. I know that I am but a reflection of the company I keep.

3. **Respect for Successful People.** I often hear people talk about what faults they find with great or particularly successful people. These criticisms are often rooted in jealousy and self-hate. A friend's father once told me to love people for what I respected in them and hold compassion in my heart for their short-comings. If I could do that for them, I could do it for myself. This is the seed for greater self-confidence.

   I have found that what I hate in others I become; and what I love in others I become.

   Respect people you want to be like. Learn from their strengths and their weaknesses. If you want to be a great doctor, respect and study great doctors. If you want to be a great crook, study great crooks. Holding onto resentment for others only turns the resentment on ourselves, and we lose the opportunities for learning from both their successes and their failures.

Since I was so shy, I studied the great speakers. I studied John Kennedy, Mikhail Gorbachev, Martin Luther King and Dr. Helen Caldicott. They have their strengths and their weaknesses. When I hold understanding in my heart, I can learn more than when I discount them for their flaws.

4. **Using Each Day Wisely.** Follow this rule: "My future is created today, not tomorrow."

   There was a time in my life when no matter how much money I made, I always came up just a little short every month. My solution was to "Put it on the card." Because it was so easy, it soon became a habit. But before I knew it, my payments to the credit card company were higher than my income. One day it all came crashing down. I had ruined my credit rating. Once the computer got my name as a bad credit risk, the whole game of living on borrowed money came screeching to a halt. Again, it was a miserable experience, but it offered an opportunity for an important lesson, one I'm glad I learned. This lesson in money applied as well to how I spent my time and my health as it did to dollars.

Today, with the aid of 20/20 hindsight, it is easier to see other people doing the same thing I used to. I use the following simple three words to explain how wealthy people and poor people differ in their use of time. It all ties into the words:

PAST PRESENT FUTURE

Though we live in the present, each day offers us an opportunity to determine our past, as well as our future. I meet people who are in dire poverty, dragging their past with them wherever they go. I also meet people who spend a little more each day than they earn, in this way spending their futures. When they continue on such a path, pretty soon the past becomes such a burden that life turns into sheer drudgery.

There are also people who are very skillful at "breaking- even" with the present. They never go into debt, yet they never get ahead either. There is nothing really wrong with that habit, as long as your health holds out and there are people to put you up when you're older. People who break even each day never create much of a future to move into. Each day turns out to be pretty much like the one before.

It finally dawned on me that if I wanted to have a bright future, full of freedom, I'd better pay for tomorrow today and not create any debt that would haunt me in the future. I made a decision that I'd take a part of each day and dedicate it to creating the kind of tomorrow I desired: "My future is created today, not tomorrow," I reminded myself.

I began to exercise a little so that I'd feel good today, and then exercise a little more for tomorrow. I also worked a little for today, and a little for tomorrow. And I would study for what I needed to know today, then study a little more for tomorrow. The results were that ten years after my disastrous financial holocaust, my wife and I are able to enjoy the rest of our lives in freedom—freedom from the struggle of having to earn a living. We took a little each day to build our corral.

Today we are able to enjoy one of the most precious gifts the Great Spirit can give—our lives together and the freedom to be of service to this planet through our work. It was a hard ten years, but it was well worth it.

For those of you who are in a financial bind today, I encourage you to do a little each day for tomorrow. Earn enough to pay off the past; earn a little more for the future. A friend of mine goes out each evening to earn a minimum of ten dollars for his tomorrow. He washes windows, mows lawns, paints rooms or does other odd jobs in his neighborhood. Once he has his ten dollars, which takes almost no time at all, he puts the money in his secret savings account. My wife and I did a similar thing when we had nothing.

Remember, you don't need a lot of money to start building your wealth. But it does require that you use your God-given resources to make the most of every precious day.

20

I Deserve a Raise

...each generation wastes a little more
of the future with greed and lust for riches...

—DONALD ROBERT PERRY MARQUIS (1927)

While flying from Oregon to Arizona a while ago, I was the only passenger in the forward cabin and struck up a conversation with one of the flight attendants. Noticing how pleasant and cheerful she was while carrying out her duties, I asked her how she liked her work. "I love this job," she replied, then paused. "I just hate the company. They don't treat us fairly."

"What is it that you don't like about the company?" I asked.

"First of all, we have no labor contract," she said. "They keep telling us to wait, but it has been over a year now. I don't know how much longer I will put up with this." She was clearly angry.

"So what is it that you want from the company?" I asked.

She looked at me as if I was from Mars. "More money, of course. And more benefits and greater promises of job security would be nice, thank you."

I began to feel like the acting chairman of the company she worked for.

I responded by telling her that according to the reports I had read, her company was in serious financial trouble.

"Well, it isn't my fault," she said. "I just want what was promised."

The pleasantness between us was quickly disappearing.

"When I joined this company fourteen years ago," she explained, "we were told that we would get raises over time if we had good performance reviews. Well, I have had excellent performance reviews and I've put in my time. The flight attendants before me got their raises, so why don't I get mine? My husband and I aren't hurting, but we aren't getting ahead like we had planned either. I deserve my raise!"

I nodded.

She shook her head in disgust. "The guys at the top get paid millions. They all have golden parachutes for leaving this sinking business and yet we don't even have a contract. It's not fair. We're not the ones who misdirected this company and overloaded it with debt. I'd like to quit but I'm too old. I don't want to start over in something new for less pay. I really feel trapped."

When the flight ended, I thanked her and wished her luck. There was so much I wished I could have said to her, yet I realized there are millions upon millions of people just like her all over the world. She is just one honest, hard-working person who has been affected financially and professionally by a fear-based, misinformed educational system.

This misinformation of the educational system is not only affecting the airline industry. It is hitting everyone from farmers to computer manufacturers. It is hitting industries born in the Agrarian Age and industries of the Information Age. Those who go on to seek new information and adopt new ways of thinking will gain the ability to do very, very well. But those who hang on to what our schools taught will continue to struggle, and many will perish financially or professionally.

The idea that I deserve a raise is obsolete. Any person or company subscribing to that line of reasoning is a dinosaur. The idea that we should get a pay raise for seniority was possible during the Industrial Age and during the high-flying '80s when money was cheap and credit was easy. But those days are gone. In the era of the '90s we're in the midst of a three-way collision between the Agrarian Age, the Industrial Age and the Information Age. And this collision is sending shock waves all over the globe. To survive and even prosper in this environment we have to learn how to think innovatively. We will barely survive if we cling to tired old ideas. We all need to reposition ourselves for the new millennium. This means re-educating the entire country to let go of old ideas that are no longer serving us and make room for new thoughts that are evolving on planet Earth.

Individuals, organizations and nations who can do this quickly will do well financially and professionally. The next decade for them will be bright and abundant. Those who fail to change will suffer needlessly. There will continue to be much chaos where the old ways of thought and the new ones collide. The rich will get very rich, widening the gap between themselves and their less fortunate brothers and sisters. And the poor will not only get poorer but angrier. How long this chaos lasts will depend on our educational system's willingness to change.

In an ideal economy, a person receives a raise for an increase in productivity; the more you give, the more you get. But between 1900 and 1973, people got raises not because they produced more, but because machines and cheap power sources kept production expenses down. As oil prices came down, company profits soared and workers demanded higher pay, their fair share of the profits. The modern machines that accelerated production, and which ran on the cheap oil, were being produced all over the country and everyone was happy. But in the process people got lazy. They grew to expect this gravy train to go on forever. The educational system started treating this economic situation as if it was a fundamental truth that was "normal" and would never change.

Then came the Yom Kippur War in 1973. The price of oil skyrocketed. To afford the increased price of oil, businesses cut back on inefficient people. They reorganized, assigning bigger work loads to fewer people. It was the only way for many businesses to stay competitive. Suddenly, homeless people appeared on the streets because government cutbacks, due to reduced tax revenues, cut down on public assistance.

People in upper management and people with expertise in the new technology that had emerged started getting paid more. Along with the maturing of the Baby Boom, real estate in certain high production areas of the country became more and more scarce and the prices shot up 300 percent and even more.

Europeans, Japanese and Arabs, seeing an opportunity to profit from this economic climate, flooded the U.S. market with money. With so much money floating around, young professionals, who'd never known anything else, started acquiring what seemed to them to be inexpensive, luxury items—cars, condos, electronic gadgets of all kinds. The problem was that while there was money, there was no corresponding increase in production.

People began to fall into the habit of getting paid more, simply for doing the same old thing day-in and day-out, year after year. Prices were always going up and people felt pressured to buy right now, before the prices increased. So they bought on credit. Then the bubble burst. With everyone out on a very shaky credit limb, and with the economy slowing down, the money lenders shut the credit door. The cost of borrowing money went up and up. Credit became harder and harder to get.

All along the way, the consumer cost of oil has risen. Today, we still don't have a cheaper alternative to replace oil. And those people, companies and governments who aren't able to produce are going broke.

The sleigh ride is over—at least for a while. In the midst of the cutbacks and the shifting economy, people have gotten scared. And with fear has come greed that has destroyed whole economic systems, leaving millions of people in poverty, or hovering very close to it.

Greed as we define it in the present economic climate is "taking more than you give." In order to do well in the 1990s, we'll all have to produce more just to break even. Pay raises are going to be few and far between. Doing the same old thing will guarantee economic decline for individuals, as well as companies and whole nations.

The problem is, we do not educate people to produce more. By reinforcing the ethic that you will do well if you just do as you are told, make no mistakes and don't make waves, we are just asking for trouble. If we don't learn the skills required for our present economic climate, the world is going to pass us by. Our current teaching methods are training people to be obsolete by the time they're 35, planning their futures around raises that will never come, all the while falling behind financially.

What causes this? Why are so many people's standards of living deteriorating? Why are so many major companies shrinking instead of growing? Why are so many hard-working employees being laid off? Why is the West losing ground to the Orient? How is it that the Japanese buy our golf courses, motion picture studios, hotels, and paper companies?

One big piece of the answer is that we want to make more money without doing anything differently. We want to get richer without having to acquire any more knowledge. To receive more, we must give more, and to produce more, we need new information. This lack of information has brought down civilization after civilization throughout history.

We have to stop confusing money with wealth. In the Information Age, wealth is what a person knows. Today, information is more important than material resources such as gold, land and money. The reason that the flight attendant can't get her raise is because the company isn't increasing its production. You can't keep afloat in a technical world if you expect more but don't do anything differently.

I remember studying American history in my fifth-grade class. My teacher smirked as he told how Peter Minuit bought Manhattan Island from the Indians for the equivalent of $24, paid in cloth and glass beads. I was 10 years old when I took the test for that section of study. The teacher asked us questions like these:

1. In what year did Peter Minuit buy Manhattan Island?
2. What was the name of his trading company?
3. How much did he pay in guilders?

What should we have learned from the real estate transaction between the Indians and Minuit back in 1626? We might have learned how to learn from our mistakes. We might have explored the external pressures that influenced the transaction to discover the economic principles involved. We might have used this event in history to illustrate the difference between money and wealth—that perhaps the Indians' decision was a wise one, given their belief system at that time. Surely any of this would have been more valuable to students than having them memorize dates and terms that could easily be looked up in a history book if you ever needed that information later on. Here's just a few suggestions about what we could have learned from the story of buying Manhattan from the Indians:

1. **The links between information, technology and the power of violence.** The Indians knew the Europeans had superior weapons and would force them off Manhattan Island whether they were paid for the land or not. They knew their days were numbered. Call it the "Rambo system of commerce," the use of force to gain power. That same system creates urban gangs today that are both dangerous and effective as they fight for "trading posts" within our cities. The same fundamental principles are at work throughout the world, and we should be able to recognize and understand the price we pay for such thinking.

2. **The use of information and technology in business.** While the Indians had a wealth of land, the Europeans had wealth in the form of information and technologies to produce glass beads and cloth. So, Peter Minuit took something that was of little real value to him—the cloth and beads, which his information allowed him to easily produce, and traded it for the land, which the Indians had in great, seemingly endless abundance. We might have learned from this that it is information and technology that allow us to create real wealth. We could also learn here that money is not necessarily wealth, but only the end result of wealth.

If we still want to laugh at the Indians for being "taken" by Peter Minuit, just stop and take a good look around. Today, it is no longer the European trading trinkets for Indian land, it is the Japanese and others selling us electronic gadgets and using our own money to gain control of our real wealth. The players have changed, but the principles haven't.

We are selling off our children's wealth today for paper trinkets called money. A few are getting rich at the expense of millions in our present and future generations. It's like killing the goose that lays the golden eggs, and then hoarding the eggs. If we'd just take care of the goose, we'd have unlimited eggs!

The fundamental flaws of our economic system have their roots in ideas first popularized by Thomas Malthus, an English economist, in the early 1800s. Malthus studied the quantities of natural resources (coal, iron, gold, etc.) around the world and then compared them to the world population. Given the information he had at that time, he concluded that there would soon be too many people for too few resources. He then defined economics as the allocation of scarce resources. Today, Western economics is still based on this definition of scarce resources—but it is an outmoded idea.

Japan, meanwhile, based its economics on some very different ideas. That country has few natural resources. Their greatest wealth is in labor and information. Today, these resources are even more valuable than the resources upon which Malthus made his calculations. We in the U.S. lose economically not because we lack natural resources but because we are still operating as if Malthus had the final word.

Malthus' theories have been refined and elaborated upon, by theories such as Keynesian economics, but the popular thinking is still wedded to

Malthusian scarcity. Why we keep misleading our young people is criminal. Just go to most college economic classes and you will find some scarcity-oriented professor working for limited pay, educating our brightest minds to accept his ideas or fail.

Check your own private thoughts right now. How often do you think there is not enough of something? Do you think that there is not enough money? Do you think that there is not enough food to feed the hungry? Do you think that there is not enough love or time? Or, as Malthus believed, that there are not enough natural resources?

Malthus observed that the world's natural resources are finite. He did not foresee the infinite amounts of information and technology yet to come. With the use of information and new technologies, we often end up getting better performance while using up fewer of our natural resources. For example, it took 175,000 tons of copper to complete the first transatlantic communication cable between Europe and America. As soon as it was completed, our space program put a quarter-ton satellite aloft that out-performed all that copper, rendering the cable obsolete. Adding technology to resources, we have been constantly able to do more with less.

The Japanese are beating us in business because they continue to give the public better products for less. They are following the principle of ephemeralization, more commonly known as doing more with less. To survive in business today, only companies that continue to deliver greater performance at a better price will stay in business. The idea that you can simply charge more is obsolete. Today, the rewards go to the efficient, not the arrogant.

The problem today is not scarcity, but abundance. Businesses have inadvertently done so much more with so much less that there is now too much—and this is driving down prices. Just go to a shopping mall and look at quantity and quality of clothes available at excellent prices. Yet our car makers raised their prices over 20 percent from 1985 to 1990. And they wonder why their sales are off! If they want to stay in business, auto makers will have to lower their prices or give us a superior car, or both. A failure to do so will mean that more workers will lose their jobs while those at the top parachute from the sinking company with a bundle of cash. Leaders are focusing on money instead of the ability to do more with less. They are starving the goose and making off with the eggs.

Lester Thurow of MIT once described capitalism as a system of failure. It is a system where the minority, who are efficient, will always replace the majority, who are inefficient. The idea of brand loyalty or national loyalty is obsolete in our present global economy. It is now a market driven by consumers' demands for better products at lower prices. No matter how loudly we cry "Buy American," the reality is that in today's global market the rewards go to those who are efficient, who deliver quality at a low cost.

Right now Japan and the Orient are the most efficient in electronics. They continue to sell us consumer goods, which get better every year. And because they get better every year, the previous year's model is soon obsolete and the price goes down. The problem is this: They are selling us their electronic trinkets which represent little or no long-term wealth, in return for our hard-earned money. Next, they are purchasing the real wealth of our country—our future growth industries such as entertainment and recreation—and they are even hiring our children to work in them.

All the Japan-bashing in the world isn't going to correct our problems. We aren't suffering from the inability to produce. Anything but! Our only scarcity is new thinking. The same problem that defeated the American Indians, the Maoris of New Zealand, the Hawaiians of Hawaii, the Aborigines of Australia and many other indigenous peoples—a lack of information—is beginning to beat us down in the West.

People who believe in scarcity get greedy. Our businesses and governments are run by greedy people. Because people think there is not enough, they begin to act desperate and commit desperate deeds.

Malthusian theory, the idea of scarcity, also creates a "me first" mentality, a "survival of the fittest" attitude which in turn leads to imperialism. Wipe out the weak because there is not enough. Grab their resources so our people can live. In the name of this social Darwinism, we have slaughtered millions of indigenous people. While in Vietnam I realized that I was caught up in just such a campaign; I too felt there is not enough. When I talk to management in the U.S. Forest Service, they too think in terms of scarcity. For them, this justifies the destruction of our forests—a resource which we should have been nurturing years ago instead of raping it for quick profits.

If we are to evolve, we must change how we think. This idea of survival of the fittest is cruel and inhumane. And yet it continues to be the "hidden curriculum" throughout our educational system. Our schools continue to classify, categorize, play God and pit one child against the other in a vicious game of survival of the fittest, played out in classrooms throughout the country.

Our educational system has fully subscribed to the Malthusian Theory. Recently a school district near Portland, Oregon, voted themselves a large pay raise. In some cases, as much as a 30 percent increase for tenured teachers. While I am happy that teachers earn more money, I am sorry to say that they are pricing themselves out of a job. Maybe not them personally, but teachers of the future will ultimately find it harder to earn more and to find security. How can I say that? Simple. The teachers are asking for a raise without a corresponding increase in productivity. The truth is that S.A.T. scores are going down, dropout rates are going up and both kids and parents are unhappy.

If teachers think their jobs are secure and that they can simply demand more money because our government protects them, they only need to look to the U.S. Postal Service for a different reality. The postal service thought they had a monopoly (scarcity) because they are a government service. As the need for speed increased in our business world, our postal service has refused to respond to the needs of its customers. Federal Express and other private mail services were born only because our postal service is arrogant—they thought they were the only show in town. People are willing to pay for speed and greater service, something government departments aren't especially known for.

Businesspeople jumped in where the postal service failed to provide good service. And now, with fax machines costing less than the average color TV or sound system, it's going to get even worse for the Post Office. If they raise their postage rates any more, without an improvement in service, they'll be out of business. Our postal employees can continue to expect raises without an improvement of production only because our government protects them. How much longer this inefficiency will be tolerated remains to be seen.

The same thing that is happening to our postal service is going to happen to our public school system. Its days are numbered. Education is the only business I know where the customer is blamed when it fails. People are getting increasingly angry with spending their tax dollars on a system that for the most part just isn't producing.

I recently met a teacher who said I had no right teaching since I did not have a teaching certificate. She wanted to know what gave me the right to teach. I told her, the free-market system. If my adult students did not think they received value for their time and money, they would not recommend my classes to their friends and I'd be out of business. She then wanted to know how I could charge as much as I did. Again, I replied that people are willing to pay to get more done in less time. She then said how awful it was that people were profiting from education, completely unable to see that those profits were directly dependent on satisfied customers—people will pay for goods and services that they feel truly benefit them.

Every time I hear educators requesting more pay for less teaching, I have to ask what world they are living in. As the young pilots in the movie *Top Gun* said, "I have the need for speed." Teachers should have the same need, should experience the same urgency. The world is moving too fast for them to keep plodding along at their current pace. Most educators do not realize that private educational organizations like mine would not make so much money or have so much business if the public educators were doing their job effectively.

One reason our instructors make more money than public school teachers is that we teach 50 to 1000 people at a time. We teach people more in less time with more fun. The educational system's teachers want to teach fewer children, provide less information in more time, and charge us taxpayers more money. If they keep succeeding in getting their demands met, they'll soon be out of a job.

Education is the single largest industry in the world. Businesses alone spend billions of dollars for educating their employees in handling new technologies. Meanwhile technological advancements, and the teaching of the same, have been virtually ignored by righteous public educators.

Ignoring technology can be costly, as the Swiss discovered not long ago. Within a 15-year period, 65 percent of Swiss workers lost their jobs because they hadn't kept an eye on LCD technology—a technology that, ironically, they invented. Instead, they relied on their belief that the world would always come to them for their precision craftsmanship. Now the only way they can make watches expensive is by putting gold around them. Once again, arrogance loses to technology.

Educators need to recognize that technology can and is replacing them. Television, computers and educational video games are proving to be far more effective as teaching tools, presenting far more information than any teacher can, and presenting it in ways that are fun and engaging to even the youngest students. Meanwhile, all too many teachers continue to believe their jobs are secure because of tenure or unions. Numerous others feel safe because of reports that indicate there will be a teacher shortage in the future. What teachers don't realize yet is that great teachers are already on video and that mediocre teachers will soon just become glorified babysitters. If I were a traditional teacher, I would change my thinking and begin looking for new answers.

A constantly changing technology will continue to change how things are done in the future, and these will continue to change how we support ourselves, the value of our labor and the value of what we know. Along with it, the question of whether or not we deserve a raise will continue to change.

The relatively new industry of video rentals provides a good example. With the onset of video rental stores, movie theatres saw a decrease in business. Video rentals provided more for less, and rental stores became the craze. But today we're seeing the growth of still another technology, with cable television taking over a larger and larger portion of the video rental business. Even at the time of this writing, there is talk of cable television libraries where on any night a subscriber can choose from hundreds of films. That's going to be tough on both the movie theaters and the rental stores but there can be little doubt that this new technology will succeed. No more will we have to go to the trouble to return videos. The selection will be almost unlimited, and no doubt the cost will continue to decline.

Just as written communication has gone from Pony Express to FAX machines, business travel will soon be done via video telephones. This will provide a way for businesspeople to conduct face-to-face, long-distance business from their offices or homes. At the same time, however, it will decrease business for the airline industry, as well as other travel-related businesses such as hotels and motels, rental cars, taxis, restaurants, and all the ancillary services involved. All this is just another example of how technology continues to move forward, providing more for less and changing the face of our economy.

Every time a new technology develops, job opportunities change. New products require new knowledge, new information, new services, and unless we're able to deliver we may discover that the activity that supported us yesterday no longer exists. Given this picture, I would advise the flight attendant who wants a raise the same as I advise everyone else: Look ahead for new answers. The days are numbered when people or organizations can simply say "I deserve more money," without giving better performance in return.

If you want to get rich, start each day by asking yourself, "How can I do more for less?"

21

Who Causes Poverty?

When a fellow says it hain't the money but the principle o' the thing, it's th' money.

—"Kin" Hubbard (1926)

One of America's business leaders was recently interviewed on a television special concerning the downturn of our auto industry. He talked about the flagging U.S. auto industry and how his company alone was being forced to lay off thousands of workers. This CEO, the leader of one of our largest automobile manufacturers, started blaming the Japanese for his company's problems. About then, I turned off the television set. When he started blaming the Japanese for his company's problems I knew that I had nothing to learn from this man. He was either ignorant or lying—and in either case, his approach to his company's problems revealed why our auto industry is in such shambles.

Our business leaders are not weeping for their own shortcomings or asking what they are doing that isn't working. Nor are they weeping for those they had to lay off or for the countless others they are putting in financial jeopardy. No, they are looking for scapegoats, turning their backs on the problems that need to be solved right here in our own country and blaming the Japanese instead. How could such a well-educated man blame the problems of our own country on his competition?

If we were all doing our jobs right we would have no competition in this country. There is no reason for us not to be the most successful country in the world. Back in the first quarter of this century, Henry

Ford understood economic principles that our industrial leaders seem to have forgotten today—or perhaps never knew. While other auto makers of Ford's time were building very expensive cars for the rich, Ford understood that he should make cars available to the masses. Instead of treating the car as a scarcity, available only to the wealthy few, he built a car that was both dependable and affordable. The shock waves of business growth brought unprecedented prosperity for many, not just a few. Just take a moment and reflect on what became possible due to humans being able to drive places in their own cars. Roads, gas stations, repair shops, drive-in soda stands, motels, car radios, shopping centers, suburbs, the ability to stay in touch with friends and relatives who live hundreds of miles away.

Henry Ford had his faults, shortcomings and blind spots. At one and the same time he was both a "great spirit" and a mediocre mind, embodying in one man something that Albert Einstein once said: "Great spirits have always encountered violent opposition from mediocre minds." However, Ford understood the principle of ephemeralization—doing more with less. If Detroit was willing to follow this principle now we could still provide better cars for a better price—and win back our market share from the Japanese. But instead of thinkers like Henry Ford, our industries are now run by business school graduates who were educated in Malthusian economics; they are trying to make money with money rather than making money through new, more effective principles of production.

Our wealth as a nation is in our potential productivity, represented by our knowledge and our other human resources—our creativity and inventiveness, our capacity for learning new things, our problem-solving abilities, our inherent capacity for working together cooperatively. Yet we have put money first and have turned our backs on our real wealth. Stockholders' profits have become a higher priority than the worker in the factory, and thus the great American ship of industry has begun to settle beneath the waves.

In our desperation, we scream for more tariff protection from the Japanese and other overseas competitors. But tariffs only push up prices, which sends shock waves throughout the global economic community, making everything more expensive. We don't get more jobs in our country; just the opposite, we lose them. When Detroit finally decides to do its job and starts providing a better car for a better price, it will once again dominate the market. Raising prices without raising quality only creates poverty for all of us in this country.

My intention here is not to pick on the auto industry. I use them as an example only because they symbolize the kind of thinking that is threatening the entire nation. In virtually every major industry across the land we are finding the same problems. Poverty is the end result—and it is a problem that cannot be solved until every one of us stops blaming our competition and start looking at how we are creating our own poverty right here at home.

The Waves of Unemployment

That automobile executive who was bashing the Japanese that day, blaming them for our shortcomings, did have one thing right —that the thousands of workers his company was laying off are only the tip of the iceberg. Each worker laid off would have a major financial impact on an average family of four. In turn, massive layoffs affect grocery stores, gas stations, doctors, accountants, retailers, ballet and piano teachers, pet shops...the list is endless. A layoff of thousands impacts tens of thousands, maybe millions of people. The loss of a paycheck ripples through a community like the ripples created when a stone is dropped in a pond. Everyone from the local grocer to the local politicians is affected. When hundreds are laid off it is like the waves on a lake. When thousands are laid off it is like the waves of the ocean, one pushing another until the entire sea is in motion. Tens of thousands laid off can be like a hurricane, cutting a wake of devastation through the entire nation.

The storms of unemployment in this country have been building for a long time. In the beginning it affected only those in entry- level jobs. Now it has spread to middle and upper management, and even to the college-educated in top research and development positions. In 1991, white-collar workers accounted for only 8 percent of the work force, yet they accounted for 16 percent of the total number unemployed.

If people get laid off from one job and are re-employed elsewhere in a week or even a month, the economy is not in such bad shape. But when people are getting laid off and are still without work six months or more later, that's a good sign that our economy is in trouble. So the real measure of what's happening in the employment picture is how many unemployed people we have who have been laid off, who have looked for work and have not been able to find a new job. What is the picture here? As of September 1991, the number of unemployed but qualified workers who have given up looking for work was over a million.

Many of the people looking for jobs are college-educated. The 1991 college graduating class had difficulty finding full-time employment. No longer are companies routinely sending out scouts to look for workers. Only 33 percent of the undergraduate class found work, and about 67 percent of our college graduates had not found full-time employment by the time they left campus. On top of that, many of the children who were born in the 1970s won't earn as much as those born during the baby-boom generation.

The ship is going down slowly. History is repeating itself. Rome is burning and everyone is fiddling. In 1959, John F. Kennedy, then a senator, warned America of this. He was speaking to coal miners in the state of West Virginia who were out of work. He said that there is something terribly amiss when people who want to work cannot find jobs to support their families. He warned us then that it might soon creep into our white-collar sector, but no one listened. His prediction has come true.

And what is behind all the layoffs? The answer is both simple and complex. Our business leaders, most of our economists, and all too many of our business school leaders are still trying to run the country from the Malthusian position of scarcity. This principle of scarcity is robbing us of our real wealth—which is still as powerful as it ever was. We must change this pattern, change our thinking, as individuals and as a nation, if we are to realize our potential again.

I am convinced that the Great Spirit, or God, created this world so that all people could enjoy prosperity and abundance. If you follow that principle—abundance over scarcity—you will do well financially and feel good about yourself because the choices you make will benefit not just you and your family but many more around you. If you follow what is taught in our schools, you may become rich, but many others will become poor. And while you may have money, you will most likely end up feeling poor too.

Even our Information Age industries, long thought to be the most durable industries in the country, are bumping up against the barriers created by Malthusian economic principles. IBM and Apple are now laying off people by the tens of thousands because they did not follow the principle of doing more with less.

Greed and the Principles of Scarcity

Greed grows out of scarcity, and with greed comes an abuse not only of our real wealth—our human resources—but of the natural resources upon which we depend for our well-being. Nature, God, the Great Spirit has been generous. What we need the most to survive, we have in abundance. The number one item for human survival is air. God provided an abundance of air. Yet, our greed is polluting our air with fossil fuel emissions and chemical pollutants just to save a few bucks. Our number two necessity for survival is water, and we have that, too, in abundance. But once again, greed is destroying our water.

The third need is food. With technology, we can provide massive amounts of food, yet we pay farmers not to produce in order to keep the prices high. We do this even as millions of people starve. Greed. The price you pay at the supermarket could be at least 35 percent lower if we allowed farmers to produce and trade instead of paying them not to produce. We violate God's principles out of the greed that we learned in our schools.

Now our people struggle long hours to pay the high prices we've created, while we lose the market share anyway. We yell at our politicians and they monkey around with interest rates, still mistaking money for wealth. The ship of fools sails on, locked on a deadly course, while the rich get richer and the poor get poorer. Poverty hits the weak while the rich hoard money that they confuse as wealth. Our real wealth goes unnoticed, untapped, unappreciated.

We have our values backwards. In this game of winners and losers, no one wins.

Environmental Pollution and Poverty

As far as environmental destruction is concerned, again, greed is the major culprit. Our higher standard of living is based on inexpensive energy in the form of gasoline and electricity. The problem is that the generation of this energy is horribly polluting; gasoline and oil, coal and nuclear power for electricity spill millions of tons of pollution into our atmosphere every day.

The automobile is a major contributor to environmental problems. Nobody would deny that. The air pollution caused by cars is a critical problem that must be solved. But let's not forget that earlier in history, the car was actually heralded for solving a huge environmental problem of a different kind. At the turn of the century, as cities boomed and people left the farm to seek jobs in factories, the horse was causing a massive pollution problem. Horse urine and manure, with their accompanying odor, health, sanitation and disposal problems were becoming a critical issue in every major city. Someone once estimated that if we still had horses doing the work that trucks and automobiles do each day in our cities, every major thoroughfare would have to be cleared of the equivalent of five feet of horse manure every week!

And what would our lives be like without electricity? Without electricity we would not live as long. Electricity not only makes life easier and more entertaining, it prolongs life via refrigeration, purification of our water and by supporting medical technology. The irony is that the price for these benefits is the destruction of our natural environment—at least that's true according to how we're doing things now.

One of the solutions offered is conservation. But, once again, this is a solution derived from a position of scarcity. I say use more power, but change our source of energy. Look for cleaner, more efficient sources. Create them according to the principle of more for less. Can it be done? It can. The Orient has several billion people all wanting the "good life" that we have and they will get it, because Japan, and others, will figure out a way to do it with alternative sources of power.

For twenty years now we have had the ability to transport electricity over great distances (4000 miles). The reason we don't has more to do with politics than technology. It is technically possible to shut down inefficient, highly-polluting electrical generators that pepper the landscape of our nation and use the more efficient power plants farther away. The reason we don't do this is, again, because it would mean a loss of jobs. Each utility company does not want to close down, so they lobby our politicians and the plants stay open. We all lose so that a few can win. If those clinging to their jobs could think beyond scarcity, they would realize that they, too, would be much better off in a healthier and more prosperous world.

The changes will come anyway. Japan already leads the world in solar electrical generation technology. They soon will be able to put solar panels in the great deserts of the world and ship electrical power thousands of miles to where we need it via a large power grid system. Russia and Europe have extensive grid systems. The U.S. has only a few.

We continue to think small and protect old industries instead of developing new, more appropriate technologies that could meet the challenge of today. We plan only for the short term and we all pay for it in the long term.

Australia today could lead the world in exporting inexpensive electrical power since the country is set up with a great desert in the middle. They could ship it right to southeast Asia, predicted as the next economic boom area of our planet. If Australia began to ship power, money would come in and not only would the Australian standard of living go up, but the standard of living of the developing countries would go up, too.

As economies expanded in those regions, millions of poor people suddenly would have money. Those who had once been beggars would become customers. Third, world health would improve. The need to cut down trees for firewood would decrease. There would be a reduction in infant mortality as refrigeration cut down on bacterial infections. Modern medicine would become available and life expectancy would go up. Birth rates would drop due to income growth. For people who think poverty curbs population growth, it doesn't. It only increases it. People have more babies when they feel threatened. When the standard of living is high, birthrates go down.

I predict that the first country to switch entirely to renewable, nonpolluting electrical power will be the next economic world leader.

Poverty's Spinoff Problems

In America, we wonder why the birthrate among our inner-city teens is rising. It is because they don't feel secure. There seems to be a genetic code that when survival is threatened, the species produces more offspring to insure the survival. When the species feels secure, then birthrates drop. One interesting thing about poverty and intelligence is that the primary cause of lower intelligence is malnutrition. If we continue to let poverty run its course, our national IQs will drop anyway no matter how much we teach and test our children.

In America, industry claims to care for our forests and thus, plants trees. What actually happens is that they rape the land, destroying thousands of other plants and animals (sub-species) that make up a complete ecosystem and then replace it with a single crop mono-culture called trees. They kill thousands of life forms and replace one. What they do not tell us is that the reason they rape the land is because it is cheaper—for them. They make money while robbing the nation of its true wealth and our future health.

We have cut down 90 percent of our own forests and then have the nerve to tell South America to stop cutting down trees in their country. We would not need to cut down any more old-growth timber had we replanted and started tree farms years ago. Again, we sacrifice our wealth for money.

Meanwhile, our nuclear power committees are trying to tell us that nuclear fuel does not pollute our air. They are lying to us. Just look at Chernobyl. Radioactive waste lasts for tens of thousands of years. We pay the nuclear power industry for a flash of electricity now, but we destroy the future of our planet for thousands of years to come. Why? So a few can make some money. The only thing presently scarce on our planet is original thinking that is not clouded by an abundance of scarcity and greed—but this, clearly, is a human-created scarcity, not a natural one.

A Change of Thought

We must start thinking in terms of abundance instead of scarcity. My main reason for saying this isn't just the "power of positive thinking." Much more is involved. To make this change of mind is the only thing that will end poverty. Every time we have applied our minds and our creativity, bringing information and new technology to our finite resources, we have expanded our resources, not diminished them. As early as the 1940s, for example, chicken was considered to be a rare food delicacy for many families, only eaten as a Sunday meal. Today, there is too much chicken. I know the growing methods are under scrutiny, and improvements need to be made, but it is still an example of how technology and creative thinking can increase our abundance.

A similar example could be found in the Japanese's response to worldwide gasoline prices. As fossil fuels became increasingly expensive, they responded by developing far more efficient cars, in many cases doubling and tripling gas mileage over Detroit's typical models, without compromising comfort. Abundance came not by finding new oil fields but by drawing upon knowledge and creativity to double and triple the use of what we already have.

Another breakthrough in the theory of abundance is recycling, making use of our abundant resources in what was once considered waste. When low-cost, non-polluting, renewable energy is combined with recycled resources, there will be an economic renaissance unprecedented in the history of the world. Prosperity will go to those who think differently. Already we are seeing new industries sprouting up in the building industry, with insulation, wallboard, doors, structural trusses and ornamentation being produced with recycled materials.

I am afraid to say that the U.S. may be a latecomer in this budding industry because we continue to view the world from the point of view of scarcity. The countries that will prosper will most likely be many of the second- and third-world nations that are hungry and looking for an honest advantage. The race is on, and it will be interesting to see who gets there first. It may take the U.S. longer because they will have to wait for the old thinkers—those who still cling to Malthusian theory—to retire or die so that new thinkers in the principle of abundance can take over.

Individual Solutions

So what can you do today if you want to be wealthy? I would say this. If you are working for a company that is not seeking new ideas, get out now. If you work with people who want little more than their paycheck and raises, get out now. If your company raises its prices without any improvement in the product or service, get out now. The reason I say get out now is because you will probably have to get out sooner or later anyway, or suffer a slow economic decline just as our automakers are doing.

We are in the midst of an information revolution. Wealth will go to those who use technology to advance abundance, not to those who perpetuate scarcity. Greed and hoarding are unethical today. It may have been ethical to be greedy when there was limited information, but the explosion in information makes greed an idea whose time is past.

If we stopped teaching Malthusian economics in our schools, we could change our national vision of the future. Instead of educating people from the point of view of scarcity, we should be educating them to look for abundance in exploding technology and productivity.

Every time our leaders legislate for protecting a business from competitors so that they can keep prices high, we press our people further into poverty. This occurs because such protectionism puts necessary products and services out of reach of more people, increasing poverty. As individuals, each time we ask for a raise without a corresponding increase in quality or productivity, we add to the poverty of our own people because ultimately those kinds of demands will push up the price of the product or service we help deliver.

If you want to enjoy more of the good life, activate your gray matter and ask yourself: "How can I give more of what I have to offer for less time and money?" If you don't find a way, you can count on eventually being replaced by someone who can. It's simply a matter of principle. Information, unlike resources, is designed to be shared. If you share information, it spreads and increases. Knowledge cannot decrease, it can only increase what we have.

It is crucial at this time to educate our children to look at the world as a place of great abundance. The people who look at how much they can give are the ones who will profit. If each of us focused on how to give what we give more efficiently, we could not only make ourselves rich, but we could also improve life for everyone. If I hoard and keep my specialty only for those who can afford it, I may make money, but I also increase poverty.

When we focus on sound economic principles and use them in our daily lives we deliver more of what we each have to give—and money pours in. When we only ask the question, "What's in it for me?" life gets hard. True wealth comes by giving personal attention to how we can each make life easier for as many of our fellow humans as we can.

For people who are praying to God for more money, I say this: First open your eyes to how much the Great Spirit has already given. Look from eyes of abundance, not from eyes blinded by a belief in scarcity. Then pray that God will get out the battery cables, clip them to your ears and jump-start your brain so that you can start thinking. It is time to use the great gift God gave to you. Use your brain for thinking about how to do more good for people. If you give, you shall receive. It is one of the oldest spiritual principles in the world, and it works even in the dog-eat-dog world of modern economics. Forget what you have been taught and start thinking for yourself.

Never forget the Golden Rule: "Do unto others as you would have them do unto you." For me, that means working at my gift so that I can make life better for as many people as I can. It is a principle that works as well on an economic level as on an ethical one—and when it is followed sincerely, it ends poverty for individuals as well as whole communities.

22

Unlearning the Lessons That Keep You Down

Education...has produced a vast population able to read but unable to distinguish what is worth reading.

—George Macaulay Trevelyan (1942)

When people are progressing and finding personal fulfillment in their lives, they are like sparkling, fast-moving mountain streams, delightfully fresh and filled with energy. People who are not progressing and not finding personal fulfillment are like murky pools, no longer moving and no longer reflecting the beauty of nature.

I can remember a time, a decade ago, when the only thing increasing in my life was my rate of stagnation. The world around me was rapidly changing and my old "right" answers had become obsolete. I had a choice. I could continue to be dragged along kicking and screaming into the '90s or I could pick myself up and have the run of my life. I decided to do the latter. As Anthony Robbins stated in his book *Unlimited Power*, "For things to change... first I must change."

But how do we change? What can we do when life ceases to be a fresh mountain stream and becomes a brackish pool? Well, there are probably as many solutions as there are people. But the following seven points are my personal prescription, a prescription which got me out of the deepest rut of my life and which continues to serve me today:

1. Do Something Strange

Out of a sense of economy or simplicity most of us establish routines in our lives. We go to the same restaurants, shop at the same stores, buy the same groceries, wear the same hair style and even drive the same streets. After awhile, we grow so accustomed to the routine that we no longer even notice what we're doing. Our lives become boring because we are living them on "automatic pilot."

When we noticed this happening in our lives, my wife and I began a new policy of saying yes to something we would ordinarily say no to at least once a week. Not long ago, my wife wanted to go to an ice skating exhibition. I didn't want to go. But since it was my turn to say yes I agreed to go.

The show was fabulous, the skaters some of the best in the world—and I hated it. I fidgeted for two hours. When Kim asked me what part of the show I liked best, I replied, "The ending."

Three weeks later I turned on the TV one night and the same skaters were performing. This time, I found myself watching with rapt attention. Something had changed about the way I looked at skating. I can't tell you exactly what went on inside my mind that changed my mind but I do know that if I hadn't said yes when I wanted to say no it never would have occurred.

The next time it was my wife's turn to say yes to a no. She hates guns. I love them. We do not own any but I like to look at them. My wife has never been around guns and has no interest in doing so. I suggested that it would be good for her to go to a gun show with me and see a wide selection of them so she could perhaps reform her opinion. So we went to the gun show.

I have to say that Kim remained open-minded as we walked through the show. And now she hates guns even more! You see, the salespeople kept telling her about all the animals the guns could kill. Little did they know how much my wife loves animals! If she had any doubts about why she hated guns, they were erased from her mind that day. It was a day of learning for her because she discovered the real source of her aversion. It was also a day of learning for me because I came to better understand and appreciate my wife's values and beliefs.

One other example comes to mind at this moment that had to do with a prejudice I had toward men who wear their hair in pony-tails. I always thought they were weird, that there was something fundamentally wrong with them. I was quite inflexible about it. So for nine months I let my hair grow. Shocked that I would even consider doing such a thing I finally took my scrawny pony-tail out in public. I was totally embarrassed. What was the result? No one seemed to notice, of course.

I wore the pony-tail for about three months and began to think that men who had regular haircuts were weird. I knew at this point I had achieved my goal. My pony-tail came off, but the experience allowed me to broaden my range of acceptance of people for who they are, instead of what they look like.

2. Create New Friends

It's hard to deny the truth in the old cliché, "Birds of a feather flock together." Poor people have poor friends. Rich and wanna-be-rich people have rich or wanna-be-rich friends. Parents of young children seek others like themselves. Con-men ultimately con other con-men. Golfers play against golfers with about the same handicap.

Take a look at the birds you flock with. Ask yourself, "Where will they be 10 years or 20 years from now? What will be the quality of their lives and their relationships?" And then ask yourself, "Do I like what I see, for I am looking at me?"

We never see ourselves clearly. Even when we look in a mirror we tend to see only what we are thinking about ourselves at the moment—the reflection is distorted or enhanced by the thoughts in our minds. A more revealing way to know ourselves is to look at the world we are experiencing as a reflection of our own thoughts and feelings. In the "mirror" the world provides is the most valuable feedback we will ever get about who we are.

My most valuable mirror is my wife, Kim. When I take the time to reflect on our marriage the only words I know are "I'm one lucky man." She is beautiful on the outside and even more beautiful on the inside.

My next most valuable mirror consists of my family, friends and co-workers. I feel good when I spend time with my family and friends. And I feel good about what my co-workers and I produce at our company.

Lastly, I see who I am reflected back to me in my possessions, such as my house, cars and clothing. They are high quality and I take care to maintain them. In reality it's me taking care of me.

In the early 1980s I began to look at the people I called my friends. Frankly, I did not like what I saw. Don't get me wrong, it wasn't my friends who were the problem; it was me. I didn't like what I saw reflecting back. For example, I found I had no women as friends or equals. I only had men as friends, confidants and business partners. This absence of women friends said something about me.

But that wasn't the worst of it. I also began to see that the men who were my friends were arrogant, competitive, strong, wealthy, many of them ex-military officers who were as cold as ice inside. Most of these men ran their own organizations and ruled them with an iron hand. They ran their families in a similar manner. Many of them were routinely cheating on their wives, and a couple of them cheated in business. I saw men who, at retirement, would be very, very, very rich and powerful. But I also saw an emptiness, a void, spirits that would remain unfulfilled no matter how much money or power they accumulated. As I looked at these friends I knew I was looking at me.

I still keep up with most of my old friends but I also began to make new friends. It was difficult, yet I am happier for it today. My new friends include women, as equals and as partners. My closest friends have beautiful relationships with their spouses, are excellent in business and are committed to making sure this world is left in better condition than when they came into it. They are also involved in continuing their education and personal growth. My new friends are strong without being bullies. But most of all, I can hug and say "I love you" to both my men friends and my women friends, which is definitely not something they teach in the Marines.

We need to seek our reflections and strive to ask what are seldom easy questions. What do these reflections tell us about ourselves, about where we are in life? Perhaps it is time to expand ourselves, with new friends.

3. Attend Investment Courses

This is for people who need to open their minds and increase their incomes. Investment courses are the best sources of information I have found for this. Many of the ideas you'll find in these courses are novel, others sometimes shaky.

Go to such courses not for "final answers" but for the expansion of your thinking. For me, some of the crazier schemes are the best because they force me to think differently. But before you put your life savings into such schemes, talk the ideas over with a financial advisor you know and trust.

If you are new to the game of investing, I would advise finding a friend who invests as a hobby to go along with you. Don't let your friend's opinions cloud your own thinking. Listen and understand his or her point of view, but make your own decisions.

Investment courses are also great places to increase your circle of friends. Just as golfers have their hang-outs, investors have theirs. Find out where they are and then sit around and just listen. After awhile what they are saying will begin to make sense. You may even find a mentor. People often learn more by osmosis than by words.

During my late 20s I used to attend as many investment seminars and motivational rallies as possible. Each time I learned something, no matter how crazy or outside my own reality they were. The payoff from all these courses did not really hit until my mid-30s. In fact, it seems to me that information needs time to age, just like a fine wine.

4. Un-learn How To Read

I used to read at between 200-350 words per minute. The reason I read so slowly was that was how I was taught to read. Today I read at three different speeds—slow, the way I learned in school, medium, about 2,000 WPM and ultra-fast, about 20,000 WPM.

It took four different speed reading courses to finally be comfortable reading fast. In one of those courses I finally understood why most people read so slowly: Again, it was linked with the educational system's need to constantly test and evaluate. Children are required to read aloud not because it is the best way for young people to learn how to read, but so that teachers can be reassured how effective their teaching is. It is a test of the teacher's skill administered at the cost of the child's education.

Reading is a visual process, not an auditory one. By requiring children to read aloud, the words go from visual to auditory before comprehension. This adds one additional step—speaking the words—interrupting the visual process. It is this verbal interference that causes people to be slow readers all their lives. The testing of reading ability has no real value in educating the children, but is costing them their futures.

If you cannot read today your chances for success are greatly diminished. If you can only read slowly you are falling behind. It took me countless hours of practice to unlearn what I learned in school—yet they are still teaching this archaic method of reading today. Children are brought into the world with very fast minds; our educational system imposes a speed limit.

To better understand this concept, try this exercise. Look around the room for ten seconds without saying out loud what you saw. Then look around again for ten seconds, only this time say each item out loud as you visualize it. Now think about how much more you saw the first time you looked around the room, not having to take that extra step of saying each item out loud. This should give you a good idea of how our educational system's teaching methods for reading actually retard a child's potential reading speed by requiring the child to read out loud.

5. Change Jobs More Often

I remember being told, "If you change jobs too often, it will look bad on your résumé." But I would have to add that being incompetent later in life will look bad on your financial statement.

Everybody has a choice—either become a robot or work to learn. Employers who want robots will find robots. If you want to insure that you continue to grow and learn, don't work for robot factories. Find a job where you can discover what you do not already know. Work diligently and quietly, making sure the company gets more than it pays for. It does not matter if you are not an accountant; just working around accountants will teach you a lot. Simply listen. As I said, I suspect we learn immeasurable amounts through osmosis. When I was a rookie salesman I learned a lot just hanging around with the top salespeople.

If you really want to make your future brighter, look for jobs that challenge you. If you are terrified of sales, get a job selling. You may want to begin in retail sales, which is the easiest, then graduate to phone sales, then door-to-door If you can learn to enjoy and be successful at knocking on doors, there is nothing in life that will ever slow you down again.

Network marketing gives people valuable experience. Just be careful about the company you get involved with. Stick with it until it gets easy. Then move to a tougher sales job with a true master. Much of what my sales master taught me I still use today. This is true wealth and security, when what I know continues to support me financially.

Always keep in mind that our knowledge is our true wealth, much more valuable than money.

6. Find Emotional Mentors

Everyone who works with us has a person outside the company to talk to. For lack of a better word, it's like going to a therapist. Not that we are all crazy; that's not my point. There are two primary reasons we have people to talk with about our emotional upsets. One is to keep the organization calm, harmonious, happy and profitable. In any organization people bump into each other. Egos clash as egos always will. If we have people harboring grudges, or fighting, or gossiping behind each others' backs, efficiency drops dramatically. We might as well stop working. One policy our organization has is that if an argument does not get resolved in 50 minutes, we call time out. Then the parties involved seek outside consultation from a paid professional to clear the problem.

How many times have you been upset with something inside yourself but have taken it out on those closest to you? And how many times have you been the target of such attacks? These are part of the human experience. By keeping ourselves emotionally clean, however, everyone within the organization ends up being more productive, happier and more profitable. Our accountant will vouch for us.

This outside consulting also supports the growth of the individual. Learning can often be an upsetting process. If the learner is stuck with the upset, the learning takes longer and the rewards from the growth process are delayed. In times of upheaval, we want everyone changing quickly while remaining calm in the eye of chaos.

Each time emotional turmoil surfaces, look at it as an opportunity to clear something out of your system—instead of stuffing it back down and keeping it there with alcohol, cigarettes, food or drugs. Best of all, though, is that we let the upset go instead of taking it out on those we love.

7. Attend Seminars of Every Kind

There are thousands of seminars on a million different subjects. You might attend seminars that help in your profession. But attending seminars outside your profession can also be beneficial. Years ago I went to a seminar on flower arranging. I still do not know how to arrange flowers, yet my sense of aesthetics has improved, a skill that comes in handy when we are designing new brochures for our company.

I have found that sitting in a classroom studying something completely outside my profession often jogs my mind, giving me a completely different point of view on old problems, stimulating new ideas.

Seminars can force you to look ahead. Too many times people come to my seminars because they have run out of answers. This often means that they are in some kind of trouble and are in the midst of digging themselves out. But why wait that long? Seminars offer a good place to find new answers before a crisis caused by limiting yourself to old ideas comes up.

Think of education as a way of nurturing and exercising your brain. Just as a good, healthy workout at the gym can keep your body working at its optimal level, so a good healthy mental workout at a seminar can keep your brain working at its optimum. You don't need any more reason than that to do it.

23

If I Could Change the Schools

Learning to learn is the key. And if your kids have forgotten how, it's only because their knowledge of these primal processes has been chased into hiding by you or too much public schooling.

—HAL ZINA BENNETT (1972)

Eleven Points of Change for Education

While public school policies have accomplished much good by making education available to millions of people, it is no longer advancing fast enough to keep up with the needs of today's world. Trapped by its own dogma, it has become obsolete. The following are eleven ways that it might move forward to meet the 21st century:

Change 1: Take Your Signals From the Child, Not the Book

Too often in education, a teacher or even an entire school is forced to follow a lesson plan that is arbitrarily geared to age groups, completely ignoring the fact that children learn at different rates. For example, while one child may be ready to learn how to read at age five, another may not be ready until the age of eight. To brand a child "stupid" or a "failure" simply because he or she isn't ready to learn a subject when the lesson plan dictates, is pure folly.

In addition to different ages of readiness, there are different kinds of intelligences that each of us will normally develop to one extent or another according to our own individual gifts. In his book *Raising A Magical Child*, Joseph Chilton Pearce describes seven such intelligences:

physical, emotional, intellectual, social, conceptual, intuitive, and imaginative. While one person may excel in one of these areas, another may excel in another.

Similarly, some people are more oriented to the right brain, focusing on non-linear and less-structured activities, while others are more oriented to the left brain, focusing on linear processes such as mathematics and science.

These are just some of the ways that people differ in their readiness to learn, the rate at which they learn, how they take in information and how they best express themselves. To help young people develop their own gifts, we need to learn how to recognize these differences and seek ways to provide each individual with the greatest opportunities for success.

Change 2: Stop Setting the Teachers Up As Both Educators and Executioners

My father, who was an educator, told me that a teacher's job, first and foremost, is to educate—not fail—the child. But in our current educational system, each teacher's power is derived from the student's fear of failure. My father told me, "If a child fails, it's the system that fails, not just the child." When I was in school, I remember being more afraid than inspired by my teachers because of my fear that they would fail me.

I believe teachers should be coaches and leaders of young people, opening new doors to them, doors that will ultimately lead them down the road to a successful life. Certainly, teachers should not be the ones who shut doors in students' faces.

In our school system of the future, there would be a new contractual agreement that would include:

1. The individual student
2. Parents
3. Teachers
4. The class as a whole

The contract would state that the student would agree to study, be on time, attend classes and do the assigned homework. The parents would agree to supervise compliance of the child's contracts, as well as to attend parent-teacher meetings, fund-raisers for the school and other activities necessary for the successful functioning of an educational system.

The teacher would agree to do whatever it took to get the child successfully onto the next level. It would not be up to him or her to fail the student.

The class would be rated as a group, not individually, and all the students would receive the same grade based on the group's overall performance. This would eliminate the "survival of the fittest," winner vs. loser, nature of education that works to weed out the so-called "slow" students who, as a result, often end up living with the stigma that they aren't smart enough to be successful in life.

In China during the Cultural Revolution, many mistakes were made, as history has shown. But the participants also experimented with some educational techniques that were very effective. There was, for example, the saying "Friendship first, competition second." Millions of people were taught new skills to help make the country economically strong. When a group of young people was trained to drive a tractor, for example, that group did not graduate until every student was competent in that task. Those who learned quickly helped the slower students learn. And when the day of graduation arrived, the accomplishment of the group as a whole was celebrated rather than singling out people who were the highest achievers. What they accomplished, they accomplished cooperatively. With all its other faults, this method of education taught a sense of community and responsibility that was both productive and positive.

You may have already begun to sense that what I am proposing here would be a very exciting and dynamic process of cooperative learning, albeit controversial. Students might even want to go to school and stay in school because it would be a more interesting, caring and honest environment than the streets or sitting in front of a television.

The agreements between students, teachers and parents would allow students to be exposed to some excellent examples, as well as poor ones, of cooperation and learning—the latter coming largely but not exclusively from the adults. Students would begin to see the benefits of working together, cooperating for their mutual and collective good. If they learned cooperation at an early age, the results would range from increased self-esteem to higher quality friendships, more loving and effective families, and less crime. Human misery and loneliness would decrease. Perhaps the greatest lesson, however, would be the realization that we all have a part in orchestrating a higher quality of life for all.

A classroom scene might look like this: The fourth-grade teacher's job would be to lead the class of 30 or so students and their parents for the purpose of getting those 30 students into the fifth grade. The contracts would be read and understood and all the parties would agree to abide by them. These agreements would be a prerequisite for anyone choosing to be in the class.

If a child was not doing well in school because the parents weren't able to provide the support he or she needed, then it would be the concern of all parents because that child would affect the whole class. If one child was misbehaving, all the children and parents would have a common stake in the matter, wanting to find a solution so that the classroom atmosphere would continue to be conducive to learning. If one child was not studying, or was having difficulty with a particular subject, then the other children would learn to encourage that child and help him or her. Parents, students and teachers would all be accountable to the learning process. Gone would be the day when parents could simply drop their children off at school and wash their hands of the educational process.

Tests taken to get into the fifth grade would be taken cooperatively as a class or in smaller work teams or groups. This would allow the fifth-grade teachers to make the tests tougher and more interesting. The students would be more excited about taking tests and their involvement would be stimulated by keeping the material applicable to their lives.

If one or more students were not carrying their load, then it would be up to the class to discuss that type of negative behavior; teachers, in turn, would seek ways that everyone could learn from it. Students would learn to take responsibility for themselves and how the group was affected by both their positive and their negative interactions. This, in time, would begin to alter the "it-is-not-my-problem" attitude that permeates our society today.

In addition, tests would be run like an athletic event, with the current class competing with the next higher level. If the scores were too low, a re-test would be allowed. The students, teachers and parents would cooperatively get together and explore what the fifth-grade teachers thought was important and why. Answers, then, would become less important than the process of thinking, correcting and learning. The class would review what they missed on the test and then would do their best to comprehend what they overlooked. They would then learn from their mistakes and correct them.

If the class felt that any of the test was irrelevant or too difficult, then the parents, teachers and students could appeal as a group. This would minimize the possibility of one teacher being too tough and singling out or picking on students who are not yet able to defend themselves. Ultimately, the entry-level tests to each grade should be standardized nationwide. This would mean that students would learn faster, would enjoy the process, and would find school exciting because the tests would be more challenging. As a result, national standards would increase. There would, however, still be those who would end up at the bottom because it is inherent in any closed system. But the bottom would be a lot higher and more students overall would do better. In addition, the lessons learned would be of life-long value, focused on our goals of being rich and happy.

After the fourth-grade group demonstrated their competency on the test, the fifth-grade teacher would sit down with them and their parents to prepare for the fifth-grade year. Agreements would again be reviewed and signed, or class wouldn't begin. Right now, too many teachers are forced to accept unprepared students.

This method of teaching would eliminate most of the fear of failing. If the group passed, everyone would pass. It would be up to the group to make sure each person in the class was doing well; otherwise they would all be slowed down. Students would learn at an early age the dynamics and distinctions of group ethics, morals, legal agreements and personal agreements. They would hopefully also learn the value of keeping one's word, of telling the truth, of respecting other people's points of view, as well as their own, and of working as a supportive group where everyone does her or his best to make sure everyone is successful.

Given these changes, in a couple of generations we might have a more prosperous and peaceful world filled with happy, cooperative, compassionate, fulfilled people.

Change 3: Teach Generalized Principles

A generalized principle is one that is true in all cases. For example, the principle that by giving to others we ultimately give to ourselves is a generalized principle. So is the principle that if you teach according to the "one-right-answer" theory, you will end up with two fractionated groups, one of winners and one of losers.

If a person understood these and other generalized principles, he or she would know the common features shared by different specialized disciplines, such as music, medicine, animals, planets, automobiles, money and economics. People would grow up with a wider range of possibilities, instead of becoming more narrowly inclined as they got older. Then people from different specialties would be able to communicate openly with others, regardless of their specialties.

There is too much to know to attempt to memorize it all. Knowing some of the generalized principles would give the child an educational foundation that would continue to serve him or her regardless of what specialized area she or he might choose to study in the future.

Change 4: Teach the Principles of Money, Business and Finance

Only a few children are gifted scholastically. Not everyone is smart enough to become a brain surgeon or a rocket scientist. But everyone is smart enough to be economically secure and comfortable. If children knew that they had the native intelligence to be rich and happy, they could feel positive about their futures.

Currently, too many children leave school thinking they are stupid, that they have no possibility of building any kind of economic well being. They believe their performance in school is a forecast of their financial future. Not only low grades but the school's own propaganda that "you will never get anywhere unless you go to college" tends to be a self-fulfilling prophecy for all too many kids. "Why put any energy into school when I have no future anyway?" is a common attitude adopted by students who are the victims of this kind of negative education. In the inner cities it is the source of chronic apathy and much crime.

Poverty is first and foremost a state of mind. All the money in the world will not solve the problems of poverty unless we integrate the principles of abundance into education. This change must start with the schools since at the present time our schools inadvertently encourage Malthusian theories of scarcity and poverty. Our current system of education is teaching people to be co-dependents, addicted to money instead of teaching them how to be masters of it.

Change 5: Use Music in Teaching

Instead of attempting to have students shut off their music, teachers should incorporate it into teaching. In our classes with adults, we constantly use a mixture of classical and contemporary rock music with our studies.

Music can set the pace for cooperative learning sessions, where small groups are working together, sometimes noisily, to share what they know. Use it to actually maintain a level of concentration during a study period. (Watch teenagers and you'll discover that some of their best study occurs while they are listening to the latest rock 'n' roll group.)

Change 6: Let Students Explore

Allow students to leave school at the age of 15 if they so desire, without the stigma of failure. They would then be free to explore the world with the understanding that they could come back when they were ready and willing. I think we would be surprised at how many students would choose to stay if given the choice.

Children often study harder when they are treated with respect and they feel that education is their own choice instead of being something imposed on them by their elders. Just how teachers are supposed to teach kids who do not want to be in school, I don't know. It has been said that between the ages of 15 and 25 is a stage of life called "infinite wisdom"—that period of life when we believe we have all the answers. If kids don't want to be in school during this time, let them out into the world to explore and discover for themselves what they need to learn. Let them come back when their raging hormones are quieter, or when the glamour of getting up and going to a minimum-wage job every day wears off. Then, teachers could teach students who are willing to learn. Why should teachers have to put up with students who don't want to learn and who disturb the rest of the class?

Perhaps we should always follow the old adage: "Never try to teach a pig to sing. It wastes your time and annoys the pig."

Change 7: Teach More in Less Time

I would train teachers to teach faster. At our business school, we teach one year's worth of college-level accounting in two days. I know, most people say it can't be done. That is their paradigm. The human brain works much faster than the ability to teach it. Kids are bored with today's slow, archaic teaching methods. Instead of asking kids to stay in school longer, the system needs to start teaching more in less time. I had a severe learning disability in school. It was called boredom. I would teach teachers to be more entertaining. Most teachers are so forced to conform within the dictates of the system that they are afraid to show any real signs of life.

Change 8: Use Games to Teach

I would use games, rather than lectures, to teach. I would require all new teachers to learn teaching via physical activities. Games are not only a fun way to educate, they are also healthier. I teach adults with games and most of them love it. We use games such as ring toss, rugby, American football and volleyball to teach business. We even play men vs. women on occasion. The only ones who seem to have a problem with games are the ones who want to know things only mentally and don't want to go through the physical and emotional learning process. In a nutshell, those who resist are often the same ones who hate making mistakes and who don't want to have to think. They only want to be given the answers. Most kids need some "mass" to learn with. Our current system is 90 percent mental. It's like teaching basketball without the ball.

Change 9: Allow Freedom of Choice

During a child's education, I would allow them to choose the subjects that interested them the most—subjects that are of sincere interest to them. Let's say, for example, that a child was interested in animals. The child's whole curriculum could involve history, chemistry, math, business, art, etc., with animals as the study base. Children would then read and study harder because they would be learning about something they first found interesting. Learning could actually be fun!

The current system of education has broken subjects up into "elements" of learning. As a result, students are required to learn math, reading, science, history, etc., without a subject of interest attached to it. This is where the term "elementary education" originated—education without a subject, just the basic, boring elements.

Change 10: Encourage Lifelong Learning through Employment

Instead of encouraging students to be good employees, I would encourage them to be good on-the-job students. I would encourage them to look for jobs where they can learn instead of only earning. I would encourage them to seek employers who are willing to educate them instead of merely train them to be a member of the corporate dog pack, barking for a paycheck. These "trained" people often end up howling at the moon saying, "I deserve another pay raise even though the company I work for is going broke and half of my friends have been fired!"

Since most children of today are growing up at a time when millions will live to be over 100, why pressure them into making a career decision at 15 years of age? Would you seek career counseling from a teenager? Then why ask them to do the same for themselves? I remember when a 46-year-old friend of mine suddenly recognized that he became an accountant based on a decision he made when he was 16 years old. At that age, he barely knew what an accountant does! Today he makes too much money to quit even though he'd rather be a park ranger because he loves the outdoors and is concerned about the environment.

I encourage young kids to take 15 years to gather basic on- the-job business skills such as production, sales, accounting, organizational management and finance. This experience allows them to be well-rounded general businesspeople, with real experience. Only then can they make career choices and go back to school for more specialized training. Parents usually scream at this advice, but I say, let them scream. They're often the ones who are trapped in dead-end, financially-unrewarding jobs. I always wonder why they want their kids to end up the same way!

I definitely do not recommend kids having to choose a career specialty too early. I recommend generalizing in the younger years and then specializing later on. It is almost like postponing becoming an adult for 15 years and having a little fun—and I highly recommend having fun in life. Just think, if people take 35 years to grow up, they still will have 65 years to be an adult.

Change 11: De-criminalize Education

Why force kids to go to school? Wouldn't it be better to change the system so they would want to go?

• • •

These are the eleven points of change that I would put in the school system if I had the power to do so. Please understand, though, that I do not contend that these are by any means the only changes necessary. I do suspect, however, that these changes would certainly begin to clear up the arthritic joints of our crippled educational system. These changes would definitely be a shock to a system that needs to be shocked. But once the upset was accepted, then the long-term rehabilitation of the system could begin.

24

Should I Send My Child to School?

Let early education be a sort of amusement; you will then be better able to find out the natural bent.

—Plato (346 B.C.)

"Study hard."

"Have you done your homework?"

"If you don't do well in school, you won't amount to anything."

"Study hard, study hard, study hard." When I was a child, it seemed to me that was all my mother could say. Every time I turned around she nagged me about studying or doing my homework. I did my best to ignore her, but the panic in her voice scared and confused me. Why did she think studying was so important?

As the years went on, so did the nagging. Although I was doing okay in school, I did much better on the football field. As I sat in my room one evening putting new coins in my coin collection, my mother came in. I feared I was in for one of those heart-to-hearts. I was right.

"Do you realize you're disgracing your father? Have you forgotten he is the head of the educational system? How can you do that? As the oldest child in our family, you're not setting a very good example for your brother and sisters."

I lowered my head as she glared at me. I had heard this speech many times before, and frankly I was very tired of it.

Finally I asked, "Why do I have to do well in school?"

A look of disbelief came across her face. "So you can get a good job!" she blurted out.

There was a long silence. For the first time I understood the panic in her voice. She was afraid that if I didn't do well in school I wouldn't be hired by some company. She didn't think I would be qualified.

"If I had gotten better grades in high school, I could have been a doctor," my mother said. She was livid. "Instead, I am only a registered nurse. I get paid a lot less than a doctor, but I do a lot more work and I have just as much knowledge. It's not fair. And I don't want you limiting your future the way I did."

Upon completing her little speech, my mom left, shutting the door behind her.

My room was as quiet as a tomb, but a million thoughts roared through my head. So that was it, I thought. She was trying to warn me against winding up like her. That panic in her words was her expressing her personal frustration and fears, her insecurity and her regrets.

I sat there for a long time thinking about this. At 16 I realized that school was part of an employment process. It had only a little to do with education. I never understood my mother's panic because I knew it didn't take much education or a very high intelligence to get rich. And I knew I didn't need to be hired by some big corporation to be financially successful.

I realized that all her life my mother had believed she wasn't smart enough. But I also realized that she was way beyond smart. She was one of the most loving, caring, and kind people I ever knew, and I still think that's true today. She had lived much of her life thinking she wasn't good enough and she didn't want me to do the same.

I opened the door and saw my mom standing at the kitchen sink, lost in her thoughts. I put my arms around her and kissed her on the cheek. "I love you, Mom," I whispered. "Thanks for being worried about me."

She turned, put her arms around me and returned the hug. "I just want the best for you, son."

I squeezed her tighter and nodded my head silently, letting her know I understood.

Many years later my mom, dad and younger sister flew from Hawaii to New York to attend my graduation from the U.S. Merchant Marine Academy. On a hot summer's day I stood in my starched and bleached naval officer's uniform holding my college degree. That degree was the culmination of a dream. It was the ticket I needed for my professional third mate's license in the Merchant Marines and my commission as an officer in the U.S. armed forces. I have a picture of my mom hugging me that day. It was one of the happiest days of my life, yet I think my mom was even happier.

However, six months later I was back home in Hawaii. I had resigned from my high-paying job as a ship's officer for a large oil company. I called a family meeting to let them know of my next step. I explained that I had taken a 92 percent cut in pay, had voluntarily activated my military commission in the Marine Corps and was signed up for pilot training. I was on my way to Vietnam. My mom cried. Dad was silent. My news came just after my brother had left to go to the war zone for his first tour. I knew my parents were opposed to war, but they also understood why their sons had chosen to go.

Less than a year later while I was still in flight school, my mom died. That was one of the saddest days of my life.

It wasn't until my early thirties that I became interested in the subject of education. My dad had dedicated his life to educational research and was highly respected in the field. We often discussed how the family environment affects a child's performance in school. One day I brought up the subject of Mom's panic around studying hard and getting good grades. Dad knew exactly what I was talking about.

"I often thought about saying something to her about constantly nagging you kids to study hard," he said.

"Why didn't you?" I asked.

"Oh, I guess I actually did on occasion," he replied, smiling. "But she meant no harm and her concerns were genuine. Your grades were horrible, if you'll remember."

"Then why didn't you ever pressure me to do better? You were top-dog in education and I was making you look bad."

My dad laughed. "You certainly did try my patience. But doing well in school or achieving professional success and satisfaction were not my issues. School was relatively easy for me and I usually achieved what I wanted in the professional world. Studying hard and getting good grades to get ahead in the world were your mother's issues because she felt she never accomplished it."

Dad came from a family of educators. After high school, he completed his bachelor's degree in two years instead of four, then completed graduate studies at Stanford University, the University of Chicago, and Northwestern. At 25, he was the youngest school principal in the state. He eventually became head of education for Hawaii.

My mother came from a family of small business owners and tradespeople. Most of them were investors. In her family, education was not a top priority; money and income property were. Mom struggled through school.

It was always interesting to go to the different family gatherings. On my father's side, conversations were about education, learning, social and political reform and innovative ideas. On my mother's side, conversations were about money—how much they made on one deal, how much they lost on another, whose marriages were in trouble and how much they dreaded going to work. I learned a lot at those gatherings, and that knowledge continues to serve me well even to this day.

During one of our conversations my father disclosed some interesting trends he had discovered while he was superintendent of education. He had researched the family backgrounds of young people who received National Merit Scholarships. A large percentage of these high achievers came from families where one of the parents was upper-executive management in business, or was a Lt. Colonel or Colonel in the military.

Checking further, my father found that children from wealthy and prestigious families—those who received these outstanding scholarships—were also known to be disruptive when they were in public school and not to be particularly good students when it came to academics. When he looked at these facts he was puzzled. If in their early years these young people had poor academic records, how did they end up with National Merit Scholarships? He found his answer when he began researching expensive private, preparatory schools. He found that most of them had been set up just to handle such children—children from wealthy families who were getting into trouble in the public schools.

If the parents were high achievers who had not quite made it to the top (a colonel striving to be general or a vice-president to be CEO), it seemed their children often picked that up and carried it into their own lives.

My dad said, "I never expected you to do well in school because I was at the pinnacle of my profession. Most teachers were careful around you because you were the boss' son. Yet I did not want you to be one of those disruptive, arrogant rich kids like many of your friends. What I set out to teach you was the love of learning, respect for others, social responsibility, the ability to think for yourself and leadership. But I never lectured you or nagged you. I knew the best way to teach you was first to be an example myself."

I looked at Dad across the living room. The sun was going down and we'd soon have to turn on a light. I thought about something that had happened a few years back. A friend of my father's had mentioned to me that my dad had been honored as one of the top ten educators in the United States. My father had never even told me about this. All my life people had told me, "Your father is a great man." I had heard this often but it had never sunk in until then.

There I was, in my mid-thirties, Dad in his mid-sixties, and I was just beginning to understand in my heart all that he had taught me and how he had chosen to teach me. At that moment I knew what a great father I had been blessed with, and what a brilliant man he really was.

Many incidents from my youth began to make sense to me at that moment. I remembered often wishing my dad would say to me, "Study hard. Be a doctor or a lawyer." I would simply have done it out of my love for him. But he never pressured me to do or become anything in particular. Even when I failed my sophomore year of high school he didn't scold me, though I expected him to. Instead, he looked at what I needed to learn, encouraged me to make it up in summer school and tutored me when necessary.

There was the time he and Mom took two years off to work for the Peace Corps. Doing so meant that the family income went way down. Their decision to do this greatly upset me because the cut meant we could not keep up with my friends' families. Dad talked to me about our responsibility to the planet and its people. Even when he financially backed one of my early business ventures, which I swore could not fail, but did, he comforted me, never saying a thing about his life's savings. Instead, he asked me what I had learned and if I was a better businessperson because of it. At perhaps the lowest point in my life, my dad was still there, investing in my education.

The evening that we sat together and discussed these things was one of the most important of my life. We talked for a long time about the trials of our family, our accomplishments, our goals. Then finally the conversation became a little lighter as we discussed our golf games.

Toward the end of the evening he turned to me and said, "I'm glad you made it, son. I had my doubts at times. I certainly never thought you'd become a teacher."

I had to laugh at that one too, considering how much trouble I'd given my teachers when I was young.

Then Dad looked at me and said something I suspect every child wants to hear: "I'm very proud of you, son. I've always been proud of all you kids. You were all so very different from one another. But your success in school or in the world never had anything to do with the love and pride I have felt for you all."

Dad and I hugged, something we rarely did while I was growing up. I thanked him for being a great dad and a great teacher.

My father had a lot to say about education later that night and in the days following. On the subject of S.A.T. (Scholastic Aptitude Test) scores, he said: "In our educational system they are used to determine which kids are smart and which ones aren't. The test determines how well a child is suited for subjects relative to being a professional scholar, which involves studying more and more about less and less. If you aren't interested in being a scholar, the system isn't interested in you. What if the child has other aptitudes? What about mechanical, financial, athletic, or an aptitude for working with people or animals? These are mostly ignored. The S.A.T. only measures a person's ability in scholarly endeavors."

"Eggheads," I said. Dad cringed but he agreed with me.

"That's why our educational system, from elementary to the highest levels, isn't working. Only the people with good S.A.T. scores survive, and they don't necessarily know how to teach or run a school system. Yet we exalt and revere them because they thrive in the 'scholastic environment.' They're not interested in people skills or mechanical skills because few of them have those skills themselves. They often view education as a long process of elimination that weeds out all the trash and undesirables who aren't like them. And just as golfers like other golfers, eggheads like other eggheads.

"Don't get me wrong, scholarship is important—but so are other aptitudes that make up what it means to be a human. Everyone has different aptitudes and that's what makes our society function. It would be much more beneficial if our system helped each student identify his or her own aptitudes and gifts, rather than judging them only according to their scholastic aptitude or lack of it. I have a feeling everyone would be able to find more satisfying work as adults if they had gotten to know and respect their own aptitude when they were very young, rather than being made to feel stupid or inadequate because they weren't scholars. But unfortunately, American scholars have brainwashed us all into believing that scholastic aptitude is the only one that's important. If you don't score well, our school system abandons you. In Japan they do their best to educate students along the lines of each child's aptitude. Japan is much more humane than we are, and it shows up in their businesses.

"Of all my four children, your brother is probably the smartest," my father continued. "But he did the poorest in school and came out the most battered. Now, had we placed a Ford V-8 engine in front of all of you, instead of books, he would've gotten straight A's. You would have failed. Put a screwdriver in your hand and you would use it as a weapon or sell it for a profit. Your sisters would also have done poorly. They are great in art and spiritual aesthetics, but neither one has any significant mechanical aptitude. The only reason your brother did poorly in school was because he didn't have a high scholastic aptitude like the rest of you. But never forget that he is brilliant mechanically."

"Is that why you never pushed us to do well in school?"

Dad nodded. "How could I have known where to push you? I believe the child has to discover his or her own natural aptitude. Had I pushed you in the direction I wanted you to go, instead of respecting your process of discovering your own gift, I would have been getting in the way of your finding your own destiny. All I could really do was love you and encourage you whether you were up or down. I was always on your side, no matter what you did in life. Your mother and I knew we were your first teachers and we wanted to set an example that you could be proud of. You kids gave us the courage to be the best we could be."

These long conversations with my father came in the last years of his life. Sometimes I find myself wondering what, if anything, I would have done differently had I understood these things when I was much younger. Knowing how arrogant I was as a kid, the truth is I probably would have done things pretty much as I did. The bottom line is that the lessons he thought were most valuable did get through to me—and this had to do with his respect and love for his children. His and my mother's interest in us was never doubted and that interest was tremendously important, supporting us in ways that continue to be valuable and deeply appreciated.

Passing the Wand

Today when concerned parents ask me if they should send their kids to school, I answer with a question: "What kind of school do they attend at home?"

To quote Lee Iacocca, chairman and CEO of the Chrysler Corporation, "In a completely rational society, the best of us would be teachers and the rest of us would have to settle for something less."

Fortunately or unfortunately, our parents are always our first teachers. All adults, whether rocket scientists, firemen, public officials or bums in the park, are teachers to our young. Our very existence—whether prince or pauper, saint or crook—teaches children something. And all of us could be doing a better job.

So when parents point the finger of blame at the educational system, I remind them that, like it or not, they are a part of the system. We may not be able to change the entire school system, but we do have a choice about what we, as individuals, are teaching children, whether they are ours or someone else's. If we want to change education, each of us first needs to ask what we ourselves are teaching all children. Soon these children will grow up to be teachers themselves. Our actions and deeds today will determine tomorrow's education.

The following are questions I ask parents before they charge off to attack the rest of the educational system:

1. **What does your marriage teach your kids?**
    a. Do you and the child's other parent (and/or step-parent) work together for your child's good?
    b. Do you and your spouse honor your marriage vows?
    c. Does male treat female, and vice-versa, with respect and equality?

2. **What are your attitudes toward education?**
   a. Do you secretly hate school?
   b. How often do you voluntarily attend educational or cultural events?
   c. How much do *you* read? What do you read?
   d. How much and what kind of television do you watch?
3. **What are your attitudes toward work?**
   a. Do you hate your work?
   b. Have you given up improving yourself professionally?
   c. Are you and in a rut?
   d. Do you keep your job only for security?
4. **What are your attitudes toward money?**
   a. Do you think or talk about it as if it were evil?
   b. Do you save and invest?
   c. Do you educate yourself relative to money and finance?
   d. Do you say "money is hard to get?"
   e. Do both parents work just to be able to "keep up with the Joneses?"
5. **Do you and/or your spouse have any addictions?**
   (Children of addicts often become addicts or marry addicts. It doesn't matter if the addiction is alcohol, drugs, sex, work or money.)
6. **How do you use your free time?**
7. **What do you contribute to make the world a better place?**
8. **How much of your free time do you spend with your child, and how do you spend this time?**
9. **Do you explore new ideas and experiences, or do you stay with what is socially acceptable, traditional or what the crowd is doing?**
10. **How intimate and safe is it for family members to communicate with each other in your home?**
    a. Are some subjects taboo? (The usual taboos are sex, AIDS, criticism of parents or teachers, and money.)

b. What emotional tone is most used in conversation? Is it love and trust, hostility and anger, subtle or not-so-subtle put-downs?

11. **If you are asking your child to do something, what is your "emotional investment" in it?**
(Many parents live vicariously through their children. They might want their kid to be the athlete, movie star, model or business tycoon that they weren't.)

• • •

No doubt about it, education starts in the home. And if you don't know exactly what that school is teaching your kids, maybe the questions above will provide some clues about what you could improve or change. Instead of telling your children what kind of people they should be, first be the kind of person you want them to be.

Education today is primarily an employment-preparation process. Too much emphasis is put on studying hard, getting good grades and going to a good school so students can get a good job and make a lot of money. The question we all need to ask is, "What has happened to learning in the process?"

Economic fear and the love of money have replaced learning. Schools are fundamentally training grounds, producing workers for the rich. When many of our best universities were founded they were not founded for the purpose of higher learning. They were founded to provide knowledgeable but compliant employees who would dutifully do as they were told. R. Buckminster Fuller called Harvard, "J.P. Morgan's school of accounting."

If you are pressuring your children to study hard, take a careful look at what is motivating you. If you want them to study hard, then let them study what they want and what they are most interested in. If you want them to study hard to get a good job, then tell them that.

When a business says, "We hire only people with college degrees," they are often saying they want someone who is disciplined, who will do as they are told and who will work hard. If that is the game you want your children to play, explain all of this to them. Give them as much information as you can so that they can make choices and take responsibility based on facts rather than emotion. Don't confuse education with your fears of your child's employability. And don't top that off by blaming the school system for not educating your kids. Tell your children you want them to go to school for the money and the job security, probably the same thing you did—or wished you had. Treat school as job preparation, but also emphasize, that "real" education is probably going to come from other sources.

If our national S.A.T. averages are falling it is only because our kids are reflections of the adults in our society. Too many adults are more worried about money than education. Too many don't even know there is a difference between "going to school" and "getting an education." They put more emphasis on looking good than on striving for quality of life for their families, for society and for the world.

I have no children of my own but I was once a kid myself, and I know the power of having an adult in my life who supports me in exploring my natural aptitudes. My wife and I have many friends with children, and sometimes they ask what we would recommend in terms of what to tell them about school. We tell them not to confuse their children by calling school "education." We also tell parents that if their children want to learn about money, go ahead and teach them how to work hard to create true wealth rather than just going after a paycheck. Let children explore this world and gather the experiences that with time will mature into real wisdom about creating wealth. Better yet, provide your children with the very best education they can get—learn about creating wealth yourself and give them your success as a model of what you want them to learn.

Buckminster Fuller and many others, including me, have long advocated apprenticeship programs instead of academic-oriented schools. I believe that one of the worst mistakes we ever made in public education was getting rid of the trade schools and classes that taught practical crafts. Instead of getting rid of such programs, we would do well to have business and industry cooperate by bringing in the latest technologies, staffing such classrooms well, and giving schoolchildren hands-on experience with the very latest inventions and processes. If school is to be effective at preparing people for employment, be honest and provide appropriate support to do just that for any student so inclined.

Several times during my own adult years I apprenticed with people who were outstanding in their fields. And I have to say that I learned more in just a few months with them than I could have learned in a lifetime of school.

If you want to make sure that your children get the best education possible, look at yourself first. As adults, we are each the most important part of the educational system. Who we are and what we do educates our kids more than mere words will ever do. As a friend in the contracting business once told me, "You can only build as high as the foundation is strong."

25

What to Tell the Children

We can secure other people's approval, if we do right and try hard; but our own is worth a hundred of it...

—Mark Twain (1894)

Many parents ask me what they should tell their children about school. They realize the system is in need of change, but they also feel their children need to be going to school. Here are the key messages you should be communicating to your kids:

1. **Education Is a Lifelong Process.**
   Going to school is just a part of that process—sometimes one of the smallest parts. There are many valuable skills to learn from school, but never stop pursuing the things you want to learn. Think for yourself. Make educational choices that will help you develop your own special gifts.

2. **School Is Primarily an Employment Process.**
   It is designed to prepare you to earn money (but not necessarily to create real wealth) and to operate acceptably in the area of life we call work.

3. **It Is a Game of Winners and Losers.**
   Play hard and play fair. Always have compassion and humility when you are winning and the courage to get back up when you've been knocked down. Be kind to all students regardless of their popularity, their academic rating, or the difficulties they face in their

lives. Take time to reach out to kids who are on the fringe. Not only is it a humane habit to have, but it also gives you the opportunity to learn about different people. As classmates of Albert Einstein found out, the class nerd might just turn out to be the next Nobel Prize winner.

4. **If You Start, Commit to Finish.**

   Learning to accept challenges. Having the tenacity to do your best and finish what you start are lifelong skills worth cultivating. Quitting when things get tough is not a habit one wants to develop. Discipline, particularly in the face of adversity, is a valuable asset in this world.

5. **Schools Are Great Places to Learn How to Find Information.**

   As long as you are going to be there, make the most of your time at school. Learn how to locate specific information. Many teachers are good researchers. Use them wisely by asking them questions about where you might go to get information, on virtually any and all questions that might occur to you, and to some that might not. Practice keeping your mind open to subjects you know nothing about. Instead of saying no to opportunities that are offered, try saying yes and watch what happens. It is often those areas you think you're going to hate that turn out to be the most personally fulfilling.

   Depth of knowledge is far more important than getting the "right" answers in order to pass a test. And you can achieve this depth only if you know where to go for information. Learning to do this quickly and efficiently is a skill that will serve you for the rest of your life, regardless of the jobs or professions you choose in the future.

6. **It's Better to Look Stupid Than to Be Stupid.**

   If you don't understand something, ask for clarification. If the teacher wants a volunteer, volunteer. People learn more by participation than by being silent and attempting to look cool. Be willing to make mistakes—they are the primary way we learn. Make many of them. If school is boring, then get entertained by being willing to participate. Be respectful but have fun.

7. **Take Advantage of Being Young.**

There are adventures and opportunities that are best accomplished while you are young. Plenty of time remains after school to be a serious, career-oriented stick-in-the-mud. Helen Keller once said, "Life is a daring adventure or nothing." Let your curiosity be your guide. Enjoy your youth. This will help you to have a youthful adulthood.

8. **Seek the One "Right" Answer—But Don't Stop There!**

Figure out what answer the teacher expects, but then find a minimum of two more answers. Having the ability to find multiple answers to problems in life will provide you with options. These options are the key to freedom. After all, there are no right answers in life; there are only multiple choices. A life without choices can quickly turn into a misery.

9. **Believe in Yourself.**

Don't take labeling and grading too seriously. It is done for the benefit of the teachers. It does not mean that you are smart or that you are dumb. Everyone learns in different ways and at different rates. Your grades in school don't determine what you are able to do in the future. Follow your dreams no matter what anyone tells you!

10. **"My Love IS Forever."**

Tell your children that no matter how they do in school, they are very special to you. Remember that school is only a game. Assure your kids that school and grades will come and go, but you will always love them.

26

Embrace Your Own Genius

I know of no more encouraging fact than the unquestionable ability of man to elevate his life by a conscious endeavor.

—HENRY DAVID THOREAU

"Your best friend Robby is a genius. Why aren't you?"

My mother used to ask me that all the time. Robby was, and still is, a genius. He was also my best friend. When we were in elementary school he was using a slide rule while I was still attempting to master the fine art of finger counting. I haven't seen him in over 25 years, but when last I heard he was awarded his doctorate degree in space science and was sitting in an observatory on some mountaintop, gazing at the stars.

Our community made quite a fuss over this young genius. The school administrators, the teachers, the parents and the kids all watched him anxiously. In fourth grade he took college math courses just for entertainment. But when educators wanted him to skip several grades, his family steadfastly opposed that idea. While Robby's mind was brilliant, he was really just like the rest of us—physically, emotionally and socially he was still a ten-year-old. We graduated together and went our separate ways. I went in search of money and Robby went on to become a star among the real stars.

I remember a friend of my mother's once asking me, "Don't you ever feel stupid next to Robby?"

I couldn't believe she would ask such a question. I replied, "I don't need to be with Robby to feel stupid. I feel that way on my own every day I go to school."

Actually, I don't recall if I felt stupid compared to Robby. I don't think so. We were simply the best of friends. He helped me in math and science and I taught him how to play baseball. Our parents were also great friends, and I sense now that it was their attitude about Robby that never made his brilliance seem any big deal. Also, my dad was responsible for Robby's curriculum in the gifted kids program, and I knew that he believed every child has his or her own unique gift.

Though I got certain pressures from my mother, I remember how my father encouraged me, my brother and two sisters to explore our own gifts. Dad never once said, "I want you to be a teacher or a doctor." He allowed us to find our own answers and interests.

I remember my father once saying to me that some kids excelled in school because that was where their gifts were; he also told me that school wasn't where everyone found their gift. I don't think it was any surprise to my father that I never found my gift in traditional education and as far as he was concerned, it was just fine that I was less than a star student.

In 1983, as I sat listening to a talk by R. Buckminster Fuller, I heard something screaming through my brain. Bucky said that in every human there is a genius. I had heard that concept before, and although I thought it was a great theory, I felt it wasn't one of those geniuses he was talking about. At that moment, I became aware of a belief that had been stored in my brain for a great many years, all but hidden from my awareness. It was the belief that since I had not done well in school, I was not smart.

I knew I was a little smart—just not as smart as someone else. No one in particular, just someone else. This thought pattern had influenced my actions most of my life. As a result, I was always coming up second best because that is how I thought of myself. I was playing out a script I had written for myself, acting as if it was the absolute and final truth. And because I thought I was second best, I experienced the world accordingly.

Bucky said, "Look into the eyes of a newborn baby and you will see the spark and the soul of a genius."

Bells and whistles went off in my head. Years of unanswered questions were instantly clarified. A few days earlier I had visited my friend's week-old baby, and as I held the child in my arms, it looked up at me and smiled. The child's eyes were wide, bright and full of wonder, amazement, excitement and anticipation of this gift called life. The child smiled its toothless smile, drooled and squirmed a little in my arms. Though I was a stranger, the child's eyes expressed love, without fear or reservation. There was communication between two souls. The spark I saw in that child's eyes was the spark of love—and in that moment the genius in both of us met.

I left my friend's home very disturbed; something inside me was churning. Bucky's words clarified my confusion. It became clear that every child is born a genius—a genius of something. And I wondered, "If everyone is born a genius, what happens?"

In time, I realized that this spark of genius is smothered by those who nurture, educate and love us the most—our parents, families, teachers and friends. Whether carelessly, maliciously, innocently or ignorantly, this spark can be snuffed out.

Bucky died soon after that lecture, on July 1, 1983. I was in the middle of a company meeting when I heard the news. Something burst inside me and I began sobbing uncontrollably. As an ex-Marine officer, crying in front of my peers was definitely not considered normal behavior, but I couldn't stop. And I didn't feel I had to try. My partners and staff members waited with quiet compassion. An hour later, the meeting resumed.

Bucky and that baby had rekindled something within me. Even though I knew my parents, family and friends had faith in me and loved me dearly, something was missing. After making so many mistakes, losing everything, fighting to get it all back, and worst of all, feeling stupid, my spirit had been crushed. A certain spark I'd had before was gone. I asked myself what was missing. The answer was that I had lost faith in myself.

Holding onto the belief that all people are geniuses, I decided to find out what caused this genius to hide—both in me and in other people. My study took me all over the world to work with thousands of people. My findings were not pretty. I discovered that the genius born in every child is greatly diminished before the child even begins school. Sadly, our teachers hardly have a chance to restore and ignite the flame. How and why our best teachers persist is perhaps nothing short of heroic.

That being the case, I started asking another question: How do adults revive their lost genius?

It appears that every one of us came into this world with a wide array of potential interests. Since my parents never pressured us to be or do anything in particular, we were free to explore anything we wanted, always knowing we could report back to home base for guidance, correction and love. A friend of mine, on the other hand, knew very early on that he was being groomed to take over the family business. I do not sense that he ever developed fully as a person. Nobody ever asked him what interested him, truly interested him; it probably never even occurred to anybody in that family. And, since his career was set he never explored his own interests to find out who he was. Though he was smart enough, crisis after crisis hit the family business after he grew old enough to take over, and I've often wondered if this was because he really didn't fit in and in his heart really didn't want to be doing what he was doing .

During my study I tracked down people who were considered geniuses in their fields. I met and interviewed doctors, lawyers, policemen, teachers, social workers, religious leaders, entertainers and many more. I classified my geniuses, famous or not, according to the quality of their work. These people pushed the known boundaries in their fields. They pushed themselves beyond personal beliefs and paradigms.

There was one principle I found operating in each of these people, which was:

They used what they LOVED to solve problems they HATED.

All of these people were using their gifts—those that came naturally to them—to solve problems that bothered them deeply or in some way totally captured their attention.

One genius I met was a young mother who loved children. What she hated, and what challenged her the most, was the cruelty to which runaway kids are exposed. As a result, she gave up a high-paying job to teach runaways the skills they need to reenter society. She had no government funding because she refused to play their game. How she accomplishes what she does is beyond me, but the results she gets with these young people is fabulous and certainly far better than any government program I have seen. In the process she has become one of the most beautiful and powerful women I have ever met. She simply glows. Her knowledge and wisdom in this field of education are beyond brilliance; one can't help but wonder if they are divinely inspired.

As I looked closely at my own life, I realized that of everything I liked to do, I had spent the most time studying money, finance, business and economics. No one ever had to motivate me to read books on these subjects. My interest in them was innate. Yet, every time I made lots of money I also became bored and somehow found a way to lose it. Making money, I figured out, was only exciting for me when I did not know how to do it. Kind of like driving a car. While I was learning, it was fun, but I wouldn't want to be a taxi driver my whole life. I needed to find something that would give purpose to my money-making.

After some soul-searching, I touched upon something I hated deeply; I hated cruelty and poverty. While I was not certain how I was going to implement this discovery, I felt that I at last had a direction. I began to teach what I loved—money and business—with the hope of reducing poverty and cruelty in the world. That's what I'm still doing today. And now there are people who are calling me a genius!

I know I will never end poverty and cruelty on my own. And the chances are that I will never live to see the day that everyone lives in harmony. But I know that I'm doing what I was meant to do. Once I had my personal combination of Love/Hate, my motivation and interest in life skyrocketed. It became a wonderful psychosis—my definition of psychosis being "attempting to achieve something that isn't realistic."

It is this wonderful psychosis that keeps me high on my life, that gives me a purpose and a mission which I love thinking about, working months on end, and traveling thousands of miles for. Like Jason and the Argonauts, I am in pursuit of my own Golden Fleece. No one has to wake me up in the morning or ask me to work overtime. I don't really care how much money I make and I'm usually too busy to spend it anyway. I know I may never capture the prize that drives me on, but I love the adventure of pursuing it and wouldn't trade my way of life for anything.

A few years ago someone thanked me for what I do and called me a genius. It was the first time anyone had called me that. I had never even imagined that anyone would ever describe me that way. I have to tell you, I was both embarrassed and humbled.

As sweet as it was, that compliment also reminded me that there is genius in everyone. It is the part that drives you to seek a better life, even when you cannot figure out exactly what that means. Realizing your genius and bringing it to life in the real world only takes a little willingness and a little courage. The problem with most of us is that we don't think our own gift is any big deal. We're too close to it. It's almost invisible to us most of the time. We don't always recognize our own gift because we're standing right in the center of it. We're like the proverbial fish who asks, "What's the ocean?" unable to understand that he's swimming in it.

For me, making money was like that, so simple I didn't think my talent for it was anything special. It wasn't until I realized how much pain poverty causes, and how cruel people with money can be to those who don't have any, that I began to appreciate and cultivate my gift.

Now I ask you: What is your gift? What comes easily to you? And how can you use your gift to solve some of the problems here on planet Earth?

There is certainly no scarcity of problems to solve. If you work in earnest, not caring what anyone else says, continuously refining and improving your gift to make this world better, your genius will emerge. I promise you it will.

Or you can live your life like most other people, simply earning a living and taking vacations, wondering why this world is so screwed up, all the while asking, "Why doesn't someone do something about it?"

It has been my experience that a person who does not find a way to give his or her gift back to the world will suffer through life with a sense of incompleteness—like awakening every morning to a void and a longing that nothing can fill.

You were born a genius. The school system may or may not have recognized it. Maybe your parents didn't either. And maybe even you are blind to it today. But believe me when I say that there really is something special and magical about you. As the country-rock band America once sang: "You can do magic." Do you have the courage to fully embrace who you are? The world is in need of people like you who are willing to give their gift.

Look closely at the word "genius." It really says, "genie-in-us." It's there if you have the courage to look. So here's to finding and embracing the "genie-in-you."

EPILOGUE

Sure, Anyone Can Criticize! Here's What We Are Doing

Our colleges ought to have lit up in us a lasting relish for the better kind of man, a loss of appetite for mediocrities.

—William James (1907)

"I was told I needed to have a master's degree if I wanted to do well in life. So I spent two more years getting my Master of Fine Arts. At graduation, they told me 'Good Luck.' I now have my master's degree, three kids to feed and a husband who is not doing much better financially than I am. Now I'm selling real estate just to keep food on the table. That was eight years ago. I'm still selling real estate because I make too much money to quit. I wonder why I spent so much time getting my advanced degree. Why did the university never teach me about business? I see my classmates from art school, and they are working very hard and are still broke. Do we all need to go through this process?"

The year was 1989 and the person speaking was a real estate agent in one of my classes. Though I was moved by her story, it was one I had heard a thousand times before. My educational company thrives because public education fails to prepare people for the real world. We teach people very quickly what traditional schools should be teaching in the early grades.

When I think about our own students, I often find myself wondering how many millions of people are out there struggling to survive financially simply because they did not have the opportunity to learn the simple, basic principles we teach. I should be grateful for the shortcomings of public education since our teachers earn very good money because of it. But somehow I am anything but happy about this because I know that our company alone cannot help all the people who struggle painfully and needlessly throughout their lives simply to make a living. Perhaps what we have discussed in these pages will help to change this, to encourage public education, to offer courses that teach people not only how to survive but how to prosper in this society.

Each time I see people struggling financially, it triggers something in me—memories of how it felt to be in the place where they are. Many people told me that if I wanted to succeed in the business world I'd have to go back to school and get my MBA. If I didn't, I was dead meat. Chances for advancement were slim in the company where I was employed at the time—and I was working my way up the ladder in a company that was coming apart at the seams. It had been hit hard by the first wave of Japanese competitive products, and to get a promotion you had to sell your soul, sing the company song and kiss a lot of you-know-what.

I came to the conclusion that I had three options: I could play the corporate game, I could go back to school and get my MBA, or I could start my own company.

I first decided to try the MBA route. I went to night school to find out if it had changed. It hadn't. It was boring and slow. And by then I knew enough about business to know that most of what was being taught was either irrelevant or off the mark. I woke up in classes to find my notes all blurred and smudged because in my sleep I had drooled all over them.

As I began working on my MBA in earnest, I discovered very quickly that my instructors had no practical experience. They were great with textbook knowledge, but they had no idea how to handle real-world problems. At first I argued with them, but I soon discovered that arguing only hurt my grades. Six months later, after studying the text, taking tests and sleeping quietly in the back of the room, it became clear that I was wasting my time and money. I decided to start my own company.

That's when my real education began. Running my own company was painful, with long days and immeasurable emotional turmoil. At the core was the financial risk—involving hundreds of thousands of dollars. But I'd do it again without a moment's hesitation. That education took me from rock bottom at the age of 34 to financial independence by age 43.

I'm not any smarter than anyone else. In fact, I'm sure that there are thousands of educators out there who are a lot smarter than I. But in starting my own company, losing it all, then starting all over again and this time succeeding in ways I had only dreamed, I learned three things very quickly:

* *First, how to be a generalist in business.* Because I'm a generalist, I can specialize in any product or service I want and change when I want or when the market dictates.

* *Second, how to operate with or without money.* I know many people who are trapped because they are co-dependent upon (or addicted to) money since they do not know how to create it.

* *Third, mastery of the art of making mistakes without catastrophic consequences.* Of the three, I've got to say I value this last knowledge the most because it allows one to continue learning, thus eliminating the constant fear of chasing after the illusion of security, such as clinging to "right" answers or mistaking money for wealth.

Today, by pushing hard, falling down, getting up, learning and correcting, I gain knowledge every day. This simple willingness to look for new ideas, take risks, and make mistakes on a daily basis gets me further and further ahead. Most people cling to their often low-paying jobs only because they are afraid of failing should they try something different. Even worse, the fear of making mistakes prevents people from discovering their own potential or experiencing the greatness inside themselves.

As I climbed out of my financial hole and discovered a truly successful way to live, my story got around and people started asking me to teach them what I knew. I agreed. And soon I discovered that teaching really excited me. In 1974, I began studying the great teachers to find out what they knew that allowed them to be so successful at what they did. I found great ones in and out of traditional education.

In every class I attended I observed the instructor as well as the response of the class. And in every class I detected the same thing—that the value of the information was only as good as the students' willingness to go through a trial-and-error process until the information they'd taken in had passed from their minds into what athletes call "muscle memory." From the study of peak performance I learned about the process of moving from intellectual understanding to "unconscious competence," that is, the ability to do and correct an activity without thinking.

Although many instructors alluded to the importance of practice, they failed to teach the art of practice itself. At this point I realized something that Dr. Buckminster Fuller had attempted to tell me. He said it was the "thought" itself that holds people back. In other words, a thought such as "don't make mistakes" can actually cripple people for life—unless they are able to unlearn this thought. For hundreds of years our educational system has inadvertently fused into our muscle memories the silent and insidious thought that we must not make mistakes. We are brainwashed in the belief that making mistakes makes us bad people.

These silent killers of action exist as part of our daily habits and behavior. Even though we may be surrounded by people—including ourselves—who are fundamentally learning by trial-and-error, we continue to blind ourselves with the same old false belief that something is wrong with making mistakes. We see a child learning to walk by struggling, standing, falling, getting up and falling again. But we still fail to realize that we are watching the principles of learning in action.

The messy part of learning is rarely revealed; like the audience at a great theater event, we see only the successful end result, not the months of rehearsals when every person involved in the production went through endless errors and corrections. If we dig deep enough, however, we discover that Thomas Edison put together thousands of experimental light bulbs before he struck upon the right combination of filament metal, gas, and other material. Without the 9,999 mistakes he made along the way, Edison might never have invented the light bulb.

The path to knowledge—which requires the freedom within ourselves to make mistakes—is the only way to gain true wealth and financial success.

Because we have been taught to focus only on positive outcomes, without looking at the process that led up to it, we have a tendency to overlook the fact that successful action doesn't come quickly or painlessly. That's what keeps millions of people looking for get-rich-quick schemes. They see the lottery winners on television or the reports of the big winners in Las Vegas. All of these are con-games—designed to draw in more losers.

Westerners have become lazy, addicted to get-rich-quick schemes. The educational system's practice of punishing students for making mistakes and requiring students to memorize right answers nurtures this disease as do few other influences in our society. Schools end up turning students off to the very process that could teach them how to improve their lives.

The next time you watch a professional athlete whom you truly admire, think about how many mistakes they had to make to get where they are today. Professional golfers have made millions more mistakes than a person who has never even picked up a golf club. Pro golfers spend hours each day practicing. They swing the club, watch the result and then correct and learn more. They are forever refining their skills. The difference between amateurs and professionals is that *professionals get paid to practice!*

Magic Johnson once said in an interview on *The Arsenio Hall Show* that he felt he learned most by making big mistakes in big games. He did not like making mistakes but he knew that when he did, then went forward by correcting himself, he became better and better in his sport.

People in jobs they don't like, working only for paychecks and not taking on new challenges, rarely have opportunities to grow, learn more, and increase their knowledge, and thus their earnings. The longer they work at jobs where they do not learn, the farther they fall behind financially. They grow more dependent, less able, and often more desperate as the world changes around them and they remain the same.

The more I observed this, the more I became convinced that I had to learn how to teach people the art and science of making mistakes. I decided there was a need for a new science, which I call "unlearning." People had learned how not to make mistakes; now they needed to learn how to make mistakes successfully.

At the cutting edge of "unlearning" was Marshall Thurber. Next to my father, he was the best teacher I ever had. Marshall was an enigma in the education world. He graduated from top universities in the United States, achieving accolades and exceptionally high grades, yet rarely attended classes. An attorney by profession, he had become a multi-millionaire by his twenties. Marshall, also a student of Buckminster Fuller's, was researching the "cutting edge" of education.

In the late '70s, Marshall paid the Bulgarian government $25,000 to allow Georgi Losanov, the father of "SuperLearning," to come to the U.S. for six weeks in order to teach Marshall how to teach. The result was a hybrid style of teaching, combining Fuller, Losanov and Marshall's styles with others, to provide a powerful new paradigm to teach people at very high speed.

Marshall created several different educational programs. But traditional educators and corporate trainers thought he was pushing the limits too far. Nonetheless, Marshall and his partner, D.C. Cordova, made a profound impact on the lives of thousands of people in the U.S. during the late 1970s and early 1980s. I was one of them.

In January, 1980, I took their course **Money and You.** That single course changed my life and redirected my business career. I had signed up for the class expecting a course about business and investment tips because I wanted to make more money. What I found was a course made up of approximately 15 percent lecture, 60 percent games and 25 percent debriefing of the games. The course had much more to do with discovering ourselves than it did about money, yet in the process I learned more about money than I ever dreamed possible.

Before I attended **Money and You,** I had heard about Dr. Fuller's generalized principles of the universe. I understood them intellectually. But after I took the course I began to grasp the profound power and simplicity of these principles. I was beginning to understand them physically. I began incorporating them into my very being and developing a degree of "unconscious competence."

In his lifetime, Dr. Fuller set out to discover the generalized principles running through all things. Some people call these "universal truths." While our educational system attempts to teach us specialized facts and data that often become obsolete even before we've had an opportunity to try them out, Bucky thought it more advantageous to teach universal principles that could be applied throughout our lives, no matter what specialty we might pursue. His belief was that if people understood the generalized principles, they could apply them to any subject of interest, be it teaching, business, mathematics or horses. The principles would always be the same; only the context of their application would change. Now, while I understood the concept intellectually, it wasn't until I took **Money and You** that I really "got" it.

Money and You taught me to look upon my mistakes as valuable learning experiences. Although I had just lost everything, I was still going along with the program I'd learned in my previous education, that making mistakes was bad. So there I was, sitting in the class, looking like nothing was wrong and pretending I hadn't made any mistakes.

Because the course is about learning from our mistakes, I soon found out why I had lost my wife, my business and all my money. The course helped me translate my horrifying "learning experiences" (which I was ashamed of) into valuable lessons, knowledge and wisdom. When the course was over I could hardly wait to get back to the world of business—which was certainly not the attitude I had come in with.

Within a year, the money was pouring in, with greater ease than I could ever have imagined, just by applying the lessons I had learned from my mistakes and the generalized principles that the course had taught.

At the same time that my business started turning around for me, I also set out to become a kinder, more compassionate man so that perhaps I would be fit for marriage. I have to confess that this took a little longer than getting my money back. But in 1986 I married a beautiful woman, and to our surprise, we found that the generalized principles also work to make our marriage intimate, fun, exciting and successful.

When Marshall left the education business to pursue other interests, my wife, Kim, and I teamed up with D.C. Cordova to continue the work of the organization.

Today our organization has six primary courses, all utilizing the best methods of leading-edge teaching that we can find. Because we are considered to be "fringe" education, we do not recommend our courses for the masses, the traditionalists or people with rigid points of view. While we can teach anyone, regardless of prior educational background, work experience, age (over 15), sex or race, a sincere desire to learn and a flexible mind are essential. If there is a typical person our courses are most suited for, it would be a professional educator or business owner between the ages of 30 and 65 who is looking for enhanced business relationships and life skills.

We do not recommend employees attend unless their bosses attend first, or the employee is already contemplating starting his or her own business. Many people experience a different way of learning, doing business and communicating. If the organization they return to is not changing, many leave the company out of frustration after attending our courses. This is not our intent, yet I must report it does happen often and those who go through the process frequently end up making career moves that allow them to fully utilize their own genius. Our courses are designed for people who have some authority within their organization so that they are better able to enhance the environment for those with whom they work. Our six primary courses are:

1. **Money And You** (Part-1): 3-1/2 days in duration.

   This is the course Marshall Thurber created and designed. Since it is about generalized principles, which are timeless, the original material has been held intact. It is the prerequisite for most of our other courses. It encompasses the big picture of business, the science of learning from mistakes, Dr. Fuller's generalized principles and how to operate win-win in an often win-lose world. For many, this course is exciting and life-changing. For others, it is too much of a departure from their usual way of thinking and learning.

   For me, **Money and You** was the most personally challenging course I have ever taken. It is not a course I would recommend for people, male or female, who want to follow the macho ethic of "toughing out" every difficult issue with a stiff upper lip and silence. Neither is it for people who play victim roles in life, blaming their personal shortcomings on other people or circumstances. It is for people who want to get rid of what isn't working in their lives, who want to move on to take risks, to make mistakes, to try different ways of thinking and to move on to find new ideas. The end result is usually improved self-confidence and increased courage to meet every challenge life might offer.

2. **Creating Wealth** (Part 2 of **Money and You**): 3 days in duration.

   Creating Wealth completes what **Money and You** begins. **Money and You** is the big picture about money, work, life's purpose, cooperative organizations and learning. **Creating Wealth** is more specifically targeted on subjects of finance, leverage, cash, credit, systems, organization and planning. These often confusing and boring subjects are made lively and exciting by playing entertaining and instructive games that challenge anyone, regardless of their level of expertise relative to money and finance. A 19-year-old kid can learn right next to an investment banker with 20 years of solid experience: Both will be challenged and both will learn.

Many certified public accountants encourage their clients to attend this course because it demonstrates to businesspeople what CPAs have difficulty explaining to them about money and finance.

The principles of finance, credit, and cash that are taught in this course allowed me to make my life's purpose my life's work, earn all the money I needed and become financially independent.

Anthony Robbins, author of *Unlimited Power*, has had a great impact upon **Creating Wealth**. Robbins' information adds a powerful new dimension to a person's ability to achieve financial goals by overcoming personal fears and limitations. Rich people are not necessarily smarter, they just have better habits. Many people who take this course find out how to break old habits that have kept them from becoming wealthier.

Money and You is a prerequisite for taking **Creating Wealth**. The energy required to complete both courses, how-ever, is very different. While **Money and You** is especially difficult for "tough" macho men, **Creating Wealth** is very challenging for women. But women who complete the course report greater self-confidence and set out to achieve more financially and professionally.

3. **Powerful Presentations:** 3 days duration.

In a study reported by Columbia University some years ago, hundreds of people were questioned about their worst fears. Not unsurprising to many of us, the majority of people feared public speaking much more than they feared death. Since most people already know how to speak, we do not go into how to give a speech. This course is about confronting and going through personal fear so that your personal power can come through in front of a group.

Money and You is recommended, and often required, before a person takes this course. Since our method of teaching is unconventional and based on experiential learning, **Powerful Presentations** is not recommended unless people know what they are getting into. None of our courses are for the faint-of-heart, this one especially so.

4. **The *Excellerated* Business School for Entrepreneurs:** 16 days.

   This is the course for people who want to learn the generalized principles of business as quickly as possible. It covers marketing, finance, investments, accounting, negotiations, organization, team building and planning—all at highly accelerated pace. People are rarely bored; they are constantly challenged to keep up, no matter what their experience or background. Ultimately, most students report a tremendous boost in self-confidence which, when combined with business knowledge, improves their success in the real world.

5. **The Excellerated Business School for Teens**

   This program is for teens between the ages of 14-18. This school is modelled on The Excellerated Business School for Entrepreneurs, which has operated successfully for the past 15 years. Based on research, and feedback from thousands of graduates of our courses, the subjects taught will be beneficial for teens to prepare them to be budding, successful entrepreneurs, businesspersons, leaders or managers. This School may even prepare kids to take care of their parents in the manner to which they have become accustomed!

6. **Global Leaders' Forum**

   This is an ongoing instruction program for people who want to enhance their ability to teach. Originally set up to train instructors for our programs, it is now open to anyone interested in learning our methods of *excellerated* learning and teaching.

   People come from all over the world to attend and participate in this program. It enhances a person's ability to teach while accelerating her or his personal abilities to learn.

6. **Corporate Education Programs**

   Our **Global Leaders' Forum** attracts business and professional people who want to train to be educators. Many use our teaching style and technology to reposition their own companies for the 21st century. A few of these business and professional leaders have been specially trained to extend some of the latest team and business technology to other companies. What makes our corporate education programs different is that most of our instructors own their own companies. They are more than consultants or trainers. They understand the problems facing companies today. They have made the necessary changes themselves in their own companies—changes that are necessary if a business is to survive in the next decade.

What Makes Our Teaching Different?

The following is a description of our method of teaching, and some of the reasons we are able to teach faster to a broad spectrum of backgrounds. I use the subject of accounting for an example because most entrepreneurs hate accounting. It is also the downfall of most small business owners because they don't understand cash flow accounting. We teach in two days what traditional schools teach in one year. Education needs to teach faster—not keep students longer.

1. **We only have people who want to be in our classes and are willing to pay.** I do not know how traditional teachers can teach anything to students who don't want to be in school. Occasionally, we have companies who require their people to attend our courses. We discourage this. Because our classes are based on people learning from their mistakes, individuals who are not excited about "getting-off-it and getting-on-with-it" in their learning usually have a tough time. If you are attempting to drag a stubborn mule, neither you nor the mule is going to get very far.

2. **Everyone who goes to our Business School has gone through Money and You.** Not everyone likes our style of teaching. I would venture to say that the programs are designed for only a small segment of the population.

   Taking **Money and You** gives people a sense of our style of teaching with minimal expense in time and money. It introduces them to our culture. This benefits our Business School because everyone coming in already has some degree of trust in our work. In my experience, education is most difficult without trust.

3. **We only have instructors who are, firstly, entertaining and charismatic.** Secondly, they are successful in the real world, not merely

teachers/preachers telling students how to do it without being able to do it themselves. And thirdly, they are well-versed in high speed teaching. The person who teaches the accounting section, for example, is a CPA, owns his own businesses, worked for years for a Big 8 accounting firm and is a powerful and fast teacher.

4. **Our teachers do not grade students.** At the end of every course at our Business School, the students grade the teachers as to how much they learned and how useful they think the information is. Teachers who do not do well are not rehired. Our accounting instructor received a standing ovation at the end of one of his two-day sessions. I had never seen students cheering their accounting instructor before.

5. **Education or business background is not a factor.** We break the room into groups of five before the accounting section begins. In every group of five is a student who is an accountant by profession or a student who is already very good at accounting. The rest of the students have varying experience in accounting, from proficiency to pure hatred of the subject. The people who are proficient are there to support the less proficient as the class rolls along. It is like a double-edged sword. Those who are good get better because they get to be teachers, and the ones who hate it learn to love it because they find out how easy it is when they are treated as equals, as well as with kindness.

6. **We use cooperative-competition.** I hear so many people say cooperation is good or competition is bad. It is just another example of limited "right/wrong," "good/bad" thinking. We teach our students to suspend judgments such as these and look at how to use certain actions to achieve different results. By the second day every group is functionally literate in the principles of bookkeeping through cash flow accounting. The finale is a competition between groups. Sometimes we bet money, like $5 per member of the group. The problems are given and then the groups race time, with accuracy, against other learning groups. The excitement is intense, the noise level is high and learning is fun and exciting. At the end the instructor posts his answers along with the groups' answers. Then the debate begins. Groups who have differing answers are allowed to question anything and anyone, including the instructor.

7. **We use music, from classical to rock, in the background.** Both teachers and students use colored markers and students are encouraged to doodle. This helps the students utilize their creativity. We have strict rules and agreements, as well as lots of freedom and latitude. It takes more creativity to work within the rules than to break them.

   The results are that the students who feared accounting learn that it is simple. Many are inspired to learn more. Those who were good to begin with get better because they coach their groups. Both parties win and no one loses.

   In two days students learn, via hands-on experience, the simple principles of bookkeeping and accounting. The main purpose is not to have them become accountants, but rather to get them over their fear of accounting. This section allows students to get one year of accounting under their belts and to be able to talk with some degree of intelligence to their accountants, instead of blindly depending on an accountant's opinion. In the end, people walk away with greater confidence and more control of their business and personal lives. Because it is fun and participatory, people seem to retain the knowledge longer. All this in two days instead of one painful, boring year!

• • •

So that, in a nutshell, is how we teach. Because we are not part of the system and not limited by its rules and regulations, we have freedom to push the furthest boundaries of learning. There are many groups like ours who are called "fringe" educators by the educational establishment because our ideas are not a part of their vocabulary. Yet we are beginning to see educators defecting from traditional school systems to us in search of new teaching methods. Our intention is to improve the science of teaching, not merely criticize a system that is doing the best it can with what it knows.

About four years ago the demand for our courses outstripped the number of instructors. As a result we began a program to train businesspeople to lead our courses. The word of our teaching teachers soon spread, and we found people wanted to learn our method of teaching, yet didn't necessarily want to teach our courses. So our program was modified to accommodate those people.

Recently I was very honored and surprised to have instructors from the University of Texas and Columbia University come to study with us. I am glad and heartened to see schools looking outside of their paradigms for new, sometimes "crazy" methods of teaching. I have found from research and experience that we have not yet come close to finding out how fast the human mind can learn. I do know that the mind works much faster than our ability to teach.

I am always pushing the boundaries of my own abilities in learning. It is exciting, challenging and frustrating. My suspicion is that we are in the stone age right now, just beginning to crawl out of our caves in the field of education.

From Chaos to Wisdom

The new science of "chaos theory" emerged in the 1970s and gained tremendous popularity in the 1980s. The science of chaos is said to be the single most significant discovery of the 20th century.

Up to now we have only tolerated chaos in our lives, wishing it would go away. Our traditional education does its best to eliminate chaos by using a linear method of teaching and thinking, whereas our style of teaching follows the principles of chaos.

In his book *Chaos,* James Gleick discusses the scientifically proven fact that information is found at the edge, or the outer boundaries, of knowing. It is not until we are pushed to the boundaries of our paradigms that learning begins. It is a process similar to the theory of "dissipative structures" that won Ilya Prigogine, a Belgian physical chemist, the 1977 Nobel Prize in chemistry. His theory bridges the critical gap between biology and physics. It explains "irreversible processes" in nature, that is, a drive toward higher and higher order of life. We are in the middle of such a process.

The planet is evolving. Unfortunately, education isn't. Steven Jay Gould, a Harvard biologist and geologist, found that evolution does not take place at the gradual pace that Darwin suggested. Gould found that change, evolution, occurs rapidly, often caused by living at the edge of tolerance. Biochemist Albert Szent-Gyorgyi, another Nobel laureate and discoverer of Vitamin C, contends that all living matter has an inherent drive to perfect itself. To perfect oneself there must be a letting go of the past. Too much of education today is refusing to let go, and as a result, is not changing with the times.

Our organization has been perfecting this style of chaotic, creative, participatory learning. We do this through simple games which encourage people to venture out to the edges of their paradigms. Our methods revive the natural desire in humans to improve and perfect themselves. Truthfully, it is sometimes a frightening process. It is the skill of our instructors to make a giant leap beyond fears they have learned in the past, so that they may evolve to discover and make use of their own potential and their own genius, allowing them to handle the present and future successfully.

Most current educational systems are still employing teaching methods that are actually counter-evolutionary, the same old stuff that's created so many of today's social and economic problems. This method is robbing people of their capacity to enjoy the wealth and happiness that are their birthright, at a time when our planet is evolving, sometimes chaotically, and usually not gradually, into higher and higher orders of living. We are currently in a renaissance of learning, but our schools are still in the dark ages.

Our organization holds that the purpose of education is to inspire further education. It is this lack of inspiration from our educational system's methods of teaching that convinces me of the depth of its failings. How schools can take a challenging and exciting process such as learning, and turn it into an experience that is boring and mind-deadening, never ceases to amaze and horrify me.

Perhaps what we and a handful of other schools like ours are doing around the world—applying teaching methods that engage every student at the highest levels of their potential —will help to spread the truth about becoming rich and happy throughout the world. That would be my fondest dream.

Thank you for reading this book.

Publisher's Note

The author's father, Ralph H. Kiyosaki, Ph.D., was given the first copy of the Australian edition of this book.

Most of Robert's life, he and his father had fought—sometimes quite bitterly—over their seemingly very different views of life. Dr. Kiyosaki had always believed that his son was only interested in money. He had thought that Robert's drive for wealth was selfish and that he was uncaring about the world's problems. However, after reading the book he changed his opinion of his son. He saw at last that Robert truly did have a higher purpose in mind—that his real interest in money had deep humanitarian roots.

Just six months after receiving the book, Ralph H. Kiyosaki passed away. This work succeeded in bringing father and son together, completing their relationship in way that Robert could only have imagined.

Bibliography/ Recommended Reading

The Abilene Paradox
Harvey, Jerry B.
Accelerated Learning
Rose, Colin
Buckminster Fuller, An Autobiographical Monologue/Scenario
Fuller, R. Buckminster
Born To Win
Bertrand, John
Chaos: The Making of a New Science
Gleick, James
Critical Path
Fuller, R. Buckminster
Dresssing to Win
Pante, Robert
The E Myth
Gerben, Michael E.
The Fifth Discipline
Senge, Peter M.
Follow Your Bliss
Bennett, Hal Zina
Intuition
Fuller, R. Buckminster
Killing the Spirit
Smith, Page
Lateral Thinking
deBono, Edward
The Learning Gap
Stevenson, Harold
Megatrends: 2000
Naisbitt & Aburdene
Paradigms: Discovering the Future
Barker, Joel
The Popcorn Report
Popcorn, Faith
Powershift
Tofler, Alvin
Savage Inequalities
Kozol, Jonathan
SuperLearning
Ostrander & Schroeder
Quantum Learning: Unleashing the Genius in You
DePorter, Bobbi
Suggestopedia
Losanov, Georgi
Super-Teaching
Jensen, Eric P.
Unlimited Power
Robbins, Anthony
Use Both Sides of Your Brain
Buzan, Tony
Using Your Brain for a Change
Bandler, Richard

Business/Financial

Danger in the Comfort Zone
Barwick, Judith M.
The Deming Management Method
Walton, Mary
The Next Economy
Hawken, Paul
In Search of Excellence
Peters & Waterman
One Minute Manager
Blanchard & Johnson
Out of the Crisis
Deming, Edwards
Passion for Excellence
Peters, Tom
Nothing Down
Allen, Robert G.
The Richest Man in Babylon
Clason, George S.
Think and Grow Rich
Hill, Napoleon

Personal/Childhood Development

Loving Relationships
Ray, Sondra
Magical Child
Pearce, Joseph Chilton
Magical Child Matures
Pearce, Joseph Chilton
Recovery from Co-dependency
Weiss & Weiss
The Secrets Men Keep
Druck, Ken

Product Information

Financial Literacy, How the Rich Get Rich

Robert Kiyosaki

Seven experts reveal their formulas for getting wealthy. One started a company worth 1.6 billion today. Two are millionaire women. One bought over 300 single family homes in less than five years using other people's money. Their stories will inspire and move you into taking action for yourself. **6 Audio Tapes and Workbook $149.00**

The Secrets of Professional Investors

Robert Kiyosaki with John Burley

Did you know that 9 out of 10 investors do not make much money, if any?

Robert Kiyosaki shows you how to be an unbeatable investor who wins consistently. In this tape set, Robert and John speak frankly on how to make large sums of money, with minimal risk. Get the hard facts on how you can get onto the fast track to wealth... and if you want, retire early. **16 Audio Tapes $295.00**

CASHFLOW™ 101
The MBA Program
($195 in the U.S.A.)

To Order these products call
1-800-308-3585
or visit our website at www.cashflowtech.com